*The American
Immigration Collection*

The Scandinavian Element
in the
United States

KENDRIC CHARLES BABCOCK

Arno Press and The New York Times

NEW YORK 1969

UNIVERSITY OF ILLINOIS STUDIES

IN THE

SOCIAL SCIENCES

VOL. III. NO. 3   SEPTEMBER, 1914

The Scandinavian Element in the United States

BY

KENDRIC CHARLES BABCOCK, Ph. D.

Dean of the College of Liberal Arts and Sciences in the University of Illinois
Sometime Fellow in the University of Minnesota and in Harvard University

---

PUBLISHED BY THE UNIVERSITY OF ILLINOIS
URBANA

TO
HARRY PRATT JUDSON, KNUTE NELSON,
NICOLAY A. GREVSTAD, AND ALBERT BUSHNELL HART
IN GRATEFUL RECOGNITION OF
UNFAILING ASSISTANCE, ENCOURAGEMENT,
AND FAITHFUL CRITICISM

CONTENTS

CHAPTER I.

INTRODUCTION.

The history of the United States, according to newer views which have largely supplanted, or progressed beyond, those of the New England school of great historians, is the history of the march of a civilization, chiefly English, across the vast North American continent, within the short period of three hundred years. It is the story of the transformation of a wide-stretching wilderness—of an ever-advancing frontier—into great cities, diversified industries, varying social interests, and an intensely complex life. Wave upon wave of races of mankind has flowed over the developing and enlarging West, and each has left its impress on that area. Across the trail of the Indian and the trapper, the highway of the pioneer on his westward journey, have spread the tilled fields of the farmer, or along it has run the railroad. The farm has become a town-site and then a manufacturing city; the trading post at St. Paul and the village by the Falls of St. Anthony have expanded into the Twin Cities of the Northwest; the marshy prairie by the side of Lake Michigan, where the Indians fought around old Fort Dearborn, has come to be one of the world's mighty centers of urban population— and all this transformation within the memory of men now living.

The progress of this rapid, titanic evolution of an empire was greatly accelerated by the desires, the strength, and the energy of multitudes of immigrants from Europe; and in at least six great commonwealths of the Northwest the Swedes, Norwegians, and Danes have been among the chief contributors to State-building. During the eighty years ending in June, 1906, among the 24,000,000 immigrants who came to the United States, the Scandinavians numbered more than 1,700,000. Whether viewed as emigrations on the eastern shores of the Atlantic, or as immigrations on the western shores, these modern *Völkerwanderungen* constitute one of the wonders of the social world, in comparison with which most of the other migrations in history are numerically insignificant. The Israelites marching out of Egypt were but a mass of released bondmen; the invasions of the Goths, Vandals, and Huns were conquering expeditions, full of boisterous, thoughtless, unforecasting energy. Even the immigration from Europe to America in the whole of the seventeenth century scarcely equalled in number the columns which moved westward in any one year from 1880 to 1890.

In this flux of humanity, mobile almost to fluidity, various in promise of utility, shifting in proportions of the good and bad, of pauper, refugee, and fanatic, or "bird of passage", sweatshop man, and home-builder, there has been such an interplay of subtle and vast forces that no just and final appreciation can as yet be reached. But some sort of tentative conclusions may be arrived at by intensive study of each immigrant group, following it through years and generations, searching for its ramifications in the body politic and social.

The student of this phase of American history must attempt the scientific method, and exercise the patience, of the student of physical nature. No geologist, for example, would think for a moment of generalizing as to the history and the future of a continent of complicated structure after a few examinations here and there of cross-sections of its strata. He must know from thoro-going observation the trend, thickness, and composition of each stratum; he must trace, if possible, the sources of the material which he finds metamorphosed; he must be familiar with the physical and the chemical forces at work in and on this material,— heat, pressure, movement, affinities, gases, water, wind, and sun. In like manner, the student of immigration as a whole, or of a section as large as that of the Scandinavians or Italians, must make careful discriminations as to previous conditions and influences, and also must notice carefully the differentiation of peoples, places, and times.

Too much stress, however, should never be laid on the character of any one group of immigrants, lest it warp the judgment upon the immigration movement as a factor in American progress. The ardent political reformer in New York City, seeing the political activity of the Irish, and the easy, fraudulent enfranchisement of newly-arrived aliens, cries in a loud voice for restriction or prohibition of immigration. The California labor agitator, feeling chiefly the effect of Chinese efficiency in the labor market, would close the gates of the country to all the eastern nations. The social worker, knowing mainly and best the degradation of the Hungarians in the mines, or of the Hebrews in the sweatshops, prophesies naught but evil from foreign immigration. From an opposite point of view, when a man travels in leisurely fashion up and down Wisconsin, Illinois, Minnesota, and the Dakotas, and finds a dozen race elements—English, German, Norwegian, or Russian—he begins to understand the real benefit to the nation of the coming of this vast, varied, peaceful army.[1] The scale of immigrants runs from the pauper or the diseased alien, awaiting deportation on Ellis Island in New York Harbor, to the rich Norwegian or German owning a thousand-acre farm in North Dakota, and to the millionaire Swedish lumberman or manufacturer of Wisconsin or Minnesota.

For more than half a century, the United States has been almost a nation of immigrants, a mixture of races in the process of combination; upon the exact nature of this combination, whether it take the form of absorption, amalgamation, fusion, or assimilation, depends future political and social progress.

The writer has for years felt a profound conviction of the vital importance of this whole problem of the alien, and a corresponding belief in the value of the investigation of each cohort in the national forces. Hence this attempt at a sympathetic study of the Scandinavian element in Ameri-

[1]Whelpley, *The Problem of the Immigrant*, 1.

can life and of its contributions to the evolution of the Northern Mississippi Valley during the last sixty years.

In such a study, the Norwegians, Swedes, and Danes, like all other citizens of foreign birth, must be judged by the character and preparation which best fit men to contribute to the permanent progress of a self-governing people. What are the signs of readiness for full Americanization? The fundamentals are manliness—Roman virility—, intelligence, and the capacity for co-operation, ennobled by "dignified self-respect, self-control, and that self-assertion and jealousy of encroachment which marks those who know their rights and dare maintain them";[2] devotion to law, order, and justice; and a ready acquiescence in the will of the majority duly expressed.[3]

Such qualities in America have been the especial possession of that sub-race of the Caucasian stock which the later ethnologists call the Baltic, in contradistinction to the co-ordinate sub-races, the Alpine, and the Mediterranean or Ligurian. This Baltic race has for centuries occupied the British Isles, the northern plains of Germany, and the North European peninsulas, being found in its purest state in Norway, Sweden, and Scotland. The people of this sub-race, asserts the writer of an admirable article on racial characteristics, are mentally "enterprising and persevering, and cheerfully dedicate most of their time and thought to work. . . . They are liberally gifted with those moral instincts which are highly favorable to the creation and growth of communities, altho not always so favorable to the individual who possesses them; they are altruistic, fearless, honest, sincere. They love order and cleanliness, and attach considerable importance to the dress and personal appearance of individuals."[4] While the other Caucasian sub-races do not lack these qualities, their most dominating characteristics are different; for example, one may

[2] J. R. Commons, "Racial Composition of the American People," *Chautauquan*, XXXVIII, 35.

[3] R. Mayo-Smith, *Emigration and Immigration*.

[4] G. Michaud, "What shall we be?", *Century*, LXV, 685.

exemplify the artistic or the idealistic side of human nature.

As related to the progress of civilization in America, all immigrants fall into three classes: those who powerfully re-enforce the strength and virtue of the nation, those who supplement its defects with desirable elements, and those who lower its standards and retard its advancement. Hence, those immigrants will be presumably the most desirable to America who come from the regions where the purest Baltic stock now exists, that is, north of a line running east and west through Brussels, and especially in north-central Germany and the Scandinavian peninsula.

Measured by character and training, the Baltic race in America stands up well to the test, not only in the foreign-born alone, but in the second and third generation born on American soil. If generations of ignorance, mental inertia, social depression, political passivity, shiftlessness, and improvidence stretch behind the immigrant, if his religion be chiefly a superstition or strongly antagonistic to the principles of the Republic, and if he be physically inferior and long inured to the hardships of a low standard of living, just so far is he an undesirable addition to American population. But, on the other hand, if his home-land show a very low percentage of illiteracy; if his life has been saturated with the ideas of thrift and small economies; if he hold himself free from domination by priest, landlord, or king; and if his history be the story of a sturdy struggle for independence, he should be rated high and welcomed accordingly, for it is of such stuff that mighty nations are made.

The student of Scandinavian immigration in the nineteenth century is not left to conjecture in his endeavor to estimate the probable result of the injection into American society of this foreign-born element. Before the second generation of English and Dutch settlers in America in the seventeenth century had grown to manhood, the Swedes began a colony upon the Delaware River; and their descendants are still a distinguishable part of the popula-

tion of the lower Delaware valley. This beginning of
Swedish immigration to America is particularly instructive
because the settlements undertaken in the period of the
Thirty Years War drew their recruits from the same classes
of Swedish society as the movements of the nineteenth century, and developed under substantially similar conditions
and along much the same lines.

The Swede of the seventeenth century and the Swede
of the nineteenth century are essentially one in character,
for two hundred years have wrought less change in him
than in his cousins of Germany and England. The accounts
of Stockholm, its people and its surroundings, written in
the early seventeenth century, might serve, with very little
modification, to describe the large features of the Sweden
and the Swedes of today. Great progress has of course been
made in two centuries, but in political wisdom, high moral
courage, and benevolent purpose, Gustavus Adolphus and
his advisers were distinctly in advance of the first two
English Stuarts and their courts.

Perhaps no better illustration of this difference could
be found than in the plans for the beginnings of the colonies
on the James River and on the Delaware River. The
scheme for a colony on the Delaware was originally out-
lined by the great Gustavus himself in 1624, but sterner
duties took his energies; and after the fatal blow on the
field of Lützen, it devolved on his daughter, Queen Chris-
tina, and her faithful minister, Oxenstjerna, to carry
out his plan for establishing a colony which was to be "a
blessing to the common man," a place for "a free people
with wives," and not a mere commercial speculation or a
haven for aristocratic adventurers and spendthrifts.[5]

The first company of immigrants arrived in 1638, and
year by year additions were received. So early as the middle of the seventeenth century, Sweden had a touch of the
"America fever," and when an expedition left Gothenburg
in 1654 with 350 souls on board, about a hundred families

[5] *Argonautica Gustaviana*, 3, 16.

were left behind for want of room. Perhaps only the transfer of the colony, first to the Dutch and then to the English, prevented the Swedish immigration from attaining large proportions two and a half centuries ago. The Swedish flag floated over New Sweden notwithstanding the protests of both the Dutch and the English, until the conquest of the colony by Governor Stuyvesant in 1655, and then it disappeared from the map of America.

In spite of threats, subjugation, and isolation, the prosperity of the early colony continued, and by the end of the seventeenth century it numbered nearly a thousand. No injustice in dealing with the Indians provoked a massacre, for these protégés of the Swedish crown, before William Penn was born, carefully and systematically extinguished by purchase the Indian titles to all the land on which they settled. Their piety and loyalty built the church and fort side by side, and long after they became subjects of the king of Great Britain they continued to receive their ministers from the mother church in Sweden. In fact, pastors commissioned from Stockholm did not cease their ministrations until they came speaking in a tongue no longer known to the children of New Sweden.

This Swedish colony, planted thus in the midst of larger English settlements, continued for many generations to add its portion of good blood and good brains to a body of colonists in the New World, which too often needed sorely just these qualities. The Honorable Thomas F. Bayard, who lived long among their descendants, wrote in 1888: "I make bold to say that no better stock has been contributed (in proportion to its numbers) towards giving a solid basis to society under our republican forms, than these hardy, honest, industrious, law-abiding, God-fearing Swedish settlers on the banks of the Christiana in Delaware. While I have never heard of a very rich man among them, yet I have never heard of a pauper. I cannot recall the name of a statesman or a distinguished law-giver among them, nor of a rogue or a felon. As good citizens they helped to form what Mr. Lincoln called the plain people of the country,—and I have lived among their descendants and know that their civic virtues have been transmitted."[6]

Their thrift and comfort and sobriety attracted the attention of Thomas Pascall, one of the Englishmen of Penn's first colony, who wrote in January, 1683: "They are generally very ingenious people, live well, they have lived here 40 years, and have lived much at ease having great plenty of all sorts of provisions, but they were but ordinarily cloathed; but since the English came they have gotten fine cloathes, and are going proud."[7]   Penn himself declared: "They have fine children and almost every house full; rare to find one of them without three or four boys and as many girls; some six, seven and eight sons. And I must do them right—I see few young men more sober and industrious."[8]

[6]Mattson, *Souvenir of the 250th Anniversary of the First Swedish Settlement in America* (1888), 44.

[7]This letter, printed as a broadside in England about 1683, was furnished me by Mr. George Parker Winship of the Carter Brown Library of Providence, Rhode Island.

[8]Janney, *Life of William Penn,* 246-247.

CHAPTER II.

SWEDES, NORWEGIANS, AND DANES

The common use of the term Scandinavian to describe Swedes, Norwegians, and Danes in a broad and general way, is one of the products of the commingling of these three peoples on the American side of the Atlantic. The word really fits even more loosely than does the word British to indicate the English, Welsh and Scotch. It was applied early in the history of the settlements in Wisconsin and Illinois, to groups which comprised both Norwegians and Danes on the one hand, or Norwegians and Swedes on the other hand, when no one of the three nationalities was strong enough to maintain itself separately, and when the members of one were inclined, in an outburst of latent pride of nationality, not to say conceit of assumed superiority, to resent being called by one of the other names; for example, when a Norwegian objected to being taken for a Swede. Thus the Scandinavian Synod of the Evangelical Lutheran Church, organized in 1860, included both Norwegians and Danes; ten years later the name was changed to the Norwegian-Danish Conference; and in 1884 the differentiation was carried further, and the Danes formed a new Danish Evangelical Lutheran Church Association, supplementing the Danish Evangelical Lutheran Church in America, which dated back to 1871.

Vigorous protests were made from time to time against the use of "Skandinavian" or "Skandinav." "Shall we Norwegians let the Danes persist in calling us Scandinavians?" wrote "Anti-Skandinavian" to the leading American Norwegian weekly of 1870.[1] He also quoted the sarcastic words of Ole Bull: "Scandinavia, gentlemen,—may I ask where that land lies? It is not found in my geo-

---

[1]*Fædrelandet og Emigranten*, May 12, 1870: "Skulle vi Norske lade de Danske fremture i at kalde os Skandinaver?"

graphy; does it lie perhaps in the moon?"[2]   But the use and acceptability of the word steadily grew; the great daily paper in Chicago took the name *Skandinaven;* in 1889, the editor of *The North* declared: "The term has become a household word . . . universally understood in the sense in which we here use it (to designate the three nationalities)."[3]

Ole Bull was, of course, right in saying that there is no Scandinavian language, no Scandinavian nation; but the ordinary reader or student does not recognize clearly that Sweden, Norway and Denmark have different spoken languages (though the Danish and Norwegian printed language is one), different traditions, as well as different governments. Almost while these words are being written, the coronation ceremony in the ancient cathedral at Throndhjem completes the process by which Norway is severed entirely from Sweden and again assumes among the powers of earth that "separate and equal station to which the laws of Nature and of Nature's God entitle them."

The physique and characteristics of the three Scandinavian peoples have been profoundly affected by the physical features of the northern peninsulas; the mountains, fjords, and extensive coast lines of Norway, the level stretches, lakes, and regular coast of Sweden, and the low, sandy islands of Denmark find a counterpart in the varying types of men and women of those countries. The occupations which necessarily grew out of these differences of surface and soil tended to give to all a strong, sturdy, hardy body; farming naturally claims by far the largest percentage, though great numbers of the men yield to the call of the sea. Both Norway and Sweden have large lumbering interests, while Norway leads in fishing industries, Sweden in mining, and Denmark in dairying.

Nature is no spendthrift in any part of the Scandinavian peninsulas; small economies are the alphabet of her

[2]"Skandinavien, mine Herrer, tör jeg spörge, hvor det Land ligger? Det findes ikke i min Geografi; ligger det maaske i Maanen?" Ole Bull, *Fædrelandet og Emigranten,* May 12, 1870.

[3]*The North,* June 12, 1889.

teaching, and her lessons once learned are rarely forgotten. Her children of the North, therefore, down to the stolidest laborer, mountaineer, and fisherman, are generally industrious and frugal, and when they migrate to the American West, to enter upon the work of pioneering, with its stern requirements of endurance, patience, persistent endeavor, and thrift, they start out in the new life with decided temperamental advantages over most other immigrants, and even over most native-born Americans.

Other characteristics common to these three peoples distinguish them strikingly from the South European. From their Viking ancestors they have inherited a love for adventure, a courage in facing the possibilities of the future. Their hatred of slavery, and their clear, high ideas of personal and political freedom, are strongly marked, and their peasantry is ranked highest on the continent.[4] Their adaptability to changes of clime, of conditions, of circumstance, has been remarkably demonstrated over and over again, in Normandy in the 11th century, in Sicily in the 12th, and in America in the 19th; yet it has not degenerated into a facile yielding to moods and whims even under the rapid changes of New World society.

The typical Swede is aristocratic, fond of dignities, assertive: he is polite, vivacious, and bound to have a jolly time without troubling too much about the far future. Yet he is not afraid of hard work; he is persistent, ofttimes brilliant, and capable of great energy and endurance. He is notably fond of music, especially the singing of choruses and the opera, and the poetry of Bellman and the epics of Tegner belong to the great literature of the world.

The Norwegian is above all democratic. He is simple, serious, intense, severe even to bluntness, often radical and visionary, and with a tendency to disputatiousness.[5] There is an unmeasured quantity of passion and imagination in

[4]N. S. Shaler, "European Peasants as Immigrants," *Atlantic,* LXXI, 649.

[5]N. P. Haugen comments on the good and bad features of this tendency in his Norway Day speech at the World's Columbian Exposition. *Skandinaven,* May 24, 1893.

him, as there are unmeasured stores of power and beauty
in the snows of his mountains and the waters of his coast.
He has the capacity for high and strenuous endeavor, even
verging on the turbulent, but he rarely has developed the
qualities of a great leader.   Like the Swede, the Norwegian
is fond of music, but it is of a different sort.   Both in his
music and in his literature, the dramatic element is strong;
no names in the realm of literature of the last generation
stand higher than those of Ibsen and Björnson, who are
first cosmopolitan and then Norwegian.

The Dane is the Southerner of the Scandinavians, but
still a conservative.   He is gay, but not to excess; the
healthiness and jollity of a Copenhagen crowd are things to
covet.   He is pre-eminently a small farmer or trader, honest and persevering, ready and easy-going, and altho not
given to great risks, he is quick to see a bargain and shrewd
in making it.   Of self-confidence and enterprise he manifests a decided lack.[6]   His country is small, open on all
sides, and near to great Powers; his interests, therefore,
have led him out from his peninsula and islands, and foreign influences have more affected him than they have his
neighbors across the Sound and the Skager Rack.   His best
work in literature and art has been done under strong
Romantic and classic impulses from the South.

Such being the qualities of the peoples of Sweden,
Denmark and Norway, the conditions of life and society in
those countries in the first half of the nineteenth century
seem on close examination quite unlikely to produce a
great emigration, in comparison with conditions in other
countries from which large numbers of men and women
migrated to America.   There were no great social, economic, or political upheavals sufficient to cause the exodus of
any class; religious intolerance and persecution were, with
few minor exceptions, neither active nor severe.   The
Napoleonic wars did not depopulate these northern lands,
nor did they, like their sister nations to the south, suffer

---

[6]Borchner, *Danish Life in Town and Country,* 3-6; Bille, *History of
the Danes in America,* 1, 7, 8.

seriously from the commercial restrictions of the Emperor of the French. Militarism did not crush them with its weight of lead and steel and its terrible waste of productive energy. Political oppression and proscription, so marked in the affairs of central and western European states down to 1850, were not features of the history of Norway, Sweden or Denmark. Though Norway protested in 1814 in no uncertain terms against the union with Sweden in a dual monarchy, she was, under the constitution of that year, one of the freest nations of Europe, " a free, individual, indivisible kingdom." In Sweden before 1840, one of the chief restrictions on the individual was potential rather than actual: a man who wished to leave the kingdom must have a passport from the king, for which he had to pay 300 kroner (about $81). He would also be under the close supervision of the state church, to which he was expected to belong.

There were, however, conditions in the home-lands as well as in America, which impelled immigration. Anyone who has travelled over the fertile prairies of the Mississippi valley and then through Norway or Sweden, will often wonder that so many people have been content to remain so long in the older Scandinavia. In Norway there were in 1910, in round numbers, 2,390,000 people on an area of 124,000 square miles.[7] Of this population, about 425,000 were gathered in the larger towns, and 250,000 were in the smaller towns, making a total urban population of 29%, over against 21% twenty years before. The remainder were scattered over the vast mountainous country or along the coast-line of three thousand miles.[8] Thousands of fishermen's huts are grappled barnacle-like to the rocks, while behind them along a trickling thread of water stretches a precious hand-breadth of soil. The greater part of the interior is one wide furrowed plateau, in whose hollows, by lakes and streams, thrifty farmers skilfully

[7] *Statesman's Year-Book, 1914,* 1141 ff.

[8] In 1880, 20% lived in towns; in 1890, 23.7% lived in towns, and 76.3% in the rural districts. *Norway* (English edition of the official volume prepared for the Paris Exhibition of 1900), 90.

utilize their few square yards of tillable land and pasture their cattle on the steep slopes. Save around Lake Mjösen, the Leir, Vos, and Throndhjem, there can scarcely be found in all Norway anything like a broad rich meadow. The farm products are almost literally mined from the rocks. "It is by dogged, persistent, indomitable toil and endurance, backed up in some cases by irrepressible daring, that the Norwegian peasant and fisher-folk—three-fourths of the population—carry on with any show of success their struggle against iron nature."[9] Yet in spite of such adverse conditions, these people have ever clung with passionate tenacity to their mountainous storm-beaten Norway, and by it have been made brave without bitterness, hardy without harshness, strong yet tender.

In Sweden the physical conditions are decidedly different. The area of 172,900 square miles supports a population of 5,600,000 (1912), of whom 50% dwell in cities of which there are now thirty with more than 10,000, Stockholm leading with 350,000. The urban population increased 166% between 1871 and 1912.[10] There are few lofty mountains and no jagged peaks, majestically dominating the outlook; the crag-set fjords are replaced by gentler bays and sounds sprinkled with beautiful islands; in some parts of the country, as in Wermland and Smaaland, are low and marshy sections, where, according to legend, the Lord forgot to separate the land and water. Agricultural conditions are less hard and means of communication are better than in Norway; closer relations exist between provinces and between parishes; information is more readily diffused, and gatherings of considerable size are held without particular difficulty.

Denmark more closely resembles Sweden than Norway, and is in still better touch with the larger world than either of the others. With an area of about 15,000 square miles,—Massachusetts, Rhode Island, and Connec-

---

[9]Wm. Archer, "Norway Today," *Fortnightly Rev.*, XLIV, 415.

[10]*Statesman's Year-Book, 1914*, 1316. The increase of urban population was five times the increase of the kingdom.

ticut, combined—it held in 1911 a population of 2,775,000.
Copenhagen and its suburbs had a population of 560,000.
The urban population was 26%.   Unlike the other two,
Denmark has several important colonies in other parts of
the world.[11]

In all three countries, as in the rest of Europe,
changes in commercial, industrial, social, legal, and religious matters were sure to be slow.   The tenure and succession in lands, the limited market for labor, the relatively
small opportunity for initiative, especially for the younger
members of considerable families,—all of these conditions
with the characteristics already described, lent added attractiveness to the call of the American West.

[11]*Statesman's Year-Book, 1914,* 789 ff.

CHAPTER III.

EARLY NORWEGIAN IMMIGRATION.

"Arrived last evening" (October 9, 1825).

"Danish Sloop Restoration, Holland, 98 days from Norway, via Long Island Sound, with iron to Boorman and Johnson, 52 passengers."[1]

"The vessel is very small, measuring, as we understand, only about 360 Norwegian lasts, or 45 American tons, and brought 46 passengers, male and female, all bound for Ontario County, where an agent who came over sometime since, purchased a tract of land."[2]

These ordinary shipping notices in the newspapers of New York City, and several other similar paragraphs, are the first entries in the chronicles of the newer Scandinavian immigration to the United States. From the cessation of Swedish immigration in the seventeenth century down to 1825, no considerable companies made the long journey from the Northlands to America, tho adventurous fellows in twos and threes came now and then, men who misliked the humdrum life in the old parishes, with its narrow opportunity and outlook, men who found the sea the only highway to novelty and a possible fortune.[3] Now, at last, the coming of a company of some size, from Norway, adding one more to the lengthening list of nationalities which contributed to the complex population of the United States, attracted more than passing attention.[4]

[1]*The New York Evening Post,* Oct. 10, 1825.

[2]*The New York Daily Advertiser,* Oct. 12, 1825.

[3]Interview with Capt. O. C. Lange (who reached America in 1824) in Chicago, 1890; Norelius, *Svenskarnes Historia,* 1.

[4]*Niles' Register,* XXIX., 115. Several extended quotations from newspapers in New York, Boston, and Baltimore, for the month of October, 1825, relating to this company of the sloop "Restoration", indicating the interest created by its coming, are printed in Anderson, *Norwegian Immigration,* 69-76.

That the sloop was not Danish, and that there is some discrepancy in the number of passengers—(and crew?)—and in the number of days in the voyage, are minor matters and easily accounted for; the New Yorker of 1825 could hardly be expected to distinguish clearly between Danes and Norwegians, when the people of the Northwest at the present time apply the name Swede indiscriminately to Swedes, Danes, Norwegians, Finns, and Icelanders. But back of the arrival of this little sloopful of Norwegians, is a story of motive, organization, and movement, more or less characteristic of Scandinavian immigration during the next two generations. The two main elements are: conditions in Norway and the United States, and the personal activities of one of the adventurous fellows already referred to.

In the region about Stavanger, in southwestern Norway, in 1825, there had been for some time a feeling of discontent with the religious conditions of the country, and a tendency to formal dissent from the established church. The direction of this tendency and the definition of the movement were vitally influenced by certain zealous and philanthropic Quaker missionaries from England. Stephen Grellet and William Allen, who visited Norway in 1818. Grellet was a French nobleman who sought refuge in the United States during the French Revolution, and there united himself with the Quakers or Friends. After residing in America for twelve years, he began making tours through Europe to propagate Quaker ideas, even obtaining an interview with the Pope, which he describes in his diary. The visit to Norway was in furtherance of his general plan. While his account of his stay in Norway does not make any mention of America, it is impossible to believe that no reference to America and to the conditions of the Friends in that part of the world, where he himself found refuge, crept into the conferences which he held around Stavanger, and that no seeds of desire to seek the New World were sown in the slow-moving minds of the Norwegian peasants whom he met.[5]

[5]Grellet, *Memoirs,* I, 321 ff.

As dissenters from the established church, these Quakers were continually subject to actual or threatened pains and penalties, in addition to those troubles which might arise from their refusal to take oaths and to render military service. Their children and those of other dissenters must be baptised and confirmed in the Lutheran Church; they must themselves attend its services and pay taxes for its support, or suffer fines or other punishment for failing so to do. Tho prosecutions, or persecutions, were really few before 1830, an episode now and then showed the dissenters what might be in store for them if they persisted, as when one of the Quakers was arrested in 1821 for burying his children in unconsecrated ground, and fined five specie dollars a day until he re-bury them in consecrated ground, and agree to follow the outward ceremonies and customs of the state church.[6] Two years before one of the Friends wrote: "There are no laws yet made in favor of Friends, so that those who stand firm in their principles act contrary to the laws of the country. Friends must be resigned to take the consequences."[7] With signs of persecution, with an increase of discontent, and with the leadership of a man possessed of first-hand knowledge about the United States, it is not surprising that emigration was decided upon.

Kleng Peerson, called also Kleng Pederson and Person Hesthammer, was a man of dubious character, who has been variously described. One has called him the "Father of the Newer Norwegian Immigration" and as such entitled to a chapter by himself; another has written him down as a tramp.[8] A softer characterization, however, makes of

[6]Richardson, *Rise and Progress of the Society of Friends in Norway,* 37.

[7]*Ibid.,* 23.

[8]R. B. Anderson, "En Liden Indledning" in the series of articles "Bidrag til vore Settlementers og Menigheders Historie," *Amerika,* April 4, 1894. Bothne, *Kort Udsigt over det Lutherske Kirkearbeide bladnt Normændene i Amerika,* 822.

him a "Viking who was born some centuries after the Viking period."[9] He appears to have been a sort of Quaker, either from conscience or convenience. His leaving his home parish of Skjold near Stavanger, and his emigration to the United States in 1821 in company with another Norwegian, are attributed to motives ranging from a commission from the Quakers to find a refuge for them in America, to a desire to escape the rich old widow whom he married, and who was tired of supporting him in idleness.[10] Certain it is that upon his return to Norway in 1824, after three years of experience in the New World, the sentiment favoring emigration from Stavanger soon crystallized.

By midsummer of 1825 a company of fifty-two persons, mostly Quakers from the parish of Skjold, was ready to journey to America. They purchased a sloop and a small cargo of iron which would serve as ballast and which might bring them profit in New York, tho this was probably a secondary matter.[11] On the 4th of July, 1825, they set sail from Stavanger, and after a somewhat circuitous voyage of fourteen weeks, which was not very long, as such voyages went, they made their landing in New York, October 9th, numbering fifty-three instead of fifty-two, for a daughter was born to Lars Larson on shipboard.[12] This landing of the "Sloop Folk" of the "Restoration," whose story is a favorite and oft-told one with the older Norwegian immigrants, is occasionally likened to the Landing of the Pilgrim Fathers who fled to a wilderness to escape persecution and to seek social and religious freedom; but on close examination the comparison breaks down at almost every point,—motive, objective, method and result.[13]

[9]O. N. Nelson, "Bemerkning til Prof. Andersons Indledning", *Amerika,* May 2, 1894.

[10]Nelson, *History of the Scandinavians,* I, 134 B-C.

[11]Langeland, *Nordmændene i Amerika,* 11.

[12]C. A. Thingvold gives a list of the names of the "Sloop Folk," save four, which he obtained from one of the survivors, in "The First Norwegian Immigration to America," *The North,* Aug. 10, 1892.

[13]J. B. Wist, *Den Norske Invandring til 1850,* published about 1890, ventures to question seriously whether such a company ever came to the

In New York the captain and mate of the "Restoration" were arrested for having more passengers than the Federal law allowed—two passengers to each five tons of the vessel. Having an excess of twenty, the sloop was legally forfeited to the United States.[14] However, for some unknown reason, the offenders were released and allowed to dispose of their cargo. The original cost of ship and cargo appears to have been about $1950, but both were sold for $400. This inadequate sum was supplemented by the generosity of the Quakers of New York, whose contributions and assistance enabled the "Sloop Folk" to proceed inland to Western New York.

They took up land in Kendall and Orleans County on the shores of Lake Ontario, about thirty-five miles northeast of the new town of Rochester in which two of the families decided to remain. The price of the land was $5 per acre, and each man was to take about 40 acres; but as they were without cash, they agreed to pay for their farms in ten annual instalments. The reasons for selecting this region are not difficult to surmise, tho there is no direct proof of the motive. The country around Rochester was, in 1825, in the midst of a sort of Western "boom"; the Erie Canal was just finished, and the prospects of Rochester were very promising.[15] Its population grew quite marvelously; in September, 1822, it was 2700; in February, 1825, 4274; and in December of the same year, nearly 8,000.[16]

The first five years of the little colony were full of hardships and suffering. It was November of 1825 when they reached their destination; the country was all new and thinly settled; their own land was wild and could be cleared

United States! His reason is that the clearance records of Stavanger show no such name as the "Restauration," and American statistics give the total Scandinavian immigration as 35, of whom 14 are credited to Norway.

[14]*Statutes of the United States, 1819*, Act of March 2.

[15]"Rochester is celebrated all over the Union as presenting one of the most striking instances of rapid increase in size and population, of which the country affords an example." Capt. Basil Hall, *Travels in North America*, I, 153.

[16]*Ibid.*, I, 155.

only with difficulty; and nothing could be grown upon it before the following summer. Just one man among them, Lars Larson, understood any English. By united efforts several families built a log-house, where the winter was spent in a most crowded condition, worse even than the three months in the close quarters of the "Restoration". The only employment by which they could earn anything was threshing with a flail in the primitive fashion of the time, and the wages consisted of the eleventh bushel threshed. With these scanty earnings and the help of kindly neighbors, they passed the dismal winter in a strange land. "They often suffered great need, and wished themselves back in Norway, but they saw no possibility of reaching Norway without sacrificing the last mite of their property, and they would not return as beggars."[17] But at length time, patience, and their own strength and diligence gave them a foothold. The land was cleared and produced enough to support them. A five years' apprenticeship made them masters of the situation; and when at last they had the means to return to the parish of Skjold, the desire had gradually faded out. Instead of re-migration, they were persuading others to join them in the New World.

But the New Norway, or the New Scandinavia, was not to be located in the Middle Atlantic States, though a beginning was made in Delaware and in New York. Land was too dear around the older settlements even at $5 per acre; the promised land was shifted to northern Indiana and northern Illinois, where fine prairie tracts which needed no clearing could be had for $1.25 per acre and upwards. And into these newer regions went the settler and the land speculator, sometimes in one and the same person. Schemes for internal improvement sprouted on every side, and canal-building was much discussed as the best means of providing cheap transportation.[18] One of

[17]Langeland, *Nordmændene i Amerika*, 15.

[18]Ackerman, *Early Illinois Railroads* (No. 23, *Fergus Hist. Ser.*), 19, quoting an editorial form the *Sangamo Journal*, Oct. 31, 1835: "We rejoice to witness the spirit of. internal improvement now manifesting itself in every part of Illinois."

these projects was for a canal from Lake Michigan to the Illinois River, for which a land grant was made in 1827. This canal would bring great prosperity to northern Illinois, it was argued, just as the Erie Canal had developed central and western New York; the price of land would go up, markets would be accessible, and speculator and farmer would reap rich rewards.

Nor was this argument based entirely on theory, for halfway to the East, in Indiana, this progressive realization was in full blast. Harriet Martineau travelled through this part of the West in 1836, and noted with the eye of an acute and experienced observer, the rapid rise in values of farms. She estimated that a settler, judiciously selecting his land in the Northwest, would find it doubled in a single year, and cites the case of a farmer near LaPorte, Indiana, whose 800 acres, costing him $1.25 per acre three years before, had become worth $40 per acre—probably not a unique example of prosperity.[19] With these visions before them, many men moved from western New York, and along the line of the proposed canal in Illinois grew up hamlets bearing the names familiar along the great Erie Canal,— Troy, Seneca, Utica, and Lockport.

Among those attracted thither, was Kleng Peerson, who again served, perhaps without deliberate planning, as a scout for his Quaker friends.[20] On his return to the Orleans County settlers, he convinced them that a better future would open to them in Illinois, and in the spring of 1834 some of the families moved into the West and began the so-called Fox River settlement in the town of Mission near Ottawa, La Salle County, Illinois. By 1836 nearly all the Norwegians of the New York colony had removed to the West, and several tracts of land were taken up in the towns of Mission, Miller, and Rutland. The sections located seem to have been unsurveyed at the time of the first settlement, for no purchases are recorded until 1835.[21]

[19]Martineau, *Society in America,* I, 247, 259, 336.

[20]"I have complete evidence that he visited La Salle County, Illinois, as early as 1833." Anderson, *Norwegian Immigration,* 172.

[21]*Ibid.,* 174, 176 ff.

Henceforth most of the immigration from Norway was turned toward the prairie country, and whole companies of prospective settlers after 1836 went directly to the Fox River nucleus, for the region thereabouts had the double advantage of being at once comparatively easy of access and in the most fertile and promising region in which government land could be had at the minimum price.

In its new location, the twice transplanted colony of "Sloop Folk" was reasonably prosperous from the start, tho the panic of 1837 made impossible any realization of Miss Martineau's roseate estimate of probable profits. No further move of the original immigrants was made, and the Fox River Valley is still occupied by the well-to-do descendants of the Norwegian settlers of the thirties.

As a preliminary to further immigration from the three countries of Northern Europe, a definite knowledge of America and its opportunities must be developed among the peasants, and a desire to remove themselves thither must be awakened and stimulated. To whole communities in Norway, made up of simple, circumscribed people, America about 1835 was an undiscovered country, or at best a far-off land from which no traveller had ever come, and from which no letters were received; the name itself, if known at all, was a recent addition to their vocabulary. Ole Nattestad, one of the early immigrants, who was decently educated for his time and more experienced in the world than the majority of his neighbors, relates how he first heard of America in 1836, when he was a man thirty years old.[22]

The leavening process went on but slowly from 1825 to 1836, for the story of the early experiences of the little company of dissenters, obscure persons from an obscure parish, if known at all, was not likely to inspire others to follow in large numbers. With increasing prosperity in the Rochester, and later in the Fox River, colony, the tone of letters sent back to friends in Norway took a new ring: America came to mean opportunity, and now there were

[22]*Billed Magazin*, I, 83.

men speaking the Norwegian tongue to whom newcomers might go for instruction, advice, and encouragement. Old settlers still bear witness to the great influence of these letters of the thirties telling of American experiences and of American conditions. Among the most influential of these semi-conscious propagandists of emigration was Gjert G. Hovland, who came to the Rochester settlement with his family in 1831, and bought fifty acres of land, which after four years of cultivation he sold at a profit of $500. Writing to a friend near Stavanger in 1835, he spoke in terms of high praise of American legislation, equality, and liberty, contrasting it with the extortion of the Norwegian official aristocracy. He counseled all who could to come to America, as the Creator had nowhere forbidden men to settle where they pleased.[23]   Of this and other letters by Hovland, copies were made by the hundred and circulated in the Norwegian parishes, and many of the early immigrants have stated that they were induced to emigrate by reading these letters.[24]   Another man whose words prompted to emigration, was Gudmund Sandsberg, who came to New York in 1829 with a family of four.[25]

These letters scattered through western Norway from 1830 to 1840, were as seed sown in good ground. Times were hard; money was scarce and its value fluctuating.[26] The crops were often short, the prices of grain were high, and the demand for the labor of the peasants was weak; the economic conditions of the lower classes, especially in the rural districts—much the greater part of the country— were growing worse rather than better.[27]   Even the oldest

[23]Translated from Langeland, *Nordmœndene i Amerika*, 16n. This writer summarizes a letter of which he saw a copy as a young man in Norway.

[24]*Ibid.;* Anderson, *Norwegian Immigration,* 147.

[25]Anderson, *Norwegian Immigration,* 133.

[26]*Billed Magazin,* I, 18-19. Of the year 1836, one writer asserts: "En Daler ei gjældt mere end to norske Skilling," and that many lost all their property.

[27]In Anderson, *Norwegian Immigration,* 133-135, is a translation of a letter written in Hellen in Norway, May 14, 1836: "If good reports

son, who was heir to his father's homestead, was likely to find himself possessed of a debt-burdened estate and with the necessity of providing for the mother and numerous younger children.[28] The younger sons, being still worse off, were forced to try their hands at various occupations to earn a bare living. Ole Nattestad, already mentioned, was by turns before his emigration farmer, peddler, blacksmith, and sheep-buyer.[29] To many a man with a large family of growing children the possibility of disaster in the United States was less forbidding than the probability of ultimate failure in Norway.

But not to occasional letters alone was the peasant,— and the emigration movement—to be left for information and inspiration. Young men who had prospered in the new life returned to the homesteads of their fathers and became, temporarily, missionaries of the new economic gospel, teaching leisurely but effectively by word of mouth and face to face, instead of by written lines at long range. One such man was Knud A. Slogvig, who returned to his home in Skjold in 1835 after ten years in America, not as an emigrant agent nor as a propagandist, but as a lover to marry his betrothed,—an early example which thousands of young Scandinavians in the years to come were to follow gladly.[30] Whatever may have been the results of his visit to Slogvig personally, they were of far-reaching importance to the emigration movement in western Norway. From near and from far, from Stavanger, from Bergen and vicinity, and from the region about Christiansand, people came during the long northern winter, to talk with this experienced and worldly-wise man

come from them (certain emigrants about to sail) the number of emigrants will doubtless be still larger next year. A pressing and general lack of money enters into every branch of business, stops, or at least hampers business, and makes it difficult for many people to earn the necessaries of life. While this is the case on this side of the Atlantic, there is hope of abundance on the other, and this, I take it, is the chief cause of this growing disposition to emigrate."

[28]*Billed Magazin*, I, 6 ff.

[29]*Ibid.*, I, 83.

[30]Anderson, *Norwegian Immigration*, 148.

about life in New York or in Illinois—or, in their own
phrase, "i Amerika." There before them at last, was a
man who had twice braved all the terrors of thousands of
miles of sea and hundreds of miles of far-distant land, who
had come straight and safe from that fabulous vast country, with its great broad valleys and prairies, with its
strange white men, and stranger red men. The "America
fever" contracted in conferences with Slogvig and men of
his kind, was hard to shake off.[31]

The accounts of America given by this emigrant visitor
were so satisfactory, that when he prepared to go back to
the United States in 1836, a large party was ready to go
with him. Instead of the fifty-two who slipped out of
Stavanger, half-secretly in 1825, there were now about 160,
for whose accommodation two brigs, *Norden* and *Den
Norske Klippe,* were specially fitted out.[32] The increased
size of this party was doubtless due in some measure to
discontent with the religious conditions of the kingdom,
but more to the activity of Björn Anderson Kvelve, who
desired to escape the consequences of his sympathy with
Quakerism, and of the marriage which he, the son of a
peasant, had contracted with the daughter of an aristocratic, staunchly Lutheran army officer.[33] Being, as his
son admits, "a born agitator and debater"—others have
called him quarrelsome,—he persuaded several of his
friends to join the party, and he soon became its leader.[34]
The greater part of the two ship-loads, after arrival in
New York, went directly to La Salle County, Illinois, a few
stopping in or near Rochester. For several years after
the arrival of this party, the immigrants from Norway

[31]Langeland, *Nordmændene i Amerika,* 18; *Billed Magazin,* I, 83.
Langeland writes: "Tre af Nedskriverens Paarörende, som reiste fra
Bergen i 1837, var blandt dem, som i Vinteren 1836 besögte ham, og kom
hjem fulde af Amerikafeber."

[32]Langeland, *Nordmændene i Amerika,* 18; *Billed Magazin,* I, 83, 150
(Nattestad's account).

[33]Anderson, *Norwegian Immigration,* 157 ff; *Madison Democrat*
(Wis.), Nov. 8, 1885.

[34]Anderson, *Norwegian Immigration,* 155.

generally directed their course towards the Illinois settlement, which, as a result, grew rapidly and spread into the neighboring towns of Norway, Leland, Lisbon, Morris, and Ottawa.

The actual process of migration from Norway to Illinois or Wisconsin was full of serious difficulty, and to be entered upon by those only who possessed a strong determination and a stout heart. The dangers, discomforts, and hardships which everywhere attended immigration before 1850, were made even more trying, in prospect, by the weird stories of wild Indians, slave-hunters, and savage beasts on land and sea, all of which were thoroly believed by the peasants. Moreover, the church took a hand to prevent emigration, the bishop of Bergen issuing a pastoral letter on the theme: "Bliv i Landet, ernær dig redelig." (Remain in the land and support thyself honestly.)[35] Until a much later time, no port of Norway or Sweden had regular commercial intercourse with the United States, and only by rare chance could passage be secured from Bergen or some southern port direct to New York or Boston. The usual course for those desiring passage to America was to go to some foreign port and there wait for a ship; it was good luck if accommodation were secured immediately and if the expensive waiting did not stretch out two or three weeks. The port most convenient for the Norwegians was Gothenburg in Sweden, from which cargoes of Swedish iron were shipped to America; from that place most of the emigrants before 1840 departed, tho some went by way of Hamburg, Havre, or an English port.

Long after 1850, the immigrants came by sailing vessels because the rates were, on the whole, cheaper than by steamer; those men who had large families were especially urged to take the sailing craft.[36] The days of emigrant agents, through-tickets, and capacious and comparatively comfortable steerage quarters in great ocean liners were far

[35]Langeland, *Nordmændene i Amerika*, 22. He naïvely remarks that the Scandinavians have preferred to follow that other text: "Be fruitful . . . . replenish the earth."

[36]*Billed Magazin*, I, 123-124.

in the future; the usual accommodations were poor and unsanitary; the danger from contagious diseases, scurvy, and actual famine were very real, especially if the voyage, long at the best, was prolonged to four and perhaps five months.[37] The cost of passage varied greatly according to accommodations and according to the port of departure. Sometimes the passage charge included food, bedding, and other necessaries, but usually the passengers were required to furnish these. One company of about 85 in 1837 paid $60 for each adult, and half fare for children, from Bergen to New York.[38] In the same year another company of 93 paid $31 for each adult from Stavanger to New York, without board; still another, numbering about 100, paid $33 1-3 for each adult passenger from Drammen in Norway to New York; the Nattestad brothers paid $50 from Gothenburg to Boston.[39] In 1846, a large party went to Havre, and paid $25 for passage to New York.[40] The extreme figures, therefore, seem to be about $30 and $60 for passage between one of the Scandinavian ports and New York or Boston. When the cost of transportation from the Atlantic seaboard to Illinois and Wisconsin is added to these figures, it will be plain that a considerable sum of ready cash, as well as strength and courage, was necessary for undertaking the transplantation of a whole family from a Norwegian valley in the mountains to an Illinois prairie.

[37]Interview with the late Rev. O. C. Hjort of Chicago, July, 1890, whose party spent five months on the sea.
[38]Langeland, *Nordmændene i Amerika*, 25—"saavidt nu erindres."
[39]*Billed Magazin*, I, 9, 94.
[40]*Ibid.*, I, 388.

CHAPTER IV.

THE RISING STREAM OF NORWEGIAN IMMIGRATION.

The second period of Norwegian immigration, extending from 1836 to 1850, is marked by the strengthening and deepening of the emigration impulse in Norway and by its spread to new districts, and also by the deflection of the course of the rising stream in the United States. Not merely in the vicinity of Stavanger, from which a second party, made up of 93 persons from Egersund, followed the wake of the first and reached Illinois in 1837, but from Bergen and in the districts near it, the "America fever" was spreading. The letters of Hovland circulated there, and at least three men journeyed to interview Slogvig. Knud Langeland, whose little book on the Northmen in America is frequently quoted in these pages, relates how, as a young man of sixteen, his imagination was fired by reading a small volume written by a German and entitled *Journey in America*, which he discovered in the library of a friend in Bergen in 1829; how he read eagerly for several years everything which he could lay hands on relating to America; and how he gathered all possible information about the emigration from England, during a visit to that country in 1834—and then became himself an immigrant.[1]

By 1837 a goodly number were determined to emigrate, and had disposed of their holdings of land. A way opened for them to make the long voyage under especially favorable circumstances. Captain Behrens, owner and commander of the ship *Ægir*, on his return to Bergen in the autumn of 1836, learned that a large party wanted transportation to America. In New York he had seen vessels

[1]Langeland, *Nordmændene i Amerika*, 20-21. See Cobbett, *The Emigrant's Guide* (London, 1829), a typical English guide book of the period.

fitted up for the English and German immigrant traffic; he had learned the requirement of the laws of the United States on the subject; two German ministers who returned to Europe in his ship, gave him further information. He therefore fitted up his vessel for passengers, and carried out his contract to transport to New York the party which finally numbered 84, being mainly made up of married men each with "numerous family," at least one of which counted eight persons.[2] From New York the company proceeded to Detroit, where they were joined by the two Nattestad brothers from Numedal, and from thence they went by water to Chicago.

Their original intention was to go to the La Salle County settlement, but in Chicago they met some of the Fox River people, Björn Anderson among others, who gave such an unfavorable account of conditions in that colony that the majority determined to seek another location. At the instigation of certain Americans, presumably land speculators, a prospecting party of four, including Ole Rynning, one of the leading spirits of the company, went into the region directly south of Chicago and finally chose a site on Beaver Creek. Thither about fifty immigrants went, and began the third Norwegian settlement, which proved to be the most unfortunate one in the history of Norwegian immigration. Log huts were built and the winter passed without unusual hardships, tho it was soon evident that a mistake was made in settling so far from neighbors and from a base of supplies at that time of the year when the soil produced nothing. Serious troubles, however, developed with the spring, and grew with the summer. The land which appeared so dry and so well-covered with good grass when it was selected and purchased in August or September, proved to be so swampy that cultivation was impossible before June. Malaria attacked the settlers, and as they were beyond the reach of medical aid, nearly two-thirds of them died before the end of the summer. The remnant of the colony fled as for their

[2]Langeland, *Nordmændene i Amerika,* 25 ff.

lives, regardless of houses and lands, and scarcely one of them remained on the ground by the end of 1838.[3]

One of the victims of these hard experiences was Ole Rynning, who succumbed to fever in the autumn of 1838. Tho in America scarcely a year and a half, he is one of the uniquely important figures in the history of Norwegian immigration. The son of a curate in Ringsaker in central Norway, and himself dedicated by his parents to the church, he passed the examinations for entrance to the University of Christiania, but turned aside to teaching in a private school near Throndhjem for four years before his emigration.[4] He is invariably spoken of as a man of generous, philanthropic spirit, genuinely devoted to the human needs of his fellow immigrants.

Having learned by personal observation in America the answers to many of the questions which he, as a man of education, had asked himself in Norway, he took advantage of the confinement following the freezing of his feet during a long exploring tour in Illinois, to write a little book of some forty pages, to which he gave the title (in translation) : "A true Account of America, for the Instruction and Use of the Peasants and Common people, written by a Norwegian who arrived there in the Month of June, 1837."[5] The manuscript of this first of many guidebooks for Norwegian emigrants was taken back to Norway by Ansten Nattestad and printed in Christiania in 1838.[6] It plays so large a part in a great movement, that a detailed analysis is worth presenting.

The preface, bearing the author's signature and the date, "Illinois, February 13, 1838," is translated as follows:

"Dear Countrymen,—Peasants and Artisans! I have

[3]Langeland, *Nordmændene i Amerika,* 30 ff; Anderson, *Norwegian Immigration,* 195 ff.

[4]Anderson, *Norwegian Immigration,* 203-205; Langeland, *Nordmændene i Amerika,* 31. Much information regarding Rynning was derived from the Rev. B. J. Muus, of Minnesota, a nephew of Rynning.

[5]Sandfærdig Beretning om Amerika til Veiledning og Hjælp for Bonde og Menigmand, skrevet af en Norsk som kom der i Juni Maaned, 1837."

[6]*Billed Magazin,* I, 94.

now been in America eight months, and in that time I have had an opportunity of finding out much in regard to which I in vain sought information before I left Norway. I then felt how disagreeable it is for those who wish to emigrate to America to be in want of a reliable and tolerably complete account of the country. I also learned how great is the ignorance of the people, and what false and ridiculous reports were accepted as the full truth. In this little book it has, therefore, been my aim to answer every question which I asked myself, and to clear up every point in regard to which I observed that people were ignorant, and to disprove false reports which have come to my ears, partly before I left Norway, and partly after my arrival here."[7]

The body of the book is made up of thirteen chapters devoted to these questions and their answers:

1-3. The location of America, the distance from Norway, the nature of the country, and the reason why so many people go there.

4. "Is it not to be feared that the land will soon be overpopulated? Is it true that the government there is going to prohibit immigration?"

5-6. What part of the land is settled by Norwegians, and how is it reached? What is the price of land, of cattle, of the necessaries of life? How high are wages?

7. "What kind of religion is there in America? Is there any sort of order and government, or can every man do what he pleases?"

8-9. Education, care of the poor, the language spoken in America, and the difficulties of learning it.

10. Is there danger of disease in America? Is there reason to fear wild animals and the Indians?

11. Advice as to the kind of people to emigrate, and warning against unreasonable expectations.

[7]Anderson, *Norwegian Immigration,* 207-208. In making this and the following translations, Mr. Anderson used the copy of Rynning's book belonging to the Rev. B. J. Muus, the only copy known to be in America. This copy is now in the library of the University of Illinois.

12. "What dangers may be expected on the ocean? Is it true that those who are taken to America are sold as slaves?"

13. Advice as to vessels, routes, seasons, exchange of money. etc.

Rynning assured his readers, in the seventh chapter, that America is not a purely heathen country, but that the Christian religion prevails with liberty of conscience, and that "here as in Norway, there are laws, government, and authority, and that the common man can go where he pleases without passport, and may engage in such occupation as he likes."[8] Then follows this strong, significant paragraph, intelligently describing the slavery system, which undoubtedly had a powerful influence on the future location, and hence on the politics, of the immigrants from Scandinavia:

"In the Southern States these poor people (Negroes) are bought and sold like other property, and are driven to their work with a whip like horses and oxen. If a master whips his slave to death or in his rage shoots him dead, he is not looked upon as a murderer. . . . In Missouri the slave trade is still permitted, but in Indiana, Illinois, and Wisconsin Territory it is strictly forbidden, and the institution is strictly despised. . . . There will probably soon come a separation between the Northern and Southern States or a bloody conflict."

From the account given thirty years afterwards by Ansten Nattestad, it appears that a chapter on the religious condition of Norway was omitted by the Rev. Mr. Kragh of Eidsvold, who read the proofs, because of its criticisms of the clergy for their intolerance, and for their inactivity in social and educational reforms.[9] This has led some writers like R. B. Anderson to attribute large weight to religious persecution as a cause of emigration. While religious

[8]Rynning, *Sandfærdig Beretning,* 23, 24. Translated in Anderson, *Norwegian Immigration,* 214-215.

[9]*Billed Magazin,* I, 94.

repression was a real grievance and affected many of the early emigrants, the cases where it was the moving or dominant cause of emigration after 1835 are so few as to be almost negligible.[10]   At best, it re-enforced and completed a determination based on other motives. For most Norwegian dissenters, the Haugians for example, lack of toleration was rather an annoyance than a distress, save, perhaps, for the more persistent and turbulent leaders.[11]   It is hardly fair, therefore, to compare them, as a whole, with the Huguenots of France.[12]

In the years immediately following 1838, the "America Book," distributed from Christiania, went on its missionary journeys and reached many parishes where the disaster at Beaver Creek and the untimely death of Ole Rynning had never been heard of. By its compact information and its intelligent advice, it converted many to the new movement. The diary of Ole Nattestad, printed in Drammen in the same year, seems to have exerted very little influence, but the visit of his brother Ansten to his home in Numedal, in east-central Norway, a hitherto unstirred region, awakened keen and active interest in America, and again men travelled as far as 125 English miles to meet one who had returned from the vast land beyond the Atlantic.[13]

The first party from Numedal left Drammen in the spring of 1839, under the leadership of Nattestad, and went directly to New York. It numbered about one hundred able-bodied farmers with their families, some of them being men with considerable capital. From New York they went to Chicago, expecting to join Ole Nattestad at the Fox River. At the latter city they learned that he had gone into Wisconsin after. his brother left for Norway in 1838, and that he had there purchased land in the township of Clinton in Rock County, thus being probably the first Norwegian settler in Wisconsin. Accordingly the larger part

[10]Letters of R. B. Anderson and J. A. Johnson, *Daily Skandinaven,* Feb. 7, 1896.

[11]Brohough, *Elling Eielsens Liv og Virksomhed,* 10-11, 20-21, 30-36.

[12]Anderson, *Norwegian Immigration,* 50.

[13]*Billed Magazin,* I, 94.

of the Numedal party followed him to the newer region, where better land could be had than any remaining in La Salle County, Illinois, at the minimum price, and took up sections near Jefferson Prairie. Thus the current of Scandinavian settlement was deflected from Illinois to Wisconsin, and later comers from Numedal, in 1840 and afterwards, steered straight for southeastern Wisconsin. In 1839 and later other recruits for the growing and prosperous settlement of Norwegians in Rock County and adjoining counties came from Voss and the vicinity of Bergen. Possibly the difference of dialects had something to do with drawing people from the same province or district into one settlement, but in a general way the same reasons and processes operated among the Norwegian emigrants as among those from Massachusetts, Pennsylvania, and Virginia who settled in various States in sectional groups, sometimes dividing a county by a well-defined line.

Closely connected with this settlement, begun under the leadership of the Nattestad brothers, were other settlements in adjacent townships,—at Rock Prairie or Luther Valley, comprising the present towns of Plymouth, Newark, Avon, and Spring Valley in Rock County, Wisconsin, and Rock Run in Illinois. Through these settlements many new comers filtered and spread out rapidly toward the West and Northwest, reaching in a few years as far as Mineral Point, more than fifty miles from Jefferson Prairie.

Other sections of Norway than those already mentioned began to feel the effects of the emigration bacillus after 1837, and the processes illustrated by the movements from Stavanger, Bergen, and Numedal were repeated— the emigration of two or three, letters sent home, the return of a man here and there, the organization of the party, the long journey, and the selection of the new home. Thelemark, the rugged mountainous district in south central Norway, was in a condition to be strongly moved by stories of freer and larger opportunities. Long before 1837, great tracts of land in Upper Thelemark became the property of two wealthy lumber men, and the tenant-farmers were drawn more and more into work in the lumber mills, to the neglect of farming and grazing. Consequently, when logging was suspended in the hard times, and the wages, already low, were stopped altogether, great distress resulted, and emigration seemed about the only means of escape. "With lack of employment and with impoverishment, debt and discontent appeared as the visible evidences of the bad condition. That was the golden age of the money-lenders and sheriffs. So the America fever raged, and many crossed the ocean in the hope of finding a bit of ground where they could live and enjoy the fruits of their labors without daily anxiety about paydays, rents, and executions."[14]

A company of about forty, representing eleven families from Thelemark, failing to get accommodations with the Nattestad party at Drammen, went on to Skien and thence to Gothenburg, where they secured passage in an American vessel loaded with iron, and made the voyage to Boston in two months.[15] Three weeks more were consumed in the circuitous journey to Milwaukee by way of New York, Albany, the Erie Canal and the Great Lakes. Like several other parties of that year they originally aimed at Illinois.[16] But their boat "leaked like a sieve," and the stop at Milwaukee was probably precautionary. Instead of proceeding further, they were persuaded to send a committee, under the guidance of an American, into the present county of Waukesha, where they selected a tract about fourteen miles southwest of Milwaukee, on the shore of Lake Muskego.[17] Here each adult man took up forty acres at the usual minimum price of $1.25 per acre, and so began

[14] Translated from *Billed Magazin*, I, 18 ff.

[15] *Ibid*, 6-7.

[16] A shipping notice in the *Boston Daily Advertiser*, Aug. 1, 1839 reads: "Passengers,—in the "Venice" from Gothenburg, 67 Norwegians on their way to Illinois."

[17] An oft-repeated story tells how the company was persuaded to remain in Wisconsin by some enterprising Milwaukee men who pointed out to the immigrants a fat, healthy-looking man as a specimen of what Wisconsin would do for a man, and a lean, sickly-looking man as a warning of what the scorching heats and fever of Illinois would quickly do to a man who settled there. See *Billed Magazin*, I, 7.

the Muskego colony proper, the name, Muskego, however, being later applied to the group of settlements in Waukesha County and to several towns in Racine County.[18] Like the colony in Rock County, the Muskego group grew rapidly in spite of malarial troubles, and for ten years it was an objective point for immigrants from Thelemark, and a halting place for those bound for the frontier farther west in Wisconsin or in Iowa.

As the emigration movement from Norway increased, the planning of settlements and the organization of parties took on a more definite and business-like air. The process is well illustrated in the case of the town of Norway in Racine County, Wisconsin, which was one of the most successfully managed settlements in the Northwest. In the fall of 1839, two intelligent men of affairs, Sören Bakke, the son of a rich merchant of Drammen, and John Johnson (Johannes Johannesson), came to America on a prospecting tour, for the purpose of finding a place where they might invest money in land as a foundation for a colony, which they may possibly have intended to serve as a new home for a sect of dissenters known as Haugians.[19] After visiting Fox River in Illinois, and various locations in Wisconsin, they found a tract that suited them—good land, clear water, and abundance of game and fish, enough to satisfy the most fastidious. This they purchased, building a cabin on it and awaiting the coming of their friends to whom they sent a favorable report.[20] The party arrived in the autumn of 1840, under the leadership of Even Heg, an innkeeper of Leir, who brought still more money, which was also invested in land. Altogether, the money which Bakke brought with him, or received later, amounted to $6000.[21] It was all used for purchasing land, which was either sold to well-to-do immigrants, or leased to new comers. This business was supplemented by a store kept in the first cabin. Upon the death of Johnson in 1845, Bakke

[18]*Billed Magazin*, I, 10.
[19]*Ibid.*, I, 12.
[20]*Ibid.*, I, 18.
[21]*Ibid.*, I, 12.

went home and settled upon an estate owned by his father in Leir, one of the first of the very small number of men who have returned to permanent residence in Norway after some years spent in America.[22] Even Heg became the real head of the colony at Norway, Wisconsin, after the departure of Bakke, whose interests he continued to look after, and under his management a steady development followed. This settlement became the Mecca of hundreds of immigrants arriving in Milwaukee in the late forties, and "Heg's barn was for some months every summer crowded with newcomers en route for some place farther west."[23]

Another important and highly prosperous group of settlements, called Koshkonong after the lake and creek of that name, sprang up in 1840 and 1841, in the southwestern corner of Jefferson County, Wisconsin, and the adjacent parts of Dane and Rock Counties. The beginning was made by men who removed thither from the Fox River and Beaver Creek localities after investigating the lands in Wisconsin. In 1840 there were nine entries of land by Norwegians in the present townships of Albion, Christiana, and Deerfield, the usual purchase being eighty acres; the next few years saw the spread of the colony to the townships of Pleasant Valley and Dunkirk, from the influx of immigrants from Illinois and from Norway.[24] After the stress and hardship of the first pioneer years, the fortunate choice of location in one of the best agricultural sections of Wisconsin told very promptly, and Koshkonong became "the best known, richest, and most interesting Norwegian settlement in America, the destination of thousands of pilgrims from the fatherland since 1840."[25] Many of the farms are still in possession of the families of the original settlers, whose children are prominent in business, professional and political circles.

[22]*Ibid.;* Anderson, *Norwegian Immigration,* 280 ff.

[23]Langeland, *Nordmændene i Amerika,* 44; *Billed Magazin,* I, 13.

[24]Anderson, *Norwegian Immigration,* 326 ff. Anderson quotes in full a letter from the United States Commissioner of Land Office giving date and extent of each entry by Norwegians.

[25]M. W. Odland, *Amerika,* Jan. 15, 1904.

The movement of the stream of Norwegian immigrants after 1845 was distinctly in a direction westward from the Wisconsin settlements; the land farther out on the prairies was better, tho it did not have the combination of timber and stream or lake which the early settlers insisted on having, often to their detriment, since land chosen with reference to these requirements was apt to be marshy. The fresh arrivals, after a few weeks or months in the friendly and helpful communities of early immigrants, were better prepared by a partial acclimatization, by knowledge of the steps necessary for acquiring citizenship and land-ownership, and by the formation of definite plans of procedure, for the next stage in the western course of their empire. Occasionally a shrewd farmer of the older companies took advantage of the rise in the value of his farm, sold out, and bought another tract farther out on the frontier, perhaps repeating the process two or three times.[26]   John Nelson Luraas, for example, was one of those men who first spent some time in Muskego, then bought land in Norway, Racine County; after improving it for three years, he sold it in 1843 and moved into Dane County.[27] Here he lived for twenty-five years, and then moved into Webster County, Iowa, taking up new land. After a few years he went back to his Dane County property, where he spent another thirteen years; finally, as an aged, retired, wealthy farmer, he died in the village of Stoughton in 1890.[28]

Provision for religious instruction and ministration was one of the early concerns of the Norwegian immigrants, as would be expected from a people essentially religious, who moved by whole families. Nor was there much distinction between the more orthodox and the dissenters. After their magnetic center shifted to the west in 1835 and the settlements and population multiplied, a good deal of lay preaching of one sort and another went on,—Lutheran,

[26]Langeland, *Nordmændene i Amerika,* 44-45; *Billed Magazin,* I, 13.

[27]It may be well to note that the name of Dane county has no relation to Scandinavian settlement, but was given in honor of Nathan Dane of Massachusetts, author of the Northwest Ordinance of 1787.

[28]Anderson, *Norwegian Immigration,* 276.

Methodist, Haugian, Baptist, Episcopalian, and Mormon. Lay services, in fact, were the rule all along the westward moving frontier, and services conducted by regular clergymen the exception. One of the Norwegians wrote: "We conducted our religious meetings in our own democratic way. We appointed our leader and requested some one to read from a book of sermons. . . . We prayed, exhorted, and sang among ourselves, and even baptised our babies ourselves."[29]

Cut off by language from much participation in English worship—a man must know an alien tongue long and thoroly to make it serviceable for religious purposes—the men from Numedal, Vos, and Drammen, felt keenly a great need for some one to instruct their children in the Norwegian language and in the Lutheran religion after the Old World customs. In 1843, two hundred men and women in the flourishing group of settlements around Jefferson Prairie, Wisconsin, signed a petition addressed to Bishop Sörenson in Norway asking him to send them a capable and pious young pastor, to whom they promised to give a parsonage, 80 acres of land, $300 in money, and fees for baptisms, marriages, and the like.[30] Tho this petition itself seems not to have been answered, it was not long before a properly ordained clergyman arrived.

Claus Lauritz Clausen, a Danish student of theology seeking employment as a tutor in Norway, was persuaded, probably by the father of Sören Bakke in Drammen, to heed the call from America.[31] On his arrival in the West in 1843, he found the need for a pastor and preacher more urgent than for a teacher, and accordingly he sought and received ordination at the hands of a German Lutheran minister, October, 1843.[32] He proceeded to organize, in Heg's barn at Norway, the first congregation of Norwegian Lutherans in the United States, and so began a career of

[29]A letter of John E. Molee, February, 1895, quoted by Anderson, *Norwegian Immigration*, 320. (See also, *ibid.*, 396-399.)

[30]Anderson, *Norwegian Immigration*, 255.

[31]Nelson, *Scandinavians in the United States*, (2d ed.) 387 ff.

[32]Bothne, *Kort Udsigt*, 835 ff.

useful ministration which lasted nearly half a century. Not long after his ordination, its validity was called in question by strict Lutherans. The question was finally submitted to the theological faculty of the University of Christiania, which decided that "the circumstance that an ordination is performed by a minister and not by a bishop, cannot in itself destroy the validity of the ministerial ordination."[33] At any rate, Clausen's activity, general helpfulness, staunchness of convictions, and length of service, if not his ordination, make him one of the typical pioneer preachers.[34]

Another clergyman of the same class as Clausen, was Elling Eielsen, a Haugian lay-preacher who went from place to place in the Northwest from 1839 to 1843, holding services with his countrymen. He was ordained in the same month as Clausen, and, like him, in a semi-valid fashion, by a Lutheran clergyman, not a bishop.[35] Like Clausen, also, his term of labors as a Haugian apostle, passed forty years.[36]

Whatever irregularities in the ordination of Clausen or of Eielsen may have disturbed the consciences of the stricter of the Lutheran sect, nothing of the sort attached to the Rev. Johannes Wilhelm Christian Dietrichson, who arrived in 1844, fresh from the University of Christiania and from the ordaining hands of the Bishop of Christiania. He was a diligent, aggressive, zealous young man of about thirty, sent out as a kind of home missionary in foreign parts at the expense of a wealthy dyer of Christiania. For two years, summer and winter, he went back and forth in

[33]Jacobs, *Evangelical Lutheran Church,* 411.

[34]Bothne, *Kort Udsigt,* 835; Jensson, *American Lutheran Biographies,* "Clausen."

[35]Brohough, *Elling Eielsens Liv og Virksomhed,* ch. II, and App.

[36]Nelson, in his *Scandinavians in the United States,* 388, is probably mistaken in stating that Eielsen built the first Norwegian church and organized the first congregation in 1842 at Fox River, confusing the fact that Eielsen had built a log house on his own land, and held religious services in the loft, with the possibility of the formation of a congregation. Eielsen's biographer makes no mention of his organization of a regular congregation. Brohough, *Elling Eielsens Liv og Virksomhed,* 61.

southern Wisconsin ministering to the Norwegians of all ages and beliefs,—and all for the stipend of $300 yearly.[37] One of the results of these labors, was a little book, *Reise blandt de norske Emigranter i "de forenede nordameri-kanske Fristater,"* in which Dietrichson gives the earliest detailed account of the settlements in Wisconsin and Illinois before 1846. He described the origin, numbers, conditions, and prospects of each community in his wide parish. At Fox River, he says he found about 500, who were of all creeds, mostly dissenters, including 150 Mormons.

Three church edifices were erected in 1844-5, and dedicated within a short time of each other. Dietrichson dedicated one at Christiana, Dane County, Wisconsin, December 19, 1844, and another at Pleasant Valley a little further west; Clausen dedicated his church at Muskego on March 13, 1845.[38] All were simple structures, as would be expected; a plain table was the altar, and the baptismal font was hewn out of an oak log. But they served none the less as effective and inspiring centers of the religious life of the settlements. For the Muskego church, Even Heg gave the land, and Mr. Bakke of Drammen, whose protégé Clausen was, gave $400 towards construction. Dietrichson left his two churches in Koshkonong in 1845, and returned to Norway where he remained about a year. Aided by benevolent friends and by the Norwegian government, he came back to his prairie parishes in 1846 for a final stay of four years.[39] But his ways were not altogether ways of pleasantness, nor entirely in the paths of peace. The records of the church, and his own story, show that he had more than one stormy time with his people.[40] He departed

---

[37]*Minde fra Jubelfesterne paa Koshkonong* (1894), 54 ff; Bothne, *Kort Udsigt,* 839-842.

[38]Dietrichson, *Reise blandt de norske Emigranter,* 45 ff; *Minde fra Jubelfesterne paa Koshkonong.*

[39]*Nordlyset,* Sept. 9, 1847.

[40]Dietrichson, *Reise blandt de norske Emigranter,* 57-67. Some of the church records are printed in *The Milwaukee Sentinel,* July 21, 1895.

for Norway in 1850, and never again was in America.[41]

The preceding account of the beginnings and progress of the earliest Norwegian settlements in Illinois and Wisconsin has been given in some detail, for the reason that the course of these settlements, in a very broad sense, is typical of all the Norwegian colonization in the Northwest, and of the Swedish and Danish as well. In the later chapter on economic conditions, the causes which led these people to settle upon the land rather than in the cities will be discussed at length. Suffice it here to say that the average immigrant brought only a small amount of cash, along with his strong desire for land, and he consequently went where good land was cheap, in order the more speedily to get what he wanted. This meant that he would push out on the newly accessible government land in Iowa, Minnesota, and the Dakotas in turn. So the transformation of the frontier has witnessed the continual repetition of the experiences of the early Norwegian immigrants in Illinois and Wisconsin in the years from 1835 to 1850, as they are described in this and the preceding chapters. At the present time, in the remoter parts of the Dakotas, Montana, Washington, Oregon, and Utah, the same story is being retold in the same terms of patience, hardship, thrift, and final success.

[41]The following year he published a second book, *Nogle Ord fra Prædikestolen i Amerika.*

CHAPTER V.

When the Swedish emigration of the nineteenth century began, it is doubtful if many persons in Sweden knew of the existence of the descendants of their compatriots of the seventeenth. The last Swedish pastor of Gloria Dei Church in Philadelphia died in 1831, and there is no evidence that any immigrant after 1800 turned his steps toward Philadelphia or the valley of the Delaware expecting to join the third or fourth generation of Swedes there.[1] Before 1840, in New York, Philadelphia, and a few other places, a Swede might now and then be found. One of these adventure-seeking young fellows was Erick Ålund, who reached Philadelphia in 1823; another was O. C. Lange who arrived in Boston in 1824, and by 1838 found himself in Chicago, probably the first of that mighty company of Swedes which has made Chicago the third Swedish city in the world.[2] Olof Gustaf Hedström, who left Sweden in 1825, and his brother Jonas, were influential early arrivals.[3] But the number of such men could not have been large, for ignorance as to America was quite as dense in Sweden as in Norway, the name being all but unheard of in parts of the kingdom.[4]

Sixteen years elapsed after the "Sloop Folk" landed in New York, and five years after they located in their second American home, in Illinois, before the Swedish immigration

[1] Winsor, *Narrative and Critical History of America*, IV, 488.

[2] Interview with Capt. O. C. Lange in Chicago, March, 1890. He stated that he was the only Swede in Chicago in 1838, but that there were thirty or forty Norwegians "who were doing anything for a living, even begging,"— but Capt. Lange was an ardent Swede and despised Norwegians!

[3] Norelius, *Svenskarnes Historia*, 23-26.

[4] Mikkelsen, *The Bishop Hill Colony*, 26.

really began. The first party, or regular company, of Swedes, consisting of about twelve families, arrived in 1841 under the leadership of Gustav Unonius, a young man who had been a student at the University of Upsala.[5] It was made up of the "better folk", and included some, like Baron Thott, who were entitled to be called "Herr."[6] The immigration does not appear to have been induced by any religious persecution or discontent, but was purely a business venture of a somewhat idealistic sort, into which the immigrants put their all, in the hope that they could get a more satisfactory return than they could from a like investment in Sweden.

From New York the party went by the water route to Milwaukee, following in the wake of parties of Norwegians. There they met Captain Lange, who seems to have persuaded them to select a location near Pine Lake—a name that would certainly attract a Swede—in the neighborhood of the present town of Nashotah, about thirty miles west of Milwaukee. Here they were later joined by a variegated assortment of characters attracted by letters which Unonius wrote to newspapers in Sweden,—noblemen, ex-army officers, merchants, and adventurers,[7] so that the colony took on almost as motley an air as that at Jamestown in the first years after 1607. While they hardly could have succeeded under more favorable circumstances, they were particularly unfitted by their previous manner of living to become farmers or to undergo the deprivations and hardships of pioneering. The winter of 1841-2 was severe, and their poorly-built houses gave inadequate protection against the cold of January and February in Wisconsin;

[5]Norelius, *Svenskarnes Historia*, 2 ff. The early history of the Swedish immigration is treated in a much more complete and scholarly fashion than is the Norwegian, in the works of Unonius, Norelius, and Peterson and Johnson. For this reason, and because of the similarity of the early Swedish and Norwegian movements, the Swedish settlements are not followed up in this study with the same detail as the Norwegian.

[6]Unonius, *Minnen*, I, 5 ff; *History of Waukesha County, Wis.*, 748.

[7]"and a large proportion of criminals," Nelson, *Scandinavians in the United States*, II, 117.

their land was badly tilled, tho they labored earnestly; and their first crop fell short of their necessities. Their hope of leading an Arcadian life in America was rudely shattered. Captain von Schneidau, late of the staff of King Oscar, was a farm laborer, and Baron Thott became a cook for one of the settlers in order to get a bare living.[8] Sickness, misfortune, want of labor, and lack of money led to almost incredible suffering at the first, and some of the settlers, like Unonius and von Schneidau, went to Chicago, where the former became pastor of a Swedish congregation, and the latter prospered as "the most skilful daguerreotypist, probably, in the whole state."[9]

Frederika Bremer, the famous Swedish traveller, visited both the Norwegian and the Swedish settlements in Wisconsin in 1850, and has left a very graphic and sympathetic account of the Pine Lake colony where she spent a few days.[10] She found about a half dozen families of Swedes. "Nearly all live in log-houses, and seem to be in somewhat low circumstances. The most prosperous seemed to be that of the smith; he, I fancy, had been a smith in Sweden. . . . ; he was a really good fellow, and had a nice young Norwegian for his wife; also a Mr. Bergman who had been a gentleman in Sweden, but who was here a clever, hard-working peasant farmer."[11] At one of the houses she met twenty-one Swedish settlers. The failure of the colony, to Miss Bremer's mind, was not altogether due to circumstances; the settlers at first "had taken with them the Swedish inclination for hospitality and a merry life, without sufficiently considering how long it could last. Each family built for itself a necessary abode, and then invited

[8]*History of Waukesha County, Wisconsin*, 749.

[9]Bremer, *Homes of the New World*, II, 214-217. Miss Bremer relates how Mrs. von Schneidau "had seen her first-born little one frozen to death in its bed," and how Mrs. Unonius "that gay, high-spirited girl, of whom I heard when she was married at Upsala to accompany her husband to the New World . . . had laid four children to rest in foreign soil."

[10]*Ibid.*, 225-235.

[11]*Ibid.*, 225; Unonius, *Minnen*, II, 6 ff.

their neighbors to a feast. They had Christmas festivities and Midsummer dances."[12]

Notwithstanding the hard life of the first years at Pine Lake, the letters from well-educated and well-known men like Unonius, especially those published in the Swedish newspapers, helped to stimulate a desire for emigration in Sweden. A company of fifty, from Haurida in Smaaland, left in the autumn of 1844, part of them going to Wisconsin, and at least one family going to Brockton, Massachusetts, and beginning the considerable Swedish settlement in that city.[13] In the following year, five families were influenced by letters from a Pine Lake settler, to leave their homes in Östergötland, and to set out for Wisconsin. At New York, however, they were persuaded, probably by Pehr Dahlberg, to go to Iowa, then just admitted to the Union, where land was supposed to be better than at Pine Lake, and could be had at the same price. The route followed was an unusual one for Scandinavian immigrants,—from New York to Pittsburg, down the Ohio River, and up the Mississippi. The location finally chosen was in Jefferson County, Iowa, about forty-two miles west of Burlington; and the settlement was christened New Sweden. To it many immigrants from the parishes of Östergötland found their way in later years. The second rural settlement of the Swedes thus established was, quite in contrast to the first one, distinctly successful from the start.[14]

The first Swedish settlements in Illinois, may be traced to the efforts of the brothers Hedström already mentioned. Olof visited his old home in 1833, after an absence of eight years, and on his return to New York he was accompanied by his brother Jonas.[15] These two men influenced the course which Swedish immigrants were to

[12]Bremer, *Homes of the New World,* II, 214.

[13]Norelius, *Svenskarnes Historia,* 27.

[14]G. T. Flom, "Early Swedish Immigration to Iowa," *Iowa Journal of History and Politics,* III, 601 ff. (Oct., 1905) ; Norelius, *Svenskarnes Historia,* 27.

[15]Norelius, *Svenskarnes Historia,* 21.

take in America down to 1854, in much the same way as the Nattestad brothers had earlier affected the Norwegians. After several years, spent presumably in New York, Jonas moved into Illinois and settled in the township of Victoria, in Knox County.[16] Olof Hedström was converted to Methodism in America, and became a zealous minister of that church; in the history of Methodism in New York City and in the chronicles of Scandinavian immigration, his is a unique figure. The needs of the multiplying hosts of immigrants of all sorts, who were flocking to New York, were thoroughly understood by the Methodist authorities of that city, and Hedström was put in charge of the North River Mission for Seamen. His "Bethel Ship" work began about 1845, a time when there was great need for a helping hand to be extended to the Scandinavians, among other immigrants, for whom agents, "runners," and "sharks" were lying in wait. The Rev. E. Norelius, the cultivated and scholarly pastor and historian, who had personal experience of the kindly offices of Hedström, declares that the missionary was a father to the Scandinavian people who came to America by way of New York.[17]

With Olof Hedström offering friendly greeting, help, and advice in New York, and working in connection with his brother Jonas in Illinois, no prophetic instinct was needed to foretell the goal which would be ultimately sought by those who came under the benevolent ministrations of this Swedish Methodist preacher. The path to Illinois became a highway for multitudes of Swedes, and that State was to the Swedish immigration what Wisconsin was to the Norwegian.

Swedish settlement on a large scale began in 1846, with the founding at Bishop Hill, in Henry County, Illinois, of the famous Jansonist colony, whose history is exceedingly interesting and, at times, highly pathetic. Not only were there many hundreds of Swedes and some Norwegians grouped together in a single county, but the colony

[16]*Ibid.*, 24-26; Johnson and Peterson, *Svenskarne i Illinois*, 286.

[17]Norelius, *Svenskarnes Historia*, 21, 23-26.

was also an experiment in communism, based on peculiar religious tenets.[18]

The Jansonist movement in Sweden, which must not be confused with the Jansenist school or system of doctrine of another time and place in Western Europe, began about 1842 in Helsingland, in the prosperous agricultural province of Norrland.[19] For fifteen years there had been an undercurrent of dissent in the Established Church in that province, led by Jonas Olson, who called his followers "Devotionalists." The agitation was carried on primarily against the general ignorance of the people and the sloth of the clergy, but not until Eric Janson appeared on the scene did any organization of the dissenters take definite form. When he moved from Wermland to Helsingland in 1844 and published the high claim that he represented the second coming of Christ and was sent to restore the purity and glory of Christianity, he was received with great enthusiasm by the restless peasants, and accepted as a divinely appointed leader who should gather the righteous into a new theocratic community.[20]

The progress of the dissenting sect was so rapid that the Established Church, backed by the civil authorities, took stern measures to suppress the heresy. It must be confessed that the dissenters continued to show a fanatical spirit, and gave the ecclesiastical officers special cause for alarm. In June, 1844, for example, the Jansonists made an immense bonfire near Tranberg, and burned as useless and dangerous, all the religious books which they could lay their hands on, with the exception of the Bibles, hymn-books, and catechisms. As if one offense of this kind were

[18]The history of this Swedish settlement, with its numerous peculiarities, its prosperity and its misfortunes, has been so often written up with considerable detail, that only the outlines of it are given here. See Bibliography.

[19]Mikkelsen, *The Bishop Hill Colony*, 19 ff.

[20]*Ibid.*, 25. "The glory of the work which is to be accomplished by Eric Janson, standing in Christ's stead, shall far exceed that of the work accomplished by Jesus and his Apostles,"—quoted in translation by Mikkelsen from *Cateches, af Eric Janson* (Söderhamn, 1846), 80.

not enough to shock the pious Lutherans and everywhere stir up the zeal of the Lutheran clergy, a second burning of books followed in October, in which the Bible alone was spared.[21]

Janson was repeatedly arrested and imprisoned; his followers were subjected to the same treatment; and finally, a price was put upon the head of the pestilent arch-heretic. It was these persecutions, supplemented by letters from a Swedish immigrant in America, which turned the thoughts of the Jansonists towards the United States. So it happened that when Janson was rescued by his friends from the crown officer who had him in custody, he was spirited off over the mountains to Norway, and thence to Copenhagen, where he embarked for America. In New York he met Olof Olson, the "advance agent," who was sent out by the new sect in 1845 to spy out the better country where there was no established church, no persecution for conscience's sake, and no aristocracy.[22] Olson met Olof Hedström on landing in New York, and by him was directed to his brother Jonas in Illinois, who gave the new-comer a hospitable reception, and assistance in a prospecting tour of Illinois, Wisconsin, and Iowa. Olson decided on Illinois as the State in which to plant the proposed colony. On the arrival of Eric Janson in 1846, the exact site in Henry County was selected, and the name Bishop Hill given it after Biskopskulla, Janson's birthplace in Sweden.[23]

Janson appointed leaders for the would-be emigrants, —captains of tens and of hundreds—before he left Sweden, and under their guidance several parties made their way to Henry County in 1846, usually going by way of New York, the Erie Canal, and the Great Lakes. Nearly 1100 persons were ready to emigrate, but, like the early Norwegians, they experienced great difficulty in securing passage, being compelled to go in companies of fifty or one

[21]Mikkelsen, *The Bishop Hill Colony*, 22; Norelius, *Svenskarnes Historia*, 63.

[22]Mikkelsen, *The Bishop Hill Colony*, 24.

[23]Johnson and Peterson, *Svenskarne i Illinois*, 26; *History of Henry County, Illinois*.

hundred in freight vessels, usually loaded with iron.[24] The greater number sailed from Gefle, though some went from Gothenburg and some from Stockholm.[25]

The greater part of these emigrating Jansonists were poor peasants, unable from their own means to bear for themselves and their families the great expense of the long journey from Helsingland to Illinois. In addition to other difficulties some of them had to purchase release from military service. It was to solve these problems of poverty and expense, that Janson followed the example of other leaders of religious sects, even of the early Christian leaders, and instituted community of goods for the whole sect. The pretext seems to have been religious, but from this distance it is clear that the motive of the leader was essentially economic and philanthropic. Nothing could better attest the tremendous earnestness of these uneducated enthusiasts than their implicit obedience to the commands of Eric Janson, for they gave all they had into his care and discretion—their property, their families, and themselves. The amounts contributed to the common treasury after the sale of individual property varied greatly, of course. Some turned in almost nothing, while others gave sums reaching as high as 24,000 kroner, or about $6,500.[26]

The methods and practices of the sect are revealed, in unsympathetic and perhaps exaggerated fashion, in a printed letter, dated at New York, May 23, 1847, written by one who found himself unequal to the high demands of the new faith and its self-appointed apostle.[27] This backslider, who emigrated with the rest, tells a story that sounds strangely like accounts of the action of more recent sects and their "divinely ordained" prophets and priestesses. Janson and all his works are denounced in very

[24]Swainson in *Scandinavia*, Jan., 1885.

[25]Mikkelsen, *The Bishop Hill Colony*, 28.

[26]Johnson and Peterson, *Svenskarne i Illinois*, 28.

[27]This account is contained in a small pamphlet, signed O. S., which was unearthed in the Royal Library in Stockholm while the author was searching there in 1890 for material on Swedish emigration.

bitter terms. After a five-months voyage not more than fifty out of three hundred, says the writer of the letter, were well, and many were suffering from scurvy; but Janson's "prophets" came aboard and "tried to work miracles and heal the sick," even damning those who did not believe they were well when they were raised up. He further says that the Jansonists were warned in Illinois to use medicine or the government would take a hand in their affairs. The letter closes with a statement that more than a hundred had already left the society.

The colony had a homestead at the outset, for Janson and his co-workers purchased for $2000 a tract of 750 acres, part of which was under cultivation. By the end of 1846, new recruits brought the number in the settlement up to about 400 souls, who were accommodated in log-houses, sod-houses, dug-outs, and tents. A church was improvised out of logs and canvas, and services were held daily at half past five in the morning and in the evening. In spite of the community of goods, the first year with its crowding brought much suffering; the funds of the society were depleted by the expenses of the great journey for so many people, and by the expenditures for land.

With the coming of spring in 1847, the settlement became a hive of industry. Adobe bricks were made, a new saw-mill was erected, better houses were built, and more land was bought to accommodate the new arrivals. By 1850 the community owned fourteen hundred acres of land, nearly free from debt. The religious or economic attractiveness of the colony is evidenced by the fact that its population in 1851 reached the considerable figure of about eleven hundred,[28] nearly one-third of the total population of Henry County, notwithstanding a schism in 1848 whose centrifugal force drove upwards of 200 from the fold, and notwithstanding the epidemic of cholera in 1849 which claimed 150 victims. Among these hundreds were representatives of almost every province in Sweden.

[28]Swainson puts the number of seceders at 250, and asserts that they were drawn off by Jonas Hedström, the Methodist. *Scandinavia*, Jan., 1885. Mikkelsen, *The Bishop Hill Colony*, 33, 35, 37.

The communistic principle worked well, at least in the first years, in spite of the severity of the religious discipline. The land was thoroughly cultivated. The growing of flax became a prominent factor in the prosperity of the colony, and from this crop were made linen and carpeting which found a ready market, the product of the looms reaching 30,579 yards in 1851.[29]

The death of Eric Janson by the hands of a Swedish adventurer, John Root (or Rooth), with whom he had a quarrel of long standing, removed the prophet and builder of this New Jerusalem, but did not seriously interrupt its development. In fact it might be said to have been a benefit to the colony, for Janson was not a careful and skilful man of business, and he had involved the community in debt. To relieve this pressure of obligation, Jonas Olson, Janson's right-hand man, was sent out with eight others, in March, 1851, to seek a fortune in the California gold fields.[30]

The period of which this chapter treats ends with 1850; but inasmuch as that year marks no break in the history of Bishop Hill, it will be well here to finish the sketch of the development of that colony. On learning of the death of Janson, Olson returned at once from California and became the head of the colony after February, 1851. Improvements immediately followed; the government, which had been autocratic or theoretically theocratic, became more and more democratic under Olson. Finally, as a completion of this broadening evolution, an act of the Illinois legislature of 1853 incorporated the Bishop Hill Colony, and vested the government in a board of seven trustees who were to hold for life or during good behavior, their successors to be elected by the community.[31]

The trustees were from the first afflicted with a speculative mania, and invested in all sorts of enterprises—in grain, in lumber, in Galva town lots, in railroad and bank

[29]Johnson and Peterson, *Svenskarne i Illinois,* 335.
[30]*Ibid.,* 39.
[31]Act of January 17, 1853. The Charter and Bylaws are reprinted in Mikkelsen, *The Bishop Hill Colony,* 73 ff. (App.).

stock, and in a porkpacking establishment. Disaster after disaster followed between 1854 and 1857, when a general panic prostrated the industries of the country. The climax of the reckless mismanagement of the Colony came in 1860, and the corporation went into the hands of a receiver, only to get deeper and deeper into financial and legal troubles. Individualization of property took place in 1861, when $592,798 was distributed among 415 shareholders, and other property to the value of $248,861 was set aside to pay an indebtedness of about $118,000.[32] The last traces of communism were gone, and with the disappearance of communism went also the old religious tenets peculiar to the faith. The majority of the Jansonists joined the Methodist communion; even Jonas Olson deserted and became "an independent Second [Seventh?] Day Adventist."[33]

Difficulties continued, however, for Olof Johnson, the chief offending trustee, secured his appointment as one of the receivers. Assessment followed assessment, and when the totals were footed up the chicanery of trustees and receivers was made clear: to pay an original debt of $118,403, these ill-fated people of the Bishop Hill Colony actually expended in cash $413,124, and in property $259,786, or an aggregate of $672,910.[34] Of course a lawsuit was begun, and the "Colony Case" dragged along in the courts for twelve years, to be finally settled by compromise in 1879, nine years after the death of Olof Johnson.[35]

Besides the numerous companies which went to Bishop Hill, many others between 1846 and 1850 sought different localities in the United States.[36] Some remained in Chicago; some built homes in Andover, Illinois; others began the large Swedish settlement in Jamestown, New York;

[32]Johnson and Peterson, *Svenskarne i Illinois*, 44 ff.

[33]Mikkelsen, *The Bishop Hill Colony*, 71.

[34]Johnson and Peterson, *Svenskarne i Illinois*, 49-52.

[35]The special master in chancery found in 1868 that Olof Johnson was indebted to the Colony in the sum of $109,613.29. Mikkelsen, *The Bishop Hill Colony*, 68.

[36]Norelius, *Svenskarnes Historia*, 30-38.

while still others were persuaded to go to Texas, thus beginning the only considerable permanent settlement of Scandinavians in the Southern States before 1880, with the exception of settlements in Missouri. During these years, knowledge of the prosperous condition of the immigrants was spreading, in the usual fashion, into every province of Sweden; Småland, Helsingland, Dalarne, and Östergötland, were especially affected. Not merely were Jansonists and dissenters moved to emigrate, but men of the Established Church as well; a Jansonist's word in matters of faith, Scriptural interpretation, and religious practice was worse than worthless to staunch Lutherans, but there was no reason to doubt the accuracy of his statements regarding land, wages, prices, and opportunities in Illinois or Iowa. Even Lutheran clergymen began to lead little companies of their adherents to the "States," and no one considered it a mortal sin or eternal danger to follow in the footsteps of worldly-wise heretics.[37]

[37]Norelius, *Svenskarnes Historia,* 34.

CHAPTER VI.

THE DANISH IMMIGRATION.

The Danish immigration began much later than the Norwegian and Swedish, and its proportions were inconsiderable until after the Civil War. Not until 1869 did the annual influx of Danes reach 2,000. Tho the population of Denmark was and is somewhat greater than Norway's, yet the Danish immigration has never in any one year equalled the Norwegian, and in but seven years has it been more than one-half. As against Norway's total of nearly 600,000 from 1820 to 1905, Denmark's is only about 225,000.[1] In calculating the immigration, however, a large allowance must be made. Since the duchies of Schleswig and Holstein were acquired by Prussia in 1864 and 1866, their emigrants have of course been recorded as German. Nevertheless, taken as a whole, the movement from Denmark has lacked momentum; its proportions are relatively small; and the influence of the Danes in the United States is much less important than that of either of the other Scandinavian nationalities.

The causes of the smaller emigration from Denmark are to be found in the nature of the people and in the conditions of the kingdom itself. Generally speaking, the Danes are not highly enterprising, adventurous, or self-confident; instead of daring all and risking all for possible, even probable, advantage, they remain at home, for,

"Striving to better, oft we do mar what's well."

Want is practically unknown in Denmark outside the slums of Copenhagen. The condition of the common people has steadily improved since the beginning of the nineteenth century, when nearly all the land was in the hands of the nobility; at the present time, six-sevenths is owned by the peasants. While this change has been going on, another, of even greater significance, has taken place.

[1]See the tables in Appendix.

Improved methods of cultivation, in the course of a hundred years, have multiplied the productive power of the land by ten, which is equivalent to increasing tenfold the available area of the kingdom. No nation, except the United States and Canada, has in recent times had such agricultural prosperity.[2]

As already noted, the activity of the Mormon missionaries drew off into the wilderness of Utah nearly 2000 Danes between 1850 and 1860, and nearly 5000 more in the next decade. In the two Prussian duchies after 1866, the discontent of Danes who preferred emigration to German rule drove a large number to the United States; and as these were far from being sympathizers with Mormonism, they found homes in the middle west. Settlements sprang up after 1870 in Wisconsin, at Racine; in Iowa, at Elk Horn in Shelby County and in the adjoining counties of Audubon and Pottawatomie; and in Douglas County (Omaha), Nebraska, just across the line from Pottawatomie County, Iowa. It should be noted in this connection that all the Danish settlements save those in Utah, were well within the frontier line, and hence are not to be classed as pioneering work, for which the Danes have shown little inclination.

The efforts of the Danish Evangelical Lutheran Church in America, organized at Neenah, Wisconsin, in 1872, have been several times directed deliberately to the organization of new Danish colonies, always, of course, with a view to strengthening the church or to carrying out some of its peculiar ideas. Of the four colonies,—in Shelby County, Iowa, in Lincoln County, Minnesota, in Clark County, Wisconsin, and in Wharton County, Texas,—that in Iowa is the most noteworthy and successful. Soon after 1880, the church secured an option on a tract of 35,000 acres in Shelby County from a land company. In return for 320 acres to be given by the company to the church for religious and educational purposes when one hundred actual settlers were secured, the church promised to use

[2]Bille, *History of the Danes in America*, 8 n2, summarizing H. Weitemeyer, *Denmark*, 100.

its influence to secure settlers for the whole tract. The company agreed for three years time to sell only to Danes at an average price of $7 per acre, for the first year, with an advance not exceeding $.50 per year for each following year. The end of the first year found more than the required number of settlers, the church received its grant, and still maintains its worship, a parochial school, and a high school, in a community which numbers about 1,000 Danes. The other colonies have been less successful.[3]

The Danish element in America has always lacked unity and solidarity. Even in their European home the Danes possess no strong national ambition, and no national institution claims their enthusiastic and undivided support. The Danish church, or churches, has gripped its immigrant sons and daughters less closely than similar organizations among the Swedes and Norwegians. It is estimated that only one out of fifteen of the Danes in the United States belongs to some church, while one out of five of the Swedes, one out of three and one-half of the Norwegians, and one out of three of the total population of the country, is connected with an ecclesiastical organization.[4]

One reason for the low ebb of church influence among the Danes is undoubtedly the wranglings of the clergy over matters of theology and polity, a continuation of the factional differences between the followers of Bishop Grundtvig and the anti-Grundtvigians or Inner Mission people in the years 1854-1895. In its beginning, the Danish Lutheran Church in America unanimously adopted this resolution: "We, the Danish ministers and congregations, hereby declare ourselves to be a branch of the Danish National Church, a missionary department established by that church in America."[5] The government of Denmark

[3]Bille, *History of the Danes in America*, 26-28; A. Dan, "History of the Danish Evangelical Lutheran Church in America," in Nelson, *History of the Scandinavians*, I, 166-171.

[4]Nelson, *History of the Scandinavians*, II, 49.

[5]Bille, *History of the Danes in Amerika*, 18.

recognized this relation; graduates of the University of Copenhagen, who received calls to churches in America, were ordained by a bishop in Denmark, and were appointed by the King as regular ministers in the Danish Church; and since 1884 the Danish Government has made a small annual appropriation for the education of ministers for the American branch of the Danish Church. This allowance was at first spent in Denmark, but since 1887, in the United States.[6] But with all this effort at maintaining unity and continuity, the American branch has not been united, peaceable or effective.

If the test of supporting educational institutions for their own people be applied to the Danes, the same deficiency of interest and contributions as in matters ecclesiastical, will be revealed. The attempt of the Grundtvigians to set up the peculiar "high schools" which they maintained in Denmark, for instruction of the common people in Scandinavian history, mythology, religion, language, and literature, all in Danish, was doomed to failure.[7] The first of these schools was located at Elk Horn, Iowa, in the midst of the largest Danish settlement in the United States, yet in the fifteen years after its establishment in 1878 the average attendance never reached forty. Four other schools, in Ashland, Michigan, in Nysted, Nebraska, in Polk County, Wisconsin, and in Lincoln County, Minnesota, all established between 1878 and 1888, suffered from like indifference and lack of financial help; not one averaged thirty pupils per year. Aside from tuition, the contributions of the Danes for educational purposes did not reach fifty cents per communicant during any consecutive five years up to 1894.[8] This is a poor showing alongside the three dollars per communicant contributed by the Norwegians when they were building Decorah College in 1861 to 1865.[9]

[6] Bille, *History of the Danes in America*, 18n. The appropriation was $840 per year.

[7] *Ibid.*, 21; *Kirkelig Samler*, 1878, 320.

[8] Bille, *History of the Danes in America*, 16.

[9] Bille, *History of the Danes in America*, 15; Estrem, "Historical Review of Luther College," in Nelson, *History of the Scandinavians*, II, 24.

CHAPTER VII.

A Half Century of Expansion and Distribution, 1850-1900.

While the immigration movement from Norway and Sweden was well-established by 1850, and certain to expand, it was numerically unimportant when compared with that from some other countries of Europe. In 1849 the influx from all Scandinavia was slightly more than one per-cent of the total immigration from Europe. Yet the rising stream had, by 1850, worn for itself a clear and definite channel from eastern ports like New York and Boston to such gateways to the Northwest as Chicago and Milwaukee; and through these it continued to flow out over the wilderness of the upper Mississippi Valley extending north of the Missouri and Illinois Rivers and west of the Great Lakes. For more than a half century there have been relatively few variations from this course, tho in the later decades, with an increase in the proportion of skilled laborers among the incoming thousands, certain eastern cities have detained a considerable percentage.

No other marked change in the character and quality of the immigrants has developed since 1850, nor have any new motives appeared, except in the case of the Danes, to be discussed later. In a word, the Scandinavian immigration since 1850 is simply the earlier Scandinavian immigration enlarged in numbers, with broader and deeper significance. The areas of interest in emigration in Europe gradually extended to every part and every class of the three Northern kingdoms; and the localities attractive to Scandinavians in the United States, expanded until eight contiguous States in the Old Northwest and the Newer Northwest showed each a foreign-born population of Northmen numbering more than thirty thousand. In the State of Minnesota they now reach close to a quarter of a million.[1]

[1]After 1850 the book of Frederika Bremer, *Homes of the New World,* is credited with large influence in Sweden among the better classes. See McDowell, "The New Scandinavia", *Scandinavia*, Nos. 5-8.

The total recorded Scandinavian immigration, according to the statistics of the United States, from 1820 to 1912, is in round numbers 2,200,000. According to the statistics of Norway, Sweden, and Denmark, which may be disregarded for inaccuracy before 1850, the total falls about 142,000 short of this figure, a difference which may be easily enough accounted for by persons leaving those countries for a more or less indefinite stay in other parts of Europe, before starting for America.[2] The American statistics in later years have sometimes shown larger numbers than the Swedish, but the discrepancy is accounted for by the fact that a great number of emigrants from Finland have passed through Sweden on their way to America and therefore are counted as Swedes.[3] The totals by decades with the percentages of the whole immigration for the decades, is as follows:[4]

	Denmark	Norway	Sweden	Total Sc.	Per cent of immig.
1820-1830	189	91		280	.2
1831-1840	1,063	1,201		2,264	.4
1841-1850	539	13,903		14,442	.8
1851-1860	3,749	20,931		24,680	.9
1861-1870	17,094	109,298		126,392	5.2
1871-1880	31,771	94,823	115,922	242,516	8.6
1881-1890	88,132	176,586	391,733	656,451	12.5
1891-1900	52,670	95,264	230,679	378,613	9.8
1901-1910	65,285	190,505	249,534	505,524	5.7

[2]Nelson in his *History of the Scandinavians,* I, 253 ff., gives some careful and excellent tables of statistics compiled from official publications of the United States and of the three Scandinavian kingdoms. Too much reliance should not be put upon the earlier figures derived from either source. It will also be noted that the European figures are in many cases given in even fifties and hundreds, which savors of estimates rather than of exact statistics. Nelson, p. 244, declares that these foreign statistics, so far as they go, are more reliable than the American.

[3]Sundbärg, *Sweden* (English Translation), 132; Sundbärg, *Bidrag till Utvandringsfrågan från Befolkningsstatistisk Synpunkt,* 34 ff.

[4]The statistics of Norwegian and Swedish immigration were combined down to 1868, but for convenience here the combination is continued to the end of the decade. Statistical Abstract of the U. S. (1912), 110.

The fluctuations of the annual immigration have been very great, as an inspection of the accompanying chart and the tables in Appendix I, will readily show. The addition of other lines to this chart indicating the fluctuations in the numbers of immigrants from Germany and Ireland, demonstrates that these rather striking variations were chiefly caused by conditions and prospects in America, rather than by circumstances in Europe. In 1849 the total immigration of Norwegians and Swedes passed 2,000, and even reached 3,400, but the terrible scourge of cholera in that year under which so many of the Scandinavians in the West fell, caused a falling off of more than half in 1850. After the panic of 1857, the Danish immigration fell from 1,035 to 252 in one year, while the total from the Northern lands fell steadily from 2,747 to 840 in 1860.

The Civil War disturbed comparatively little the conditions favoring Scandinavian immigration, for the Northwest was never in danger of invasion, and nominal prices for farm produce ranged higher and higher. Furthermore, the Homestead Act of 1862 gave new and cumulative impetus to the immigration which sought farming lands.[5] So from a total of 850 in 1861 (the statistics of Norway show 8,900 emigrants for that year, and those of Sweden, 1,087), the numbers gradually increased, in spite of the war, to 7,258 in 1865. The panic of 1873 did not affect the Scandinavian movement so immediately and seriously as might at first thought be expected, probably because the Northmen were seeking farms in the West, and also because the farmers as a class are about the last to feel the effects of financial crises like that of 1873. As the depression deepened, letters from America to Northern Europe lost their tone of buoyancy and enthusiasm; the eastward flow of passage-money and prepaid tickets almost ceased. At the same time a series of good crops in the three Scandinavian countries caused a rise of wages about 1873, doubling them in some instances.[6] Consequently the current

[5]*United States Statutes at Large* (1861-2), 392 ff.

[6]Young, *Labor in Europe and America*, 676,—quoting and summarizing from a report to the Secretary of State by C. C. Andrews, United States Minister to Sweden, Sept. 24, 1873.

of immigration lost force and volume for several years, the totals dropping, in round numbers, from 35,000 in 1873, to 19,000 in 1874, and to 11,000 in 1877.

After the high-water mark of 105,326 in 1882, reached during the revival of business from 1879 to 1884, the totals did not again fall below 40,000 Scandinavian immigrants per year, until after the industrial and financial stagnation of 1893 to 1896; 62,000 in 1893 became 33,000 in 1894, and 19,000 in 1898. With the prosperity of the first years of the new century in the United States, the number again passed 50,000, reaching another climax in the 77,000 of 1903.

In general, the variations of the curves for the three nationalities under discussion have been nearly co-incident, as for example the high points in 1873 and 1882, and the low points in 1877, 1885, and 1898. The Danish immigration did not rise proportionately with the other two, especially in 1903, probably because of the democratizing of land-ownership in Denmark, and because of the remarkable improvement in methods of cultivation in the course of the nineteenth century.[7] No such decided improvements took place in the other peninsular kingdoms.

Another feature of the fluctuation is entitled to some consideration. In proportion to the population of those nations, the emigration from Norway and Sweden since 1870 has been very large, and such drafts as were made in the years 1882 or 1903 could not be expected to keep up. The periodicity of the ripening of a good "crop" of eligible emigrants for the great American West seems to have been since 1877 from five to eight years. In this connection it is a noteworthy fact that the population in each of the Scandinavian kingdoms, notwithstanding the great emigrations, has steadily tho slowly increased since 1850.[8] For

[7] J. H. Bille, "History of the Danes in America", *Transactions of the Wis. Acad. of Sciences, Arts, and Letters,* IX, 8 n., citing H. Weitemeyer, *Denmark,* 100.

[8] For Denmark, the increase has been about 1% per year since 1870; Sweden shows a slightly smaller increase, falling as low as ¼% in 1890; Norway has a still smaller average increase than Sweden, estimated by Norwegian authority "1865-1890, .65%". The same writer adds: "The

the last decade of the nineteenth century, the figures for the increase were, Denmark, 16.6%, Norway, 10.6%, Sweden 7.3%, United States 20%.[9] In this statistical distribution, account must also be taken of the Scandinavians of the second generation, born in this country of foreign-born parents, since this element, racially speaking, is just as much an alien stock, with its inheritance of tendencies, temperament, and passions, as were the original immigrants. The census of 1910 enumerated among the foreign-born and the native-born of specified foreign parents:[10]

	Foreign-born white	Native white having both parents born in specified country	Total
Danes	181,621	147,648	329,269
Norwegians	403,858	410,951	814,809
Swedes	665,183	546,788	1,211,971
	1,250,662	1,105,387	2,356,049

To these must be added still another group, made up of those persons having a father born in Norway, Sweden, or Denmark, and a mother born in one of the other two countries, in other words, persons of pure Scandinavian descent. The number of such in 1910 was 72,152. It does not include, be it noted, those persons of equally pure Norse blood whose parents, one or both, were born in the United States. The minimum number of Scandinavians, then, in the United States in 1910, who must be taken into account in all calculations and estimates of power and influence exercised by that factor of the population, is 2,428,201. If it were desired to bring the estimate up to date, the immigration of 1910-1913 and an approximation of the increase of the native-born, would have to be in-

Norwegian race, in the course of the fifty years from 1840 to 1890 must have about doubled itself, which is equivalent to an annual growth of about 1.4%." *Norway*, 103; *Statesman's Year-Book*, 1900, 491, 1047, 1050.

[9] *Supplementary Analysis of 12th Census*, 31-33.

[10] These figures are drawn from the tables in the *Census Reports, 1910, Population*, I, 875 ff. The statistics generally deal only with white persons, thus excluding blacks and mulattoes of the Danish West Indies.

cluded, and the grand total of persons of pure Northern stock would not be far from 2,700,000 at the present time (1913).

The distribution of this vast company to the different States of the Union is a consideration of primary importance. The detailed analysis of the motives, processes, and results of the occupation of the Northwestern States by the children of the Northlands, belongs in later chapters.[11] The reasons why the stream flowed to the north of Mason and Dixon's Line are a combination of climate and a fear and hatred of slavery. If the movement from Scandinavia had begun fifty years earlier, before the anti-slavery agitation became acute, the New Norway and the New Sweden of the nineteenth century, would doubtless still have been in the North and probably in Ohio, Indiana, and Michigan, for very much the same reason that the Western Reserve was a New Connecticut.

Desiring ownership of good agricultural land above all else, and finding after 1835 that the best and cheapest was to be found along the advancing frontier west of a north-and-south line drawn through Chicago, the men from Norway, Sweden, and Denmark followed their distant cousins of New England and the Middle States in the great trek into the Any-Man's-Land of the fertile upper Mississippi Valley.[12] For more than two decades after the Civil War, tho slavery no longer existed in the South, that region was still in the depression and uncertainty of the post-bellum industrial disorganization, and hence unattractive to immigrants of any class. So the tide continued to run high in the Northwest and spread wider and wider because of the traditions of two generations, and because of the attracting power of the Scandinavian mass already comfortably and solidly settled there.

[11] See chapters VIII-X.

[12] The "line which limits the average density of 2 to a square mile, is considered as the limit of settlement—the frontier line of population". *Eleventh Census, Report on Population*, I, xviii. See R. Mayo-Smith in *Political Science Quarterly*, III, 52.

The first States of the Northwest into which the Norwegians and Swedes penetrated, as has been described above, were Illinois and Wisconsin; and in the censuses of 1850 and 1860 Wisconsin held first place in the number of these aliens, showing an increase from 8,885 to 23,265.[13] In 1850, Iowa, in the "far west," ranked fourth, with 611. Minnesota, which then stretched away to the Rocky Mountains, had 4 Swedes, 7 Norwegians, and 1 Dane.[14] By 1860 Iowa was passed by Minnesota which then had 11,773, and thenceforward the Scandinavians were to keep close step with the westward march of the frontier. In 1870 Minnesota took first place, with 58,837, a position which the State has continued to hold. In 1890 she had within her borders 236,670 foreign-born Northmen, and enough of the second generation to make her Scandinavian population 466,365, or about one-fifth that of Denmark or Norway. The order of Minnesota, Wisconsin, Illinois, and Iowa held good for 1870 and 1880, but Wisconsin and Illinois changed places in the reports of 1890 and 1900. The Dakotas, as one Territory, received their first Norse settler in 1858, but when the census of 1880 was taken there were 17,869, and in 1890, when the Territory was divided into two States, the Scandinavian contingent was more than 65,000 strong.[15] Nebraska illustrated in a similar manner the widening overflow of the steady stream out of the European North; her population of Scandinavian birth which numbered only 3,987 in 1870, grew by direct entry of immigrants, and by the secondary movement of early immigrants out of the middle Northwest, to 16,685 in 1880, and to 40,107 of foreign-born in 1900. According to this last census, Nebraska counted 38,914 native persons of foreign-born Scandinavian parents, showing that the second generation did not fall much behind the first in the habit of frontier-seeking.[16]

In the rush of gold-seekers into California after 1848 were many Danes and Swedes, who gave that State in 1860

[13]For the tables illustrating this discussion, see Appendix.
[14]Gronberger, *Svenskarne i St. Croixdalen*, 3 ff.
[15]Sparks, *History of Winneshiek County, Iowa*, III.
[16]See Appendix I.

fifth rank as to the number of Scandinavians; by 1890 these numbered about 42,000, of whom the greater part were of the two nationalities just named. Another frontier region which gained from the Danish immigration between 1850 and 1860 was the Territory of Utah, for the Mormon missionaries seem to have been particularly successful in Denmark, and nearly every convert became an immigrant. Quite in advance of their invasion of Dakota, more than 2,000 Danes had settled in the Mormon Territory, and ten years later Utah counted nearly twice as many Scandinavians as Nebraska, seven-tenths being Danes.

The increasing density of this Scandinavian population in certain localities,—what might be called its vertical distribution—is strikingly illustrated in both urban and rural communities. Chicago had barely emerged from the Fort Dearborn stage when the first Scandinavians walked its streets. Yet within two generations there were found inside of her wide-stretching borders more than 100,000 Swedes, Norwegians, and Danes of foreign birth, and enough of the second generation to give her more than 190,-000, so that the city at the head of Lake Michigan was next after Copenhagen, Stockholm, and Christiania,—the largest Scandinavian city in the world.[17] By a similar calculation, Minneapolis would rank sixth or seventh.

Rockford, Illinois, received the first of its signally prosperous Swedish colony about 1853; by 1865 the city had 2,000 Swedes.[18] The census of 1910 credits Rockford with 10,000 foreign born Swedes, and a total of Swedish parentage reaching close to 19,000. One of the west-central counties of Minnesota, Otter Tail, counted (1900) more than half of its 45,000 population of pure Scandinavian blood of the first and second generation of immigrants. Polk county, newer and farther north in the same State, reveals almost sixty per-cent of the same sort of population in a total of 35,000. For some of the still newer and more

---

[17]*Svenska Folkets Tidning,* Jan. 1, 1896, estimated the totals as follows: Swedes, 100,000, Norwegians, 62,000, and Danes, 35,000!

[18]Kæding, *Rockfords Svenskar,* 27, 35.

sparsely settled counties even larger percentages might be obtained.

A closer analysis of the tables of population reveals some further facts as to the distribution of the different nationalities. The Swedes are the most numerous in Minnesota, Illinois, Iowa, Michigan, Nebraska, and Kansas; the Norwegians predominate in Wisconsin, North Dakota, and South Dakota, and nearly equal the Swedes in Minnesota where each passes 200,000. The Danes are strongest— they can hardly be called a very important factor in any State—in Iowa, Minnesota, Wisconsin, Illinois, and Nebraska; in each State they have more than 25,000. Another feature of this varying density of the three groups has to do with the cities. Chicago, Rockford, Minneapolis, St. Paul, and Duluth account for a large proportion of the Swedes of Illinois and Minnesota, and represent the later rather than the earlier stages of distribution. Outside of the cities mentioned, the Norwegians in Minnesota outnumber the Swedes by some 52,000. In North Dakota, the Norwegians are 72% of the foreign-born Scandinavian population, in South Dakota, 56%, and in Wisconsin, 60%, while in Illinois the Swedes are about 70%, and in Michigan and Nebraska, 63% and 59% respectively. The Danes reach their highest percentages of the Scandinavian foreign-born in Utah, 50%, in Nebraska, 34%, and in Iowa, 23%. Large numbers of the later immigrants, especially of the skilled Swedish laborers, have found occupation in New York and Brooklyn, Boston and Worcester, Hartford and Providence. These have raised the proportion of the Swedes in the United States living in cities of more than 25,000, to 36%, while only 28% of the Danes, and 19% of the Norwegians were similarly located in 1900.[19]

Climate, particularly the mean temperature, has also played considerable part in the choice by the immigrants from Northern Europe of the sites for their new homes, though it is an open question whether they would not have been established where they were and when they were

[19]*Census Reports, 1900, Population*, I, Tables 33 and 35.

even if the climate were different. Certain it is that the few Icelandic settlements are situated in the extreme northern part of Minnesota and North Dakota, and in Southern Manitoba.[20] South of them come, in order, the zones of densest Norwegian population, 49° to 42°, of the Swedish, 48° to 40°, and of Danish, 44° to 38°. The three nationalities thus occupy relatively the same latitudinal position in America as in their homes in the Old North.[21]

Summarizing the matter of location, the great bulk of the Scandinavian immigrants went into the Northwest, 78% of them during the first fifty years of the movement, and about 70% of the total. Out of the immigration of the different nationalities, 81% of the Norwegians are in the Northwest, 60% of the Danes, and 59% of the Swedes, the percentage of the last being brought down, in comparison with the Norwegians, by the fact that nearly 100,000 Swedes are found in Massachusetts, New York, and Pennsylvania.

The Civil War occurred before the numbers and expansion of the Norse element of the country's population had much passed a promising beginning; the 75,000 present in 1860 could not be expected to play any large and leading rôle. Yet the one dramatic and heroic chapter in the whole story of the progress of the Scandinavians in America is that dealing with their part in that great struggle, in which many hundreds of them gave their strength and their lives for the unity and safety of their adopted country no less bravely and no less cheerfully than did the native-born American. The men from Thelemark and Smaaland and the sons of Massachusetts and Michigan were inspired by the same fine and pure motives; they hated slavery and loved

[20]These are of course enumerated as Danes. Pembina County, in the extreme northeast corner of North Dakota had in 1900 1588 Danes (Icelanders). The movement from Iceland began about 1870. See R. B. Anderson in *Chicago Record Herald*, Aug. 21, 1901.

[21]G. T. Flom, "The Scandinavian Factor in the American Population", *Iowa Journal of History and Politics*, III, 88.

[22]*Statistical Atlas of the Twelfth Census;* Plates 69, 71, 73, 76; *Iowa Journal of History and Politics,* III, 76.

the flag under whose folds they realized their hopes and dreams.[23] By temperament, by religion, by education, by tradition, men of Norse parentage were fitted to participate in upholding a cause so essentially right and high.

In the short space of this volume, details of the loyal services of companies made up wholly or in large part of Swedes and Norwegians must be omitted, and the laurels won by such men as General Stohlbrand, who was made a brigadier by President Lincoln himself,[24] Colonel H. C. Heg,[25] Colonel Mattson,[26] and Lieutenant Colonel Porter C. Olson,[27] must be passed by with mere allusions.

The Fifteenth Wisconsin Regiment of Volunteers, consisting of about 900 men, whose organization was decided upon at a mass meeting held in the Capitol at Madison, in September, 1861, was made up almost entirely of Norwegians and Swedes, some of whom had been in the United States less than a year. Hans C. Heg, one of the early leaders of the Norwegian immigration into Wisconsin, was appointed colonel of the regiment and began organization at Camp Randall, near Madison, in the following December.[28] The roster of officers indicates plainly their origin, including such names as Rev. C. L. Clausen, Thorkildson, Hansen, Grinager, Skofstad, Ingmundson, Tjentland, and Solberg.[29] The regiment left for the front in March, 1862, and participated in the operations of the next three years in Kentucky, Tennessee and northern Georgia. It was mustered out at Chattanooga in February, 1865, having lost about 300, quite one-third of its total enlistment, from

[23]Mattson, *Story of an Emigrant*, 60, 94. Here is printed, in translation from *Hemlandet*, a stirring appeal "To the Scandinavians of Minnesota!;" *Fædrelandet og Emigranten*, September 29, 1870.

[24]Osborn, "Personal Memories of Brig. Gen. C. J. Stolbrand", *Year-Book of the Swedish Historical Society of America*, 1909-10, 5-16.

[25]Dietrichson, *Det Femtende Wisconsin Regiments Historie*, 26.

[26]Mattson, *Story of an Emigrant*, 59-93.

[27]Anderson, *Norwegian Immigration*, 112-127.

[28]Enander, *Borgerkrigen i de Forenede Stater*, 106; Dietrichson, *Det Femtende Wisconsin Regiments Historie*, ch. i.

[29]Dietrichson, "The Fifteenth Wisconsin, or Scandinavian, Regiment," *Scandinavia*, I, 297 ff.

deaths in battle or in the hospitals, including Colonel Heg, who was killed at Chickamauga.[30] Its record is summed up by the military historian of Wisconsin who states that it was "one of the bravest and most efficient regiments that Wisconsin sent to the field."[31]

Besides this Scandinavian regiment, there were several others in which the Norse element was large. Company C of the 43d Illinois Regiment was made up of Swedes, serving under Captain Arosenius. It was organized in the spring of 1862 and mustered out in the fall of 1865, with an honorable record of services faithfully and uncomplainingly performed.[32] Company D of the 57th Illinois Regiment, which served from the autumn of 1861 to July, 1864,[33] and Company D of the 3d Minnesota Regiment, which was mustered in at about the same time,[34] were composed of Scandinavians. A sprinkling of Swedes, Norwegians, and Danes appears in the lists of many of the regiments of Illinois, Wisconsin, and Minnesota, and many of these men rose to the ranks of commissioned officers.[35] The Adjutant General of Minnesota in 1866 estimated that of the enlistments from that State, at least 800 were Norwegians, 675 Swedes, and 25 Danes. "In numerous instances the nativity of the soldiers is omitted; and it is not easy to count correctly all the names in such publications; hence it is fair to estimate that 2,000 Scandinavians from Minnesota enlisted under the Stars and Stripes. . . . One-eighth of the total population of the State enlisted under the Union flag; while at the same time one out of every six Scandinavians in Minnesota, as well as in Wisconsin, fought for his adopted country."[36]

[30]Nelson, *History of Scandinavians*, I, 166.

[31]Quiner, *The Military History of Wisconsin* (ch. xxiii, "Regimental Histories—15th Infantry"), 631.

[32]Johnson and Peterson, *Svenskarne i Illinois*, 143-149.

[33]*Ibid.*, 155-161.

[34]Mattson, *The Story of an Emigrant*, 59-93.

[35]*Ibid.*, 62.

[36]*Annual Report of the Adjutant General of Minnesota, 1866*, ii; Nelson, *History of the Scandinavians*, I, 303-304. Similar figures for Iowa are in Nelson, II, 67.

Everywhere the story of their services in the army is creditable, and it is not strange that the survivors are proud of their war records as the badge of loyal Americanism. They did not go into the war for mere love of adventure, nor for love of fighting, for men in large numbers do not leave their families and their half-developed farms for flimsy and temporary reasons. They loved the new country they had made their own, with a love that was measurable in the high terms of sacrifice, even to the shedding of blood and to death. The stock out of which Gustavus Adolphus made brave and effective soldiers had not degenerated through lapse of time nor through transplanting.

Though John Ericsson was in no wise connected with the regular Swedish immigration movement, nor with Swedish settlement in the Northwest, the United States owes him too large a debt for what has sometimes been called the salvation of the Union through the agency of his "Monitor", to warrant the omission of his name from among those Swedes who served American freedom during the Civil War.[37]

[37]Church, *Life of John Ericsson*.

CHAPTER VIII.

ECONOMIC FORCES AT WORK.

In the many monographs and more pretentious works
dealing with various phases of the economic history of the
United States, much attention has been given to the tariff,
manufacturing, banking, currency, transportation, and
public lands. Only recently have the economic results of
immigration begun to receive the attention which their
importance deserves. For a long time the excellent work
of Professor Richmond Mayo-Smith, *Emigration and Immigration* (1890), notable for the strength and breadth of its
general treatment, was quite alone in its field. Mere statistical studies no longer suffice, and just as the census-
taking of the Federal Government has changed from the
simple, old-fashioned inventory of numbers—so many
heads, black and white, native-born and foreign-born—to
an elaborate investigation of the life problem of the population, so the meaning of immigration as a whole, and of
Scandinavian immigration in particular, requires a discussion extending beyond annual and decennial statistics
and maps of the density of settlement.

In the economic development of the Northwest, as compared with the history of the Eastern, Middle, or Southern
States during the nineteenth century, the three principal
topics are immigration, the Federal land policy, and improvements in transportation. In a peculiar manner the
last two subjects are interwoven with the story of the Norwegians, Swedes, and Danes in America. When people by
the hundreds of thousands were settled in the West, when
commerce and manufacturing arose upon the sound basis
of a prospering agriculture, then and not till then, protection, currency, and bimetallism might be accepted as real
and immediate issues.

The Scandinavian immigrants along the frontiers, like
the other pioneers all through the prairie west, were from

the first vitally interested in securing some form of cheap transportation of the produce of the farms to a good market; railroads were indispensable to the development of the agricultural areas of the Great West. Western Pennsylvania might find profit in 1794 in shipping the quintessence of its agriculture across the mountains in demijohns; the cattlemen of the South and Southwest might drive their products to market on the hoof; but at the very best these were exceptional, inelastic, and primitive methods. Many pioneer Norwegians and Swedes in Minnesota and Iowa were obliged to carry their wheat and corn forty and fifty miles to have it ground for their families, but they could not hope to haul any great amount of ordinary farm produce over the abominable roads of the West for a distance greater than forty miles and make a profit.[1] Without the hope of railroads, the vast stretches of cereal-producing land in the trans-Mississippi would long have remained virgin soil. Yet without assurance that population would rapidly increase in numbers and in complexity of life, thus giving a large traffic in both directions, no railroad company would build out into the thinly settled area.[2]

Broadly speaking, then, the real problem of the Northwestern frontier after 1850 was: how to put more and ever more men of capacity, endurance, strength, and adaptability into the upper Mississippi and Red River valleys, men who first break up the prairie sod, clear the brush off the slopes, drain the marshes, build the railroads, and do

[1] *Fædrelandet og Emigranten*, July 21, 1870; interview in 1890 with the Rev. U. V. Koren, the first Norwegian Lutheran minister permanently located west of the Mississippi. Miss Bremer in October, 1850, described the road over which the early settlers in Wisconsin went 30 and 40 miles to market: "the newborn roads of Wisconsin, which are no roads at all, but a succession of hills and holes and water pools in which first one wheel sank and then the other, while the opposite one stood high up in the air. . . . To me, that mode of travelling seemed really incredible. . . . They comforted me by telling me that the diligence was not in the habit of being upset very often !" *Homes of the New World*, II, 235-236.

[2] It was on faith in the future of the northern zone of the Northwest, based upon observation, that the Great Northern Railroad was built without any land-grant or subsidy such as the Northern Pacific and other roads demanded and got.

the thousands and one hard jobs incident to pioneer life, and then turn to the building of factories and towns and cities. Not every sort of man who could hold a plow or wield a hoe would do: Chinese coolies, for example, would hardly be considered desirable, even with all their capacity for hard work, persistence, and patience. Furthermore, it is plain now, that the West could not have looked to the Eastern States alone to send out an industrial army sufficient in numbers and spirit for the conquest of the new empire and the extraction of its varied resources at the desired speed. The demands were too severe, the rewards too remote and uncertain for the average prosperous native-born citizen. The aliens from the western side of the Atlantic, as it were by regiments and battalions, must re-enforce the companies westward-bound from the older States; in such a situation the Scandinavians were all but indispensable to rapid material progress in the Northwest after the middle of the last century.

It is not easy to realize how attractive to the Northland immigrants were the broad, level lands of the West, to be had from the United States Government on the easiest of terms, both before and after the passage of the Homestead Act of 1862. Scarcely in their dreams had they conceived of soil so fertile, so readily tilled, and so cheaply acquired. To speak to a Norwegian from Thelemarken, to a Swede from Smaaland, or to a Dane from the misty, sandy coast of Jutland, about rich, rolling prairies stretching away miles upon miles, about land which was neither rocky, nor swampy, nor pure sand, nor set up at an angle of forty-five degrees, about land which could be had almost for the asking in fee simple and not by some semi-manorial title—this was to speak to his imagination rather than to his understanding. The letters from immigrants to their old friends in Europe continually dilated on these advantages, sometime with a curious mingling of humor and pathos. One of these communications, which was printed as a small pamphlet in 1850, sets forth in large letters, that the land was so plentiful that the pigs and cattle were allowed to

run at will.[3]   What more could be asked of Providence by
a poor peasant or "husmand," owing to his landlord, for
the little strip of land on which he lived, the labor of two or
three days each week?[4]

These strictly economic advantages of soil and price
were not the only attractions for the sons of the Northlands.
Both the traveller and the prospector for a site for a settlement were deeply impressed by the general appearance of
the rolling country of the Northwest with its abundance of
streams and lakes.   During her visit to Wisconsin and
Minnesota in the fall of 1850, Frederika Bremer saw with
quite prophetic vision, the possibilities of the region:

"What a glorious new Scandinavia might not Minnesota become! Here would the Swede find again his clear,
romantic lakes, the plains of Scania rich in corn, and the
valleys of Norrland; here would the Norwegian find his
rapid rivers, his lofty mountains, for I include the Rocky
Mountains and Oregon, in the new kingdom; and both nations their hunting fields and their fisheries. The Danes
might here pasture their flocks and herds, and lay out their
farms on richer and less misty coasts than those of Denmark. . . . . Scandinavians who are well off in the old
country ought not to leave it. But such as are too much
contracted at home, and who desire to emigrate, should
come to Minnesota. The climate, the situation, the character of the scenery, agrees with our people better than
that of any other of the American States, and none of them
appear to me to have a greater or a more beautiful future
before them than Minnesota. Add to this that the rich soil
of Minnesota is not yet bought up by speculators, but may
everywhere be purchased at government prices. . . . . There

[3]A copy of this interesting little pamphlet, without signature, was
found in the National Library in Stockholm.

[4]Young, *Labor in Europe and America*, 696. Laing, *Journal of a
Residence in Norway* (1834), 151, describes the conditions in a parish,
Levanger, near Throndhjem. There fifty estates were entered to pay land
tax. Out of a population of 2465, 124 were proprietors cultivating their
own land; 47 were tenants leasing lands, and 144 were "housemen" or
tenants owing labor for their land.

are here already a considerable number of Norwegians and Danes."[5] The Swedish air-castle took material shape rapidly; during forty years the name Minnesota, even more than Iowa, or Wisconsin, was a name to conjure with among the laborers and would-be farmers of the old kingdoms.[6]

Of the peculiar fitness of the Swedes, Norwegians, and Danes for this promotion of economic progress in a great section of the country, there is practically a unanimous opinion. A dispassionate, mature estimate is expressed officially by an agent of the British Government sent out to study the question of immigration in the United States. "It is generally admitted," he states, "that physically, morally, and socially, no better class of immigrants enter the United States. In some respects they are the most desirable of all."[7] A first-hand observer of their work as western farmers wrote in 1868 concerning the settlers in a Norwegian township in Minnesota, "They open their farms quicker, raise better stock than most any other class, and quickly become wealthy."[8] In a hearing before the Industrial Commission in 1899, Hermann Stump, a prominent German, testified that the Scandinavians "are really the best immigrants who come to the United States."[9]

While the Scandinavians were admirably fitted to become substantial citizens and to develop their own

[5]Bremer, *Homes of the New World*, II, 314-315.

[6]The charm of this name was illustrated in a curious way during the journey of the writer and another American through the mountains of central Norway in the summer of 1890. One early evening they came to the cabin of a *sæter*, or summer pasture, high up on the side of Gaustafjeld, and asked to be lodged for the night. It appeared that the only room available for strangers was already occupied by two young men from Christiania; but when the conversation developed the fact that both the late-comers were from America, and one from Minnesota, the woman of the house hastened off into the next room, ordered out the two Norwegians, and announced on returning that the room was at the service of the foreigners!

[7]*Report of the Board of Trade of Great Britain on Alien Immigration to the United States*, 211, 212.

[8]Goddard, *Where to Emigrate and Why*, 247.

[9]*Report of the Industrial Commission*, XV, 22.

properties, and while the prospect of possessing a farm was the most potent and pervading influence affecting their movements after about 1850, the very high rate of wages paid in the United States, as compared with the wages in Europe, was everywhere an important factor among the immediate attractions. All of the western States, in the first decade of their growth, were exceedingly anxious to secure settlers who should take up and improve the vacant square miles, thus adding to the population and to the taxable values of the commonwealth. At the same time there was a large and steady demand for wage-labor; the farmers needed helpers; the construction of internal improvements, begun and projected, like the rapidly expanding railroad systems, could be carried on only by the aid of an abundance of laborers.[10]

These needs could not be met by any considerable migration of laborers from the eastern States, for there the development of manufacturing and of transportation by land and by sea would operate to keep up wages and so to hold the laborers. The hard labor of the Far West, therefore, must be done, if done at all, by those who had not already found places for themselves in the industrial system of the United States, and for such services a good rate of wages would be paid, or at least a rate sufficient to draw the desired labor. In 1851 the $15 per month received by some Swedes working as farm hands near Buffalo, New York, was considered "big wages."[11] At the same time laborers on railroad construction in the West were receiving $.75 and $1 per day. Whether measured as real or nominal wages, these rates were certainly higher than even the average skilled laborer could earn in Norway or Sweden.[12]

[10]Mattson, *The Story of an Emigrant,* 29 ff.

[11]Mattson, *The Story of an Emigrant,* 17.

[12]*Ibid.,* 29. For work on the Chicago & Rock Island Railroad, Mattson received $.75 per day, and paid for board $1.50 a week, but the determination of the real wages, per month, requires a liberal deduction from these day-wages, for the process of acclimatization was severe in such malarial districts as that in which Mattson worked, and few men at first worked more than fifteen or twenty days in the month.

Tho the wages in the peninsular kingdoms rose considerably from 1850 to 1875, there was still at the later date and afterwards a large differential in favor of the American scale, whether for skilled or unskilled laborers. The experienced agricultural laborer in the fields of Illinois, or Wisconsin received two or three times as much as the corresponding worker in Norway and Sweden, while in new States like Minnesota the multiple was even greater.[13] Still more marked were the differences between skilled laborers, such as carpenters and smiths, in America and Europe even after the panic of 1873.[14]

[13]The following tabulation is drawn from the statistics of Dr. Young, *Labor in Europe and America,* to illustrate the differences of wages. Personal inquiries among men from all parts of Northern Europe confirm in a general way these figures reported from Europe. The European rates are reduced to gold values, while those for the United States are in paper money values, and should be discounted 10% or 12% to put them on a par with the other rates.

Experienced agric. laborers, per day	Summer		Winter	
	With Board	Without Board	With Board	Without Board
Sweden, 1873	$ .66	$	$ .46	$
Norway, 1873	.28–.43	.42–.55	.21–.31	.55
Denmark, 1872	.54	.80	.40	.60
U. S. (Western), 1870	1.34	1.84	.97	1.40
Minnesota, 1870	1.60	2.50	1.17	1.67
U. S. (Western), 1874	1.15	1.58	.93	1.35
Minnesota, 1874	1.00	1.50	.75	1.25

[14]*Ibid.*

Mechanics and skilled laborers, per day	Blacksmiths	Carpenters
Sweden, 1873	$ .80	$ .80
Norway, 1873	.90	.85
Denmark, 1873	.85	.65–.85
U. S. (Western), 1870 & 1874	2.88 & 2.66	2.98 & 2.72
Minnesota, 1870 & 1874	3.03 & 3.00	2.92 & 2.50

Domestic servants, female, per month	
Sweden, 1873	$2.14— 8.00
Norway, 1873 (cooks)	2.42— 3.59
U. S. (Western), 1870 & 1874	9.43 & 9.28
Minnesota, 1870	8.98

The eloquence of these figures, and of the conditions behind them, was not left to do its work by chance in the private letters of immigrants or in the occasional pamphlet. States and counties, as well as railroad corporations disseminated very widely and systematically the knowledge of the opportunities open to the laborer in the great West. If he were a man who would progress from a temporary tho necessary factor in construction or in the field, to a permanent settler taking up vacant land, so much the better for the State and the corporation. Fortunately for those great railroads, which were pushing construction and receiving large subsidies in public lands, they found just such men in the Swedes and Norwegians. As the Rock Island railroad pushed across Illinois and Iowa, as the Northern Pacific built out through Minnesota and Dakota, and as the road now known as the Great Northern carried its lines from St. Paul into the Red River valley, and on across North Dakota, the Scandinavian and the Irishman supplied the demand for labor from 1850 to 1890, in precisely the same way as the Italian, Pole, Mexican, and Greek have been doing in later years.

When construction of a railroad ended, the demand for immigrants merely changed its form and became cumulative. The dividends of any railroad running out into a new country depend on the development of the tributary territory, and this is especially true of the land-grant roads which owned half of the land within ten miles of their tracks. Thus it came about that the Scandinavians were doubly valuable, first as laborers for wages, and second as independent farmers in the townships made accessible by the new lines.[15] It was, indeed, faith in human nature, and especially Swedish and Norwegian human nature, which led to the construction and profitable operation of hundreds of miles of new roads in Minnesota and Dakota after 1880.

[15]Personal interviews with a large number of Swedes and Norwegians in northwestern Minnesota, in May, 1890, brought out the fact that many of them worked in the construction of the Northern Pacific and Great Northern railroads, and then invested their savings in railroad lands in the Red River valley, where they were prosperous farmers.

One prominent railroad man estimated that each settler (presumably each head of a family) meant in the long run from $200 to $300 a year for the railroad.[16] The fulfilment of the expectations of the builders of railroads and commonwealths was often surprisingly prompt. The prophetic insight of at least one "captain of industry," President James J. Hill of the Great Northern Railway Company which built its transcontinental system without land-grant, was as sure a reliance for capital as the subsidy of the Federal Government. Speaking in 1902 at Crookston, in the center of the great Scandinavian region in northwestern Minnesota, he described in striking terms the growth of farm values, and of the railroad business in some of the towns in Minnesota and North Dakota: "I took the best towns [of the Red River valley] outside Crookston [for comparison with towns in North Dakota]. . . . I will give you the annual business. Warren's last year's railroad business with our company was $86,-000: Hallock, $94,000,—a respectable sum; Stephen, $87,000; Ada, $81,000. . . . Langdon [in North Dakota] . . . . away up towards the boundary, upon Pembina Mountain, $210,000; Osnabrock, I hardly know where it is myself, $101,000; Park River, $170,000; . . . . Bottineau, away at the west end of the Turtle Mountains, where a few years ago people said it was too far away; could not live there and could not raise anything if they did live there, $258,000. . . . Land up there [around Bottineau], worth $3, $5, and $8 an acre, and a few pieces $10 an acre, a few years ago, is worth today $25 and $30 per acre."[17]

The railroads left nothing undone to stimulate the economic desire of the Scandinavians to migrate to their particular sections of land and to the adjoining government sections. Several companies maintained for years regular immigration or land agents, besides a considerable and variable corps of sub-agents, port agents, and lecturers;

[16] Mr. Powell. General Immigration Agent of the Chicago, Milwaukee & St. Paul Railroad, in the *Milwaukee Sentinel*, Dec. 30, 1888, p. 10.

[17] *Northwest Magazine*, XX, 7, 11 (1902).

some of them paid the expenses of men representing groups of prospective immigrants, who desired to visit and report upon a particular locality. The St. Paul, Minneapolis & Manitoba Railroad advertised in "Facts about Minnesota" (1881) : "The settler—his family, household goods, live stock and agricultural implements—will be carried from St. Paul to any point on either of our lines at one-half the regular price."

Besides these efforts and inducements, the railroad companies prepared handbooks in different languages, distributed them widely throughout the East and West, and circulated them systematically in Norway, Sweden and Denmark.[18] A few of the companies even sent special representatives to Europe to work directly with the people of those countries. The Hon. Hans Mattson left the office of Secretary of State in Minnesota in 1871 to become the liberally paid European agent for the Northern Pacific Railroad whose resources he was to advertise from his headquarters in Sweden.[19] He was not, however, to organize regular parties of emigrants. A high official of one of the northwestern roads summed up the matter by saying, "There is as much competition among the railroads desiring to attract immigrants, as among dry-goods stores in aiming to attract customers."

The northwestern State governments were hardly less interested in inducing immigrants to help fill up the vacant square miles and townships than were the railroads, for developed farms meant towns, diversified industry, and greater assessment values, which, being translated, meant much-needed public buildings, institutions, and improvements. The competition of the States, for immigrants such as the Norwegians, re-enforced and parallelled that of the railroad and land companies. Wisconsin appointed a Commissioner of Emigration in 1852, who resided in New York,

[18]Such pamphlets were issued by the Wisconsin Central, the Chicago & Northwestern, the Chicago, Milwaukee & St. Paul, and the Northern Pacific railroads. Some of them were printed in Swedish, Norwegian, German, Dutch, and Polish.

[19]Mattson, *The Story of an Emigrant,* 118 ff.

and employed a Norwegian and a German assistant.[20] The following year another Act created a Traveling Emigrant Agent, and prescribed that he should "travel constantly between this State and the city of New York," to advertise "our great natural resources, advantages and privileges, and brilliant prospects for the future."[21] Pamphlets by the thousand in German, Norwegian, and Dutch were sent out in America and Europe. The office was abolished in 1855, but in 1867 another Act created an unpaid Board of Immigration and appropriated $2,000 for printing pamphlets in English, Welsh, German, and the Scandinavian languages.[22] The State even went so far, in a later Act, as to authorize the Board, in its discretion, to help with money, "such immigrants as are determined to make Wisconsin their future home."[23]

The Board was succeeded by a Commissioner (Ole C. Johnson) in 1871, whose office was in turn abolished in 1874. The story of Wisconsin's later organizations for promoting immigration ought almost to go into the chapter on politics—a new Board in 1879, abolished in 1887, renewed for two years in 1895, and revived for another two years in 1899.[24] In 1880, at the request of the president of the Wisconsin Central Railway Company, K. K. Kennan, agent of the land department of that company, was also appointed agent for the State in Europe, without expense to the State.[25]

For the same purposes, and with the same methods, Iowa had a Commissioner, 1860-1862, and a Board (of

---

[20]*Laws of Wisconsin*, 1852, ch. 432; Ibid., 1853, ch. 53; *Wisconsin Documents*, 1853, 1854, Reports of Commissioner of Emigration.

[21]*General Acts of Wisconsin*, 1853, ch. 56.

[22]*Ibid.*, 1855, ch. 3; 1867, ch. 126; 1868, ch. 120; *Governor's Messages and Documents*, 1870, 11.

[23]*General Acts of Wisconsin*, 1869, ch. 118.

[24]*Ibid.*, 1871, ch. 155; 1874, ch. 238; 1879, ch. 176; 1887, ch. 21; 1895, ch. 235; 1899, ch. 279. The abolished Commissioner of 1874 declared the repeal was "conceived in vindictiveness and brought about by third-rate politicians, and followed my refusal to appoint to place in my office" certain incompetents. *Report of Commissioner of Immigration*, 1874, 2.

[25]*Annual Report of Board of Immigration*, 1880, 6.

which the Rev. C. L. Clausen was a member), 1870-1874, which sent agents to Norway, Sweden, and Denmark, where they published articles in the newspapers and stirred, up emigration sentiment.[26]

Minnesota, likewise, in 1867 created a Board of Emigration, and Hans Mattson was appointed secretary. He proved a very efficient officer, and not the less so because at the same time, as he admits, he acted as land agent for one of the great railroad companies, whose line went through Wright, Meeker, Kandiyohi, Swift and Stevens counties.[27] Of the work of the Board, Mattson gives a convincing summary: "In the above-named localities there were only a few widely scattered families when I went there in 1867, while it is now (1891) one continuous Scandinavian settlement, extending over a territory more than a hundred miles long and dotted over with cities and towns, largely the result of the work of the board of emigration during the years 1867, 1868, and 1869. . . . . Our efforts, however, in behalf of Minnesota brought on a great deal of envy and ill-will from people in other States who were interested in seeing the Scandinavian emigration turned towards Kansas and other States, and this feeling went so far that a prominent newspaper writer in Kansas accused me of selling my countrymen to a life not much better than slavery in a land of ice, snow, and perpetual winter, where, if the poor emigrant did not starve to death, he would surely perish with cold. Such at that time was the opinion of many concerning Minnesota."[28]

The secretaries or commissioners of immigration were usually men of alien birth or extraction, and therefore intelligent and sympathetic in their labors for succeeding immigrants.[29] Probably no State gave better care, guidance, and protection to foreigners coming as settlers than did Minnesota, and naturally, with a Swede as commissioner, the Scandinavians were "preferred stock." The

[26]*Laws of Iowa*, 1860, ch. 81; 1862, ch. 11; 1870, ch. 34.
[27]Mattson, *The Story of an Emigrant*, 97, 99, 101.
[28]Mattson, *The Story of an Emigrant*, 100-101.
[29]*Ibid.*, 99, 102; *Wisconsin Legislative Manual*, 1895, 133.

work of the Minnesota commission included the appointment of interpreters to meet immigrants at New York, Montreal, and Quebec and accompany them to Minnesota; provision for temporary homes for the new-comers until they went to their chosen locality; and wide publication of newspaper articles in different languages. Pamphlets containing maps and detailed descriptions of States and counties were distributed at railroad stations and on steamers, in America and in foreign countries.[30] It would be stretching the truth a little to say that these circulars sent out by States, counties, and railroad companies were always strictly accurate and ingenuous, but they brought the desired results, not in one campaign alone, but year after year. Taken as a whole the energies of the State and railroad agents, were honorable, well-managed, and highly beneficial to both the States and the immigrants. The best evidence for this statement lies in the figures of the censuses of 1880, 1890, and 1900 for the population of Wisconsin, Iowa, Minnesota, and the Dakotas.[31]

The value of so many tens of thousands of immigrants added to the assets of western commonwealths,—so many scores of thousands of "hands," to make use of the colloquial term for labor units,—is at once great and difficult to measure or estimate. In economic terms, how much is a full-grown, healthy, intelligent, literate young man worth to a community into which he drops himself, for is he not as much a finished labor-performing machine as a new traction engine or a span of mules, either of which the assessor would set down in his books? The risks and pains and costs of up-bringing through unproductive years, of educating, of training for occupation, have all been borne by another community; the increment of wealth arising from his labor, providence, and skill will enrich the United States.

[30]See Bibliographical Chapter, under the names, Hewitt, Listoe, and Mattson, for Minnesota.
[31]See Statistical chapter, tables 5, 6, 7.

Yet it is not a fair test of the value of an immigrant to this country to measure it by the cost of his bringing up and education, either by the standards of his old home or by the American standards. Professor Mayo-Smith pointed out the fallacy in the oft-quoted estimate of Kapp, made up on this basis, that "the capital value of each male and female immigrant was about $1,500 and $750 respectively, making an average of $1125.[32] Dr. Young, formerly Chief of the United States Bureau of Statistics, chooses as a basis the "market value" rather than the "cost of production," and estimates the approximate yearly addition made by each immigrant to the realized wealth of the country in the form of farms, buildings, stock, tools, and savings, to be amount $40, which, capitalized at 5%, gives $800 as the value of each immigrant.[33] An interesting German calculation in 1881, made in much the same way as Dr. Young's, put the capital value of each immigrant at $1,200.[34] Another method of gauging the amount contributed to the earnings of the country by each immigrant, is to multiply the average daily wage of $1 by one-fifth the total number of immigrants, and that by 300, the number

[32]Kapp, *Immigration and the New York Commissioners of Emigration*, 146; Mayo-Smith, *Emigration and Immigration*, ch. vi.

[33]Young, *Special Report on Immigration* (1871), vii-ix.

[34]"According to other statistics, the average annual earnings of a workman amount to $625, and one may safely presume that every able-bodied workman contributes every year ⅕ of his earnings to the increase of national wealth. Taking into consideration the period of time of a full working capacity of emigrants according to their age, and considering the much less working capacity of females, and the cost of raising the children which they bring with them, one may fairly presume that, during the last few years, not only considerable cash capital has been taken to the United States by emigrants, but that every one of them carries to that country, in his labor, a capital which may be estimated at $1200. The total value of the labor thus conveyed to the United States during the last five years, may therefore be estimated at about $700,000,000. No wonder that the United States of America prosper." *Hamburger Handelsblatt*, March 18, 1881, quoted in translation from this "leading trade journal of Germany", in *Annual Report of the Wisconsin Board of Immigration*, 1881, 14.

of working days in the year.[35] Taking the values of the immigrant over fourteen years of age and under forty-five, as $1000, and estimating conservatively that 80 per-cent of the foreign-born enumerated in the census of 1900 reached the United States between those ages, the Scandinavians so enumerated represented a capital value of about $850,000,-000, to which the immigration from the North countries in the next five years added not less than $230,000,000. Viewed from one point, this capital was just so much given by the gods of plenty to accelerate the development of the West.

Another phase of the economic advantages of Scandinavian immigration has to do with the cash capital brought by the incoming thousands. While the first Norwegians were of the poorest class of the community, who escaped from unfavorable conditions almost empty-handed, squeezed out from the bottom of society, as it were through cracks and crevices, and while many of the later arrivals have had no other capital than strong hands and equally strong determination, the great proportion of adults have brought with them average sums variously estimated from $22 to $70 each. G. H. Schwab of New York, whose firm was general American agent for the North German Lloyd Steamship Company, estimated the average money or money equivalent brought by the Scandinavians, at $22 per head, probably including children in the calculation.[36] W. W. Thomas, Jr., Commissioner of Immigration for Maine, and later minister to Sweden, states that 900 Swedes who came to Maine in one year, besides clothing, tools, and household goods, had $40,000 in cash; and elsewhere he puts the average at $50 per head.[37] The figures from Wisconsin, which received better material than the average, would naturally run higher; in 1880 the official estimate

[35]J. B. Webber, in *North American Review*, CLIV, 435 (1892).
[36]*Forum*, XIV, 810.
[37]*Report of the Board and Commissioner of Immigration of Maine*, 1872, 6; F. L. Dingley, "European Emigration," *Special Consular Reports*, II, No. 2, 1890, 260.

of cash brought by each immigrant was "from $60 to $70."[38]
Assuming an average of 50,000 Scandinavian immigrants
per year for the last thirty years,—a safe minimum—and
an average of $50 cash per capita, the annual addition to
the cash capital of the country would be at least $2,500,000.
Whatever may be gained in this way is, however, offset
by the steady stream of remittances flowing from America
to Northern Europe, especially during the last quarter of
a century, and by the large sums spent by the thousands of
erstwhile immigrants returning to their old homes for a
winter or for a vacation.[39] Many a son, prospering in
America, has contributed regularly to the support or added
comfort of his parents or family in the fatherland; every
holiday season swells the mail sacks with letters containing
money-orders, and drafts. During 1902 at least $1,000,000
was sent to Norway alone.[40] In the last two months of
1903, it is estimated that $3,000,000 went from the United
States to the Scandinavian countries in these personal remittances.[41] Another sort of remittance which does not
immediately take the form of cash, is the prepaid ticket
for passage to an American port, sent to friends and rela-
tives to assist them to emigrate. The United States consuls
at Bergen and Gothenburg reported that about one-half
of the emigrants from Norway and Sweden in 1891 made
the journey on tickets sent from America.[42] In this connection, it should be noted that the money thus spent by immigrants is not in the nature of a permanent investment of
hoarded earnings; it is not the remittance of "birds of
passage" like some Italians, for example, who will shortly
follow it. In comparison with the millions of dollars sent

---

[38]*Annual Report of the Board of Immigration of Wisconsin*, 1880,
4. A writer in the *Milwaukee Sentinel*, Sept. 10, 1889, states, "Many of
them (Germans and Scandinavians) bring abundant means to secure large
farms and stock them well."

[39]Brace, *The Norsefolk*, 146; *Harper's Weekly*, Sept. 1, 1888; *Gamla
och Nya Hemlandet*, Jan. 14, 1903 (Malmö correspondent).

[40]*Special Consular Reports*, XXX, 116 (1903, Christiania).

[41]*Amerika*, Jan. 8, 1904.

[42]*Letter of the Secretary of the Treasury, etc.*, 1892, 45, 50, 65.

home by Italian immigrants in an average year, the Scandinavian remittances and spendings are almost insignificant.[43]

From the first, great numbers of the immigrants have come with no other capital than strong and willing hands, stout hearts, and an unchanging land-hunger. They served for a time as laborers on the older farms, in town, in the lumber camps, or in railroad construction, saving their money, learning American ways, and acquiring some English, but as soon as money enough was saved, perhaps in a year, to buy forty or eighty acres of government land at the minimum price, a yoke of oxen or a team of horses, and a few necessary farm tools and implements, the prospective farmer moved upon new land and started out for himself. Under the Homestead Act of 1862 the amount of capital required for the beginning of operations was greatly reduced, and it was under this act that the lands of the northwestern States beyond the Mississippi were so rapidly taken up.[44]

A typical illustration of the process described is found in Levor Timanson, who came with his father in 1848, at the age of eighteen, to Rock County, Wisconsin, where he worked for several years as farm laborer, carpenter, and mason. He visited Iowa and Minnesota in 1853 in search of satisfactory land; finding it at Spring Grove, in the latter State, he settled down there as a grain and stock farmer. In 1882 he owned 840 acres of land of which 550 acres were under cultivation.[45] A study of the histories of counties and townships in eastern Iowa and Minnesota, and of the biographies which usually accompany them, reveals clearly the fact that the larger part of the Scandinavian farmers resident in those counties in the sixties and seven-

---

[43]"In an average year the Italian bankers of New York City alone sent to Italy from $25,000,000 to $30,000,000. This is said to have an appreciative effect upon the money market." *Lippincott's Magazine*, LVIII, 234 (1896).

[44]"An Act to secure Homesteads to Actual Settlers on the Public Domain," *U. S. Statutes at Large*, 1861-2, 392.

[45]*History of Houston County, Minnesota*, 481.

ties spent from one to five years in Wisconsin or Illinois before moving into the Farther West.[46] They were in turn apprentices and journeymen, and finally attained to the full dignity of masters of their own estates.

The economic as well as the social importance of the tendency of the Scandinavian immigrants to settle upon the unoccupied farm lands of the West, can scarcely be over-emphasized. It gains still more striking significance when the figures showing such settlement are compared with those of some other races which have more recently contributed largely to the immigrant population; for the man who owns and develops a farm necessarily makes a permanent, long-time investment of himself and his family in a reproductively extractive industry; while the wage-earner in the mines or in lumbering is quite likely to be a "bird of passage," engaged in destructively extractive industries, with only vague notions of, or longings for, citizenship and its responsibilities. Professor John R. Commons, perhaps the best statistical authority on this subject, gives some striking figures illustrative of the farm-ward tendencies of different alien elements, showing the percentage of total number of males in 1890 engaged (1) on farms, (2) as farmers and planters, and (3) as laborers not specified:[47]

	(1) Farm Labor	(2) Farmers	(3) Laborers
Danes	40.78	27.41	13.30
Swedes and Norwegians	38.26	27.12	14.95
Germans	27.04	21.14	11.58
English	18.53	14.82	7.47
Irish	14.71	11.60	25.16
Russians	15.19	11.03	10.96
Italians	5.81	3.91	34.15
Hungarians	3.92	2.13	32.44

[46]*History of Goodhue County, Minnesota; History of Houston County, Minnesota;* Sparks, *History of Winneshiek County, Iowa.* See the numerous biographies in Nelson, *History of the Scandinavians,* I, II.

[47]*Report of the Industrial Commission,* XV, 301-302. Mr. R. C. Jones, assistant superintendent of Castle Garden, New York, estimated, according to an interview in the *Milwaukee Sentinel,* Dec. 30, 1888, that about one Swede out of a hundred went to a city.

From calculations based upon the reports of the censuses of 1870, 1880, and 1890, it appears that one out of four of the Scandinavians was in the last year engaged in agriculture; of the Americans, one out of five; of the Germans, one out of six; and of the Irish, one out of twelve.[48]

One of the very natural consequences of the tendency of the Norse immigrants to seek agricultural locations, and to seek them along the advancing frontier, is the township and even the county, particularly in Minnesota and the Dakotas[49] peopled almost solidly with the men and women of one nationality. The names of post-offices and townships, and the assessment rolls of the counties, bear witness to the density of these settlements which were made up of immigrants in both the first and second stages, composed in part of people coming from the older colonies like those in Dane County, Wisconsin, or Henry County, Illinois, or Goodhue County, Minnesota, and in part of newcomers direct from their Old World homes. About 1880, the names of those whose land abutted upon the two railroads traversing Houston County, Minnesota showed plainly this process of massing. Taken in order, the first twenty-two names were those of American, Irish, and German settlers; then followed nineteen, all Scandinavian save two.[50] Fillmore County, Minnesota, one of the older counties, largely Norwegian from its beginning, and Chisago County, on the eastern border of the same State, a stronghold of the Swedes from its first settlement, are excellent examples of the economic contributions made to the State by the Scandinavian element through its development of the wilderness into cultivated fields and prosperous villages. Of the transformation of Dakota before 1890, and the part of the sons of the North in it, a writer says: "Most of them came with just enough to get on Government land and build a shack. . . . . Now they are loaning money to their less

[48]See Nelson, *History of the Scandinavians*, I, 246.

[49]*History of the Upper Mississippi Valley*, 281, 312, 416, 440, 511; *History of Fillmore County, Minnesota*, 344, 346; *Northwest Magazine*, Oct., 1899.

[50]*History of Houston County, Minnesota*, 286.

fortunate neighbors. . . . . Every county has Norwegians who are worth from $25,000 to $50,000, all made since settling in Dakota."[51]

In comparing statistics of such counties as Fillmore and Chisago, showing their growth in wealth and productivity, as reported in the decennial census, two facts regarding the nativity and parentage of the population must be kept clearly in mind if the full significance of the work of the men of alien stock is to be appreciated: first, that the increase of the foreign born is largely made up of adults; second, that the increase of the native-born is in reality an increase of the purely Norwegian or Swedish element, the sons and daughters, grandsons and granddaughters of foreign-born parents, for the census-taker, even in 1900, did not penetrate beyond the first degree of ancestry.

The tabulation given in Appendix II illustrates the economic progress of three Minnesota counties in which the Norse factor has been strong from the early days of their settlement: Fillmore, Chisago, and Otter Tail, one of the newer counties in the west-central part of the State. From these figures some conception of the influence of the North European in one American commonwealth may be obtained. These are not unique cases, but rather are they what might be called normal counties of their class, counties whose population is made up more or less of good native-born settlers from the older Eastern States.

Several processes already discussed will be easily and forcibly illustrated by these tables. In Fillmore County, for example, the oldest of the three, the increase of the foreign-born element was most rapid in the decade 1870-1880, while during the next ten years there was a distinct falling off, due beyond any doubt to the rise in the price of lands in that county and to the opening up of new counties like Otter Tail where just as good land was to be had at the minimum rate. This falling off was paralleled in the same decade in Chisago County, while both the rise and decline in the number of foreign-born Nor-

[51]*The Northwest Magazine,* Oct., 1889, p. 32.

wegians going into Otter Tail County occur in the two later decades, 1880-1890 and 1890-1900, when the Dakotas were filling up.

The continuing additions to the acreage of farm lands and the steady transformation of unimproved areas into improved areas, indicate the extent to which the labor of alien hands was enhancing the value of the prairies even down to 1900, and presumably since that date. The figures for the increase of the cash values of the farms, including fences, etc., but not improvements, have been chosen because the increases in the total valuations of counties is not infrequently due to the rise of considerable villages and cities, and to the building of railroads, and to these enterprises in contrast with the evolution of agricultural values, the Scandinavian is a comparatively insignificant contributor. The extent to which this development of rural areas may go, is curiously evidenced in the names of the subdivisions of the relatively new Otter Tail County. Of its sixty-two townships in 1900, not less than thirteen bear unmistakable Scandinavian (Norwegian) names—Aastad, Aurdal, Norwegian Grove, St. Olaf, Tordenskjold, Throndhjem, etc.

The price which the immigrant-agriculturist was willing to pay for his coveted free-hold farm was not measured in dollars and cents alone. In a very real way, the land was to become the property of the highest bidder, tho each one paid $1.25 per acre; the land was sure to go to him who would in the long run put the most of himself into the bargain—muscle, courage, patience, pride in his family, and the future of himself and his family as over against the present. It was due in no small degree to the composite nature of this individual investment by the man from Europe's Northwest, that he so promptly and intelligently succeeded in acquiring free of debt his farm and home in the American Northwest.[52]

[52]See the testimony of John Anderson, editor of *Daily Skandinaven*, before the Select (Congressional) Committee on Immigration and Naturalization, 1891. *House Reports, No. 3472*, 51 Cong. 2 Sess., 679-683.

Another reason for his nearly uniform success lies in the fact that he was brought up to a more careful and intensive system of farming than his average American neighbor. Perhaps, too, he works harder than the American, but hard work, long and unflinchingly continued, is a fundamental condition of the success of a farmer whatever his nationality. From the Scandinavian immigrant's point of view, he does not work so hard in the United States, in order to gain a given result,—ownership of his own farm, for illustration,—as he would have had to work in the land of his birth. Personal interviews with scores of men in various parts of the Northwest confirm the opinion expressed to Miss Bremer in Wisconsin so far back as 1850, when pioneering was as hard as at any time since the "Sloop Folk" landed in New York: "About seven hundred Norwegian colonists are settled in this neighborhood, all upon small farms. . . . . I asked many, both men and women, whether they were contented; whether they were better off here or in old Norway. Nearly all of them replied, 'Yes, we are better off here; we do not work so hard, and it is easier to gain a livelihood.' "[53]

In a discussion of the competition of the immigrants with American laborers, an eminent scholar maintains that the Scandinavians of the West have succeeded where the American with a better start has failed.[54] He questions if this success is a survival of the fittest, if it has not been purchased at the expense of American labor which is forced elsewhere, because the Americans will not endure the hard work and live on the coarse fare, through which the immigrants win their success.[55] However true this might be as a generalization about immigrants as a whole, it can hardly be true of the Swedes and Norwegians, except in so far as they have been more willing than the native American to live the life of a pioneer and to stick to the

[53]Bremer, *Homes of the New World*, I, 242.

[54]Mayo-Smith, *Emigration and Immigration*, 146.

[55]*Ibid.*, quoting a letter from Fargo, Dakota, July 24, 1887, to the *New York Times*.

soil. But this cannot fairly be called forcing out American labor, or driving the American to the wall; immigrant labor went in where there was no labor of any kind. Furthermore, up to 1890, there was certainly plenty of land for all the American, or native-born, laborers who desired to devote themselves to that sort of work by which the Scandinavians were gaining their independence. If the agricultural land of the vast West be looked upon as a national asset, to be held for cautious and discriminating distribution to examined and approved settlers, then it may be that the foreigner has occupied land which might have sometime fallen to a better man.

The standard of living among the Scandinavian settlers, whether on the frontier or in the towns, has not been very different from that of their American neighbors. It cannot vary much in a sod-house on the prairie, in a cabin on a claim, or in a log-hut in a clearing, whether the occupant be of Viking or Puritan descent.[56] The food was Indian corn, sometimes ground in a coffee-mill, occasionally wheat, milk, fish, wild fowl, pork, and common vegetables; the clothing was often primitive and always rough, and in the early days, at least, "men in wooden shoes and home-made woolen jackets were no uncommon sights at their religious meetings, or even when they were locked in holy matrimony before the altar."[57] But with prosperity, Americanization, and the settling up of the region about them, they took to comforts and luxuries just as soon as they could afford them. During the autumn of 1886 the writer spent more than six weeks in the family of a well-to-do Danish farmer in central Minnesota, and made frequent calls at the homes of Swedish and American neighbors; very little perceptible difference could be observed in the standards of living, whether judged by furniture, dress, or food. In the gradations up to the

[56]Langeland, *Nordmœndene i Amerika,* ch. xi; Strömme, *Hvorledes Halvor blev Prest,*—an excellent picture of life among the Norwegians in Wisconsin and Minnesota; Foss, *Tobias: a Story of the Northwest.*
[57]*Scandinavia,* I, 142.

wealthy families of the larger towns and cities, the same statement would be true. If any modifications were to be made, it would be that Scandinavians set a more bountiful table, and give more attention than the Americans to festivals and celebrations.

The men of Scandinavian stock have by no means devoted themselves exclusively to agriculture, tho it has already been shown how dominant with them is the desire for the possession of land and the independence which that possession brings. In business—trade, manufacturing, and finance,—and in the professions, in all that differentiates the village or urban community from the rural, they have, especially since 1890, played an active part. A rising percentage of skilled laborers and of those who had in the Old World experience with business affairs, marked the immigration from Northern Europe after 1880. The accumulated wealth of the earlier immigrants sought investment in the thriving towns of the newer commonwealths of the Northwest. Villages which sprang up along railroads, became cities with the advent of other lines; water power has developed fast; the forests were to be turned into lumber and its further manufactured products. The Scandinavian villages and wards of great cities evolved their own stores, shops, factories, and banks just as they did their churches, lodges, and other social organizations, manned by men of ambition, ability, skill, and resourcefulness.

Both in the cities like Chicago, Minneapolis, Rockford, and Madison, and in the more homogeneous villages of the solidly Scandinavian counties, Norwegian and Swedish merchants and tradesmen, catering to Americans as well as to persons of their own nationality, rapidly achieved success and fortune. Seven years after landing, a Swedish immigrant is reported in 1873 to have built up in Anoka, Minnesota, the largest grocery establishment in that section, doing an annual business of $100,000.[58] In the city of Minneapolis one of the largest department stores west of

[58]*History of the Upper Mississippi Valley,* 228.

Chicago, and probably the greatest Scandinavian business house in the country, is that of S. E. Olson & Co., which does a yearly business of about $2,000,000, and in the height of the season employs more than 700 persons.[59] Scattered over the Northwest are scores of enterprising Scandinavian individuals and firms engaged in business as merchants, grain-dealers, contractors, etc., whose annual business passes $100,000.[60]

The manufacturing industries in which the Swedes and Norwegians play the more active part are those closely related to agriculture and the forest—the cutting and sawing of lumber, the manufacture of furniture, and the manufacture of agricultural implements. By foresight and shrewd investments in timber lands in Wisconsin and Minnesota, a certain Norwegian immigrant accumulated nearly a million dollars; a Swedish immigrant in like manner built up the C. A. Smith Lumber Company of Minneapolis, one of the great manufacturers of the upper Mississippi Valley, with works occupying seventy acres, employing upwards of 800 men, and with branch lumber yards situated in western Minnesota and in the Dakotas.[61]

The manufacture of furniture is the chief occupation of the Swedes of Rockford, Illinois, who comprise fully one-third of that city's population of 30,000. In 1875 fifteen Swedes organized the Forest City Furniture Company, with a capital of $50,000; ten years later, Rockford was the second city in the country in the production of furniture, and in 1893 there were more than twenty furniture companies with a capital varying from $50,000 to $200,000. Nearly all of these companies were organized on the co-operative basis, nearly all were composed of Swedes, and nearly all were earning a clear profit of 20 per-cent

[59]Söderström, *Minneapolis Minnen,* 204; Nelson, *History of the Scandinavians,* I, 466.

[60]*Ibid.,* I, 504, 467; II, 160, 164, 193, 229, 233, 248, 261; Söderström, *Minneapolis Minnen,* 202, 203.

[61]S. A. Quale, a Norwegian immigrant of 1869, and C. A. Smith, a Swedish immigrant of 1867. *The North,* May 21, 1890; Söderström, *Minneapolis Minnen,* 191.

and upwards..[62]   Other notable instances of successful Scandinavian manufacturers are John A. Johnson, whose works for making agricultural implements in Madison, Wisconsin, employed about 300 men; the great printing and publishing house of John Anderson & Company of Chicago, from which are issued the daily and weekly editions of "Skandinaven," and the Swedish-American Publishing Company of Minneapolis, publishing the widely circulated "Svenska Amerikanska Posten."[63]

The economic progress of the immigrants from the Northlands may well be gauged by the number of public and private banking establishment in the Northwest controlled by them. Surprisingly numerous are the men who, after gaining a competency as merchants, grain-dealers (one of these built twenty-five elevators along the Great Northern Railway), land speculators, and lumbermen, have turned to banking as their communities developed. The market for capital was active, ready to absorb large or small amounts; rates of interest ran from ten to twenty per cent.; the thrift and honesty of the Norse folk were equivalent to a bond. Hence small banks with $25,000 and $50,000 capital multiplied, not always on the soundest basis, it should be said, though this does not imply dishonesty. In Minneapolis, between 1874 and 1900, the names of no less than six Scandinavian banks appear, the largest becoming the strong Swedish American National Bank with a capital of $250,000.[64] Smaller cities like Sioux City and Boone, Iowa, have developed similar sound banks capitalized for $100,000. Not all Scandinavian bankers, however, have escaped the temptations of "high finance," though the total of failures is comparatively small. One of the most notorious and shameful examples of bank-wrecking in recent years occurred in Chicago in 1906, when Paul O. Stensland,

[62]Kæding, *Rockfords Svenskar*, 67, 95; *The North*, Jan. 8, 1890, July 12, 1893.

[63]Nelson, *History of the Scandinavians*, II, 209; Söderström, *Minneapolis Minnen*, 181-189.

[64]Söderström, *Minneapolis Minnen*, 206; Nelson, *History of the Scandinavians*, II, 164, 228.

for years the trusted and honored and admired president of the Milwaukee Avenue State Bank, the depository of hundreds of working men and small tradesmen, wrecked the bank through speculations in real estate, fled to Africa, and was brought back and placed in the Joliet prison for a term of fifteen years.[65]

As the regions into which the Scandinavian immigrants have gone so determinedly as agricultural settlers have gradually become more complex in their economic structure, these men and women have once more illustrated their notable capacity to adapt themselves to the new conditions and to share in new advantages. The second and third generation will probably develop much the same tendency city-ward which the Americans of the same class show so markedly; and they will take their share of the honors and emoluments of business, manufacturing, banking, the technical professions, and the so-called learned professions.

[65]The Chicago papers for August, September, and October give full details of the wrecking of the bank and the career of its president. See *Chicago Tribune*, August 9 ff., 1906.

CHAPTER IX.

The social results of the settlement of a body of aliens in any country, as compared with the economic, are far more undefinable and elusive, even when the settlement is compact and homogenous, like that of the Dutch in New York or the French in Louisiana. But when a particular element, like the Irish or the Scandinavian, in a complex population, is distributed over a wide area, with accessions running through three-quarters of a century, the problem of its social influence and importance becomes vastly more difficult. No study or observation of such a well-established racial group, outside of the purely statistical, at best can reach far beyond an impression or an individual opinion; it cannot arrive at a convincing and conclusive scientific deduction.[1] Looked at in its length and breadth, the question of social results of Scandinavian immigration takes various forms. Have the foreign-born citizen and his immediate descendants adapted themselves rapidly and vitally to the best American customs in business, politics, education, and religion? Have they learned English quickly? What has been their attitude towards such questions as intemperance, slavery, and public honesty? Are they re-enforcing the best standards of public and private morality prevailing in the communities into which they come?

Fundamental to this discussion, is the general effect of the process of immigration and new settlement, upon the physical and intellectual state of the immigrant and his offspring. It has already been pointed out that the immigrants of the nineteenth century, like those hardy souls of the sixteenth, who left England, Holland, France, or

[1] Hall, *Immigration*, ch. viii.

106

Sweden, were the more adventurous and determined men and women of their parishes, and that the incidents and anxieties of settling up affairs in their old homes and of getting off for America, would stir to quicker thinking the minds of even the slow and inert. Then came the influence of adjustment to the ways of a new and larger world, with its greater distance, its more rapid communication, its more strenuous activities, its new language, and its different climate and diet; all these re-enforced the original, quickened impulse, and of necessity affected both subtly and powerfully the mind and body of two generations.

The change has in general been for the better, tho some observers think they see a retrogression, especially in physical respects. A Norwegian physician who spent about nine months in the United States in 1892, wrote for a Christiania medical journal an article in which he declared: "That the Norwegian race in the United States is declining physically, every one, I think, who has spent some time among our emigrated countrymen there must admit. But the change is a slow one." The causes, as he saw them, were the unwholesome climate of the Northwest, the unsuitable food of the farmers, the cold, damp houses of the prairies, and the abuse of alcoholic liquors and tobacco. By way of final summary of opinions, he states that "the general rule is that, these dark sides to the contrary notwithstanding, the social conditions in America and its democratic institutions are conducive to individual thinking thereby contributing to the development of individual talent, great or small as that may be."[2]

The views of Dr. Kraft were more or less disputed by several Norwegian physicians in the United States, in *The North* for January and February, 1893. Dr. Harold Graff, writing to the periodical in which Dr. Kraft's article originally appeared, says: "With astonishing rapidity, the

[2]Dr. E. Kraft, "The Physical Degeneration of the Norwegian Race in North America," *The North*, Jan. 3, 1893,— translation from *Norsk Magazin for Lægevidenskaben;* Ch. Gronvald, "The Effects of the Immigration on the Norwegian Immigrants," appendix to the *Sixth Annual Report of the State Board of Health of Minnesota*, (1878), II, 507-534.

wide mouth and ungainly nose of the specific Norwegian peasant type become modified and disappear, the difference between the physiognomy and facial expression of parents and children being often bewilderingly great. . . . . I have interviewed some of the oldest and most experienced physicians practising in this country, and also other intelligent Norwegians who have travelled among their countrymen in the States, without as yet having heard any divergent opinion whatever. All agree that the Norwegian race in every respect is progressing in both mind and body."[3] Others, who were not so sure of the physical improvement, agree as to the intellectual quickening. In a word, if the transplanting of the tree has not certainly produced an improved trunk or foliage, it has bettered the quality of the fruit. The next logical step is to attempt to estimate the value of such fruit in the American market.

The two obvious ways of determining the influence of a foreign element, are to compare it with some other foreign-born constituent longer and better known, and to compare it with the native American. The latter is the fairer criterion, but it is not easy to ascertain and define what are the purely American characteristics with which comparison is to be made. Statistics on social matters are so incomplete that reliance must be placed upon the consensus of opinion of thoughtful, sympathetic observers and students of American life, whether they be statesmen and philosophers bred in the United States, or scholarly, penetrating foreigners like James Bryce and Alexander de Toqueville.[4] Such men of insight agree that the American ideal comprises love of freedom, independence, and equality; respect for law, government, education, and social morality (including reverence for the family and the home) ; and lastly a willingness to share the common burden and, if need be, to make a common sacrifice for the permanent welfare of the commonwealth.

[3]*The North,* Jan. 18, 1893, translating the article mentioned.
[4]Bryce, *American Commonwealth* (3rd ed.), ch. lxxx; Matthews, *American Character,* 20-34; Roosevelt, *American Ideals,* ch. i, ii.

In acquiring the use of English and in maintaining high standards of education, the Scandinavians have an unimpeachable record which no other foreign, non-English-speaking element can equal. Illiteracy in Norway and Sweden is almost unknown. Taken together, these two kingdoms have less than one per-cent of illiteracy, and among the recruits in Sweden in 1896 only .13% were unlettered, and only .63% were unable to write.[5] Personal acquaintance with many hundreds of Scandinavians, on both sides of the Atlantic, has failed to reveal to the writer a single adult who was unable to read and write.

One of the very first matters to receive attention in a Scandinavian settlement in the United States, has been the establishment of a school, and, as speedily as possible, the instruction has been given in English, partly because the school laws of most of the States would not recognize a public school conducted in a foreign language, and partly because the settlers desired to have the children know English.[6] For a year or two in some of the isolated communities, as in Arendahl, Fillmore County, Minnesota, in 1857-8, it was necessary to conduct the schools in Swedish or Norwegian; but only rarely has any attempt been made to continue systematic, regular instruction exclu-

---

[5]*Statesman's Year Book, 1900*, 1049; Kiddle & Schem, *Dictionary of Education*, 452. In the latter work, Norway, Sweden, Denmark, and Switzerland are marked with asterisks, signifying that they are practically without illiteracy. The contrast of these figures with the percentages of illiteracy of some other European countries is very striking. In 1890 the percentage of illiterates in Austria was 40%, in Hungary, 54%, in Italy, in 1897, among conscripts, 37.3% (reduced from 56.7% in 1871), and among those persons marrying, males, 32.9%, females, 52.13% (reduced respectively from 57.73% and 76.73% in 1871). For Russia the percentage is probably about 80%, perhaps as high as 90%. See *Statesman's Year Book, 1900*, 374-375, 392, 744-745. Statistical returns relating to German army recruits indicate that in 1896-7 only about .11% could neither read nor write. *Ibid.*, 592. See also, Hall, *Immigration*, 46, 48, 54, 61, 141.

[6]*History of Fillmore County, Minnesota*, 346, 463,—a Norwegian school for one year in a private house, then an English school; Sparks, *History of Winneshiek County, Iowa*, 16-17.

sively in the mother-tongue by the maintenance of year-long parish schools. The immigrants have frequently been insistent, and properly so, upon some scheme by which they might be able to educate their children in the use of the mother-tongue; but schools for this purpose have usually supplemented rather than supplanted the ordinary public school.[7] In a very few localities, like the older settlements in Goodhue County and Fillmore County, Minnesota, Allamakee County, Iowa, and Dane County, Wisconsin, parish schools are still maintained throughout the year.[8]

The church schools are more commonly a sort of summer vacation school supported either by the persons whose children attend, or at the expense of the whole congregation; in them are taught the language of the parents and the preacher, the church catechism, and something of church history; sometimes especial attention, as in the case of the Danish, Grundtvigian "high schools," is given to keeping alive the traditions of the European kingdom from which sprang the immigrants. The teacher of both the language and the doctrines of religion is customarily a student in some theological seminary of the denomination to which the congregation belongs. The Lutherans have kept up these vacation schools more consistently than any other Scandinavian church. The report of the parochial schools of the United Norwegian Lutheran Church for 1905 showed that on the average almost thirty days were devoted to the church school in each of the 750 congregations reporting.[9]

The clergy are mainly active in this mild paternalism, upon which the younger people not infrequently look with disfavor, for to the second generation it appears an unnecessary perpetuation of an un-American custom, a

[7]For a discussion of the Bennett Law in Wisconsin, see pp. 167 ff.

[8]*Beretning om det syttende Aarsmöde for den Forenede norsk lutherske Kirke i Amerika, 1906,*—"Parochialraporter for Aaret 1905."

[9]"Sammendrag af Parochialraporter", *Beretning om det syttende Aarsmöde for den Forenede norsk lutherske Kirke i Amerika, 1906,* LVI; J. J. Skordalsvold, in Nelson, *History of the Scandinavians,* I, 241.

scheme for emphasizing peculiarities and differences rather than a means of hastening the process of amalgamation. Sometimes the younger men have revolted and broken entirely with the Lutheran church, identifying themselves with American congregations, or drifting out on the wide sea of religious indifference.

The loyalty of the Scandinavians to the public school system has been of far-reaching consequence to the immigrants themselves as well as to American society. There is always a more or less strongly marked tendency among aliens speaking a foreign language to congregate in groups in the country or in certain wards in large towns and cities, and out of this tendency springs a sort of clannishness which cannot be avoided and which is not peculiar to any class, for the immigrants naturally follow the lines of least resistance. They go to those whom they know, to those whose speech they can understand, to those from whose experience they may draw large drafts of suggestion and help. But this clannishness with the Swedes, Norwegians and Danes, has been but a stage in their evolution out of which, through the gates of the English language, public schools, naturalization, and increased prosperity, they have passed to broader relations. The filling up of the Scandinavian quarters of great cities like Chicago, Minneapolis, and St. Paul, may modify the effect of their persistent attachment to the public school; but so far the public school is the great foe to clannishness, and loyalty to it one of the best evidences of the desire of these people from the Northern lands to become Americanized. In the cities of Minneapolis and St. Paul, with their large Scandinavian population, there was not in 1907 a single parish in which the parochial school lasted through the year, and only a few in which vacation schools were maintained.

In higher education the Scandinavians have allowed their denominational zeal to outrun their judgment. They have founded numerous seminaries and so-called colleges, but almost invariably as a part of the necessary equipment of a religious denomination, for how could a self-respecting sect, no matter how young or how slightly differentiated from its older brethren, permit its children to attend the schools of those whose denominational beliefs or practices had become objectionable enough to warrant a schism in the church? A few of these institutions, like Luther College, at Decorah, Iowa, Gustavus Adolphus College at St. Peter, Minnesota, Augustana College at Rock Island, Illinois, and Bethany College at Lindsborg, Kansas, have maintained an excellent standard of work and exercise a wide and beneficent influence.[10]   The great majority, however, have simply wasted resources by the multiplication of ambitious, struggling, poorly-equipped, so-called colleges, with little or no endowment, and often dependent upon the congregations of the denomination which gave them birth.[11]

One of the results of the excessive splitting-up of the Scandinavian churches is that the energies which ought to be concentrated are frittered away on unnecessary schools. A separate denominational school and a family paper seem to be indispensable parts of the machinery of every newly organized sect, no matter how young or how small or how poor it may be.[12]   The number of these institutions continually varies with the ups and downs of the denominations trying to support them.   In 1893, Mr. J. J. Skordalsvold, a graduate of the University of Minnesota, put the number of Scandinavian colleges, schools, and seminaries in the United States at thirty-six, with an attendance of about five thousand.[13]   Sixteen of these, with an attendance of twenty-five hundred, one-half of the total, were located in Minnesota.   By 1900 the sixteen had grown to twenty schools, having property worth $500,000, one hundred and

---

[10]See catalogs of these institutions.

[11]Several of the Norwegian and Swedish weekly papers supported by the different denominations publish regularly lists of donors to particular schools, stating the amount of money, or the nature of the articles given, enumerating the books, quantities of fuel, clothing, etc.

[12]Bille, *History of the Danes in America*, 20-24,—an excellent account of some of these attempts.

sixty teachers, and three thousand students.[14] In that
state, however, and in others like North Dakota, these
schools are likely to follow the same course as many of
the schools of other pioneering Protestant denominations,
and become little more than preparatory schools on the
one hand, or theological seminaries on the other, leaving
to the State university the maintenance of higher education in every field save arts and theology. Even as secondary schools, not many of them will be likely to survive
the third generation of the original immigrants, unless
they are much better endowed than any one of them is at
the present time.[15] The Red Wing Seminary (Hauge
Synod) of Red Wing, Minnesota, founded in 1878, is essentially an ordinary private secondary school with a theological course attached, and three-fourths of its work is
conducted in English.[16] Bethany College at Lindsborg,
Kansas, one of the three prosperous Swedish colleges, and
perhaps the most ambitious, is substantially an English-
speaking college, with nine departments of instruction,
and in 1912 a registration of 919. Only in the classes in
Swedish language and literature is the instruction given
in Swedish, tho "Swedish is required of all students preparing to enter the ministerial work of our Swedish Evangelical Lutheran Church."[16a] Luther College, the Norwegian institution at Decorah, Iowa, has followed along the
same course only not quite so far. Several years ago the
proportion between English and Norwegian as media of
instruction was slightly in favor of the English in the

[14]Nelson, *Scandinavians in the United States* (2nd ed.), 317 ff.
[15]*The World Almanac and Encyclopedia*, 1914, 599-609.

	Instructors	Students	Prod. Fds.	Income
Augsburg Seminary	8	173	40,000	20,000
Augustana College	31	629	414,356	101,923
Bethany College (Kan.)	44	893	55,777	93,166
Gustavus Adolphus College	23	348	75,000	35,328
Luther College	16	213	272,408	37,000
St. Olaf College	32	550	250,000	74,000

[16]Interview with Professor G. O. Brohough, August, 1906. See Nelson, *Scandinavians in the United States*, I, 179-180.
[16a]*Catalogue of Bethany College, 31st Academic Year* (1912), 54.

college classes; in the classes in the preparatory department, in the literary societies, and in the conversation of the students, English was decidedly predominant.[17] The practice of this, the oldest, and in some respects the soundest and most influential, of the Scandinavian colleges, is sure to be adopted by the lesser schools which survive their adolescence.

From a religious standpoint, the most noteworthy characteristic of Scandinavians wherever found, is their intense Protestantism. Everywhere and always they are uncompromising enemies of the Roman Catholic church, and there are barely enough Catholics among them in Europe and in the United States to prove that it is possible to convert one of them to that faith. In fact, their dislike of Catholicism is an instinct coming down from Reformation times rather than a matter of experience or close-at-hand observation; but so strong is this feeling that it colors, consciously or unconsciously, their relations in politics and society in the United States. Their distrust of the Irish is at bottom more a religious than a racial instinct, even when it takes an active form. While this dislike and suspicion are still real and large, it has undoubtedly been reduced by the breaking-up of the old rigid lines of Lutheranism, which has taken place in the last two decades in the United States.

Each of the three peninsular kingdoms of Northern Europe has an established Lutheran church, administered by bishops, which holds still the great majority of the people. Toleration has been generally practiced for a half century, the sole exception being the ban against Jesuits in Norway.[18] Of all the Protestant churches, none is more rigidly orthodox than the Lutheran, none is more unwilling to admit changes in its traditional creed; only a few years ago, the Norwegian Synod in America re-affirmed its belief in the literal inspiration of the Bible.

[17]A. Estrem, "A Norwegian-American College," *Midland Monthly*, I, 605-611.

[18]*The Statesman's Year Book, 1900*, 491, 1048, 1062.

Yet in spite of this conservatism, the Lutherans settled in the United States have invariably rejected the episcopal form of government, and have organized upon a more or less democratic basis. No matter how loyal they were to the Establishment in the Old World, a bishop has not appeared to be necessary to their happiness or salvation in the New. The Lutheran Church proper has kept within its folds a much larger percentage of Swedes than of Norwegians in the United States, the characteristic independence of the latter leading many of them even farther than mere separation from the mother-church. The persistence of the centrifugal force of dissent shows itself again and again in the violent polemics and divisions which have marked the course of Norwegian church history in America.[19] While this divisiveness may in some degree be due to the fashion set by the early settlers of whom many were dissenters, probably the deeper cause is to be found in the general freedom from religious restriction and prescription which characterizes the whole United States and especially the West.

Even the more extreme sects, in regard to belief and practice, have been recruited from among the Scandinavians both before and since their coming to this country. The Mormons were early at work as missionaries in Northern Europe and, as has been stated above, won many converts, particularly in Denmark, from whose immigration Utah mainly profited. In 1900 Utah had a total foreign-born population of 53,777, of whom 9132 were Danes; 7025, Swedes; and 2128, Norwegians. The real result of the missionary work, however, is better seen in the figures for persons having both parents born in a specified country and residing in Utah in 1900: Danes, 18,963; Swedes, 12,047; Norwegians, 3,466; total, 34,476.[20]

[19]Gjerset, "*The United Norwegian Lutheran Church*," in Nelson, *History of the Scandinavians*, I, 229-242.

[20]*Twelfth Census, 1900, Population*, Pt. I, Tables 33 and 39; H. H. Bancroft, *Utah*, 441, 431; Montgomery, *The Work Among the Scandinavians*, 8. Mr. Montgomery, the superintendent of Minnesota for the American Home Missionary Society (1886), laments the fact that very

The American churches and missionary societies were
not unmindful of the needs of the Scandinavians scattered
over the Middle West in the early days of its development,
and in zealous and effective fashion gave them aid. The
work of the Hedström brothers in New York and in the
West, already described, reflects credit on the Methodist
Church. Once at least, help came to them from an unex-
pected source: Jenny Lind, the "Swedish Nightingale,"
devoted to charity the proceeds of a concert in New York,
in November, 1850, and among the items of the distribution
of the total of $5073.20 by a committee, is "To the Relief
of the Poor Swedes and Norwegians in the city of New
York per the Rev. Mr. Hedström, $273.20. To the distri-
bution of Swedish Bibles and Testaments, in New York."[21]
Besides the Bethel Ship in New York Harbor (1845), this
same church established a Scandinavian mission in the
Rock River Conference, in Illinois, in 1849, and two others
in Iowa and Wisconsin in 1850. Three years later the
report showed two Swedish missions with four missionaries, and two Norwegian missions with four missionaries.[22]

The American Lutheran churches undertook to aid
their co-religionists, and in 1850 the Pittsburg Synod and
the Joint Synod of Ohio each sent one of its ministers into
the Northwest, but the epidemic of cholera caused them
to hurry back to their former homes.[23] The real support
of some of the immigrant Lutheran missionaries came
from the American Home Missionary Society (Congregational). One of the men thus assisted was Paul Anderson

large numbers of the Scandinavians "have become converts to Mormonism, and have 'gathered' to Utah," and adds further: "I have before me
the official statistics of the Mormon church (not easily obtained) giving
a report of their missionary work in Scandinavia for each year from
1851 to 1881. They report that their converts in these lands during these
thirty-one years reached the enormous total of 132,766 persons, and that of
these 21,000 emigrated to Utah." From a beginning of four elders of the
Mormon church at work in Denmark, Sweden, and Norway in 1850, the
force increased to sixty-one missionaries at work in 1881.

[21]Rosenberg, *Jenny Lind in America*, 79.
[22]Simpson, *Cyclopedia of Methodism*, 785.
[23]*The North*, Aug. 30, 1893, quoting from *The Workman*.

(Norland) who came from Norway in 1843, and received
a part of his education in the new Congregational college
at Beloit. He was chosen pastor of the first Norwegian
Lutheran Church in Chicago in 1848, and journeyed to
Albany, New York, to be ordained by a Lutheran minister,
but he nevertheless served under a commission from the
Congregational Society, and made reports to it for several
years.[24]

In a similar manner this Society supported for several
years the missionary labors of Lars Paul Esbjörn, a graduate of Upsala University, who was ordained a Lutheran
clergyman when he emigrated in 1849, and likewise the
labors of T. N. Hasselquist. Esbjörn was appointed a
missionary of the Society in December, 1849, on the recom-
mendation of the Central Association of Congregational
Ministers of Illinois, to whom he presented his credentials
and by whom he was examined and received into the
Association.[25] He was re-appointed year by year, making
reports from 1851 to 1854.[26] Hasselquist makes acknowl-
edgment of his obligations to the Society in a letter of
July, 1853, saying that he rejoices "in connection with
your in the highest sense benevolent Society, without
which it would have been impossible for me to do for my
scattered countrymen what I have done. . . . . . I give

[24]Jensson, *American Lutheran Biographies*, 25 ff; *The Home Missionary*, XXII, 263, 264; XXIII, 119. In Anderson's report for 1850 is an
account of a visit to Dane County, Wisconsin, where 'one of the Formal-
ists,' after five years of labor had failed to bring much enlightenment.
"There are some four thousand or more Norwegians in one settlement,
about three-quarters of whom are members of this man's church, and the
rest are sheep without a shepherd. They had had preaching there for the
last five years, but such gross immorality I had never witnessed before. . . . We have no reasonable ground to hope that a single individual
of those three thousand souls is converted to God; for all are intemperate
and profane. . . . Of all I saw (and I saw a great many) two out of
three were intoxicated, or had been drinking so that it was offensive to
come within the sphere poisoned by their breath; and of every two I
heard talking together one or both profaned their Maker."
[25]*The Home Missionary*, XXIII, 250, 263.
[26]*Ibid.*, XXIV, 238; XXIV, 287.

humble thanks to the Home Missionary Association which
out of Christian benevolence helps to build up the Kingdom
of Christ among scattered Swedes who are almost all very
poor, but still love the word of God."[27] In 1852 the Society
appointed the Rev. Ole Anderson [Andrewson?] to the
charge of the Scandinavian church in Racine, Wisconsin,
and two years later he reports to the Society from La Salle
County, Illinois.[28]

Since the Civil War and the great increase in the
numbers of immigrants, the home missionary efforts of the
Methodists, Congregationalists, and Baptists have been
carried on with persistence, if not always with perfect
wisdom. In 1911 the Methodists had five Swedish Conferences with 222 churches, a membership of about 18,000,
and property valued at upwards of $2,000,000, and two
Norwegian-Danish Conferences, with 119 churches, 6,300
members, and property worth $400,000.[29] The cost of this
work to the Methodist Missionary Society is not far from
$50,000 per year.[30] The Baptists began their proselyting
work in Norway and Sweden, and have prosecuted it steadily in the Northwest since the establishment of the first
Swedish Baptist church in Rock Island, Illinois, in 1852.
In 1912 the church reports showed 18 Swedish conferences, 374 churches, 28,000 members, and current income of
about $350,000, and also eleven Norwegian-Danish confer-
ences, 94 churches, 5,900 members, and current income of
$65,500.[31] The Congregationalists have pushed their de-
nominational interests in like manner, and in 1913 had
about one hundred churches, with rather more than six

[27]*The Home Missionary,* XXVI, 73.

[28]*Ibid.,* XXV, 77; XXVI, 268.

[29]Liljegren, "Historical Review of Scandinavian Methodist in the
United States," in Nelson, *History of the Scandinavians,* I, 208; *The
Methodist Year Book, 1912,* 42-45.

[30]Nelson, *History of the Scandinavians,* I, 337; *The Methodist Year
Book, 1912,* 90-92.

[31]Newman, *A Century of Baptist Achievement,* 126; Nelson (and
Peterson), *History of the Scandinavians,* I, 202; *Annual of the Northern
Baptist Convention, 1913,* 189.

thousand members.[32] Besides these churches regularly connected with the Congregational organization, there are about one hundred congregations of the Swedish Mission Union, and the group of independent congregations whose faith and practice are closely allied with those of the Congregationalists.[33] The Unitarian church has endeavored to organize congregations, spending $25,000 on one church in Minneapolis in sixteen years.[34] A few Protestant Episcopal parishes also exist among the Swedes, chiefly in the large cities.[35]

The three denominations first mentioned have for many years maintained, in their respective western theological seminaries, departments or professorships for the education of young men for ministerial service among the immigrants from the Northlands. At the Chicago Theological Seminary (Congregationalist) the Dano-Norwegian department was organized in 1884, with one professor and two students; in the following year a Swedish department was added, the professor being chosen from the Swedish Free Mission Church. In 1906 these two departments had each two professors and respectively thirteen and twenty-seven students, and published a religious paper, *Evangelisten*.[36] Besides the Garrett Biblical Institute (Methodist), Northwestern University has two similar departments, with thirty-one students in the Swedish, and sixteen in the Norwegian-Danish section.[37] In the Divinity School of the University of Chicago (Baptist), the same departments appeared up to 1912; in 1897 there were twenty-two students in the Dano-Norwegian Department, and thirty-five

[32]*Congregational Year Book*, 1914. Cf. Nelson, *Scandinavians in the United States*, I, 346; Montgomery, *Work among the Scandinavians* (1888), and a *"Wind from the Holy Spirit" in Norway and Sweden*, 7-8, 109-112.

[33]Söderström, *Minneapolis Minnen*, 231-236.

[34]*Cosmopolitan*, Oct., 1890; Nelson, *Scandinavians in the United States*, I, 337; Söderström, *Minneapolis Minnen*, 249-250.

[35]Söderström, *Minneapolis Minnen*, 237-241.

[36]*Year book of the Chicago Theological Seminary*, 1906; Montgomery, *The Work Among the Scandinavians* (1888), 9-12, 22.

[37]*Catalogue of the Northwestern University*, 1913-1914, 379-380, 478.

in the Swedish; for 1905, the corresponding figures were twenty-four students, with one professor and two instructors, and thirty-four students, with two professors and one instructor. Both departments were dropped after 1913.[38]

So far as the movements represented by these missionary endeavors and by the organization of schools help to furnish church privileges to those beyond the reach of other Protestant churches—since the Catholics are out of the question—they are admirable, accomplishing much good. But when they cease to be efforts to extend religious opportunities, when they are mainly devoted to swinging men and women already Christian from one denomination to another, they simply add one more factor to the inexcusable competition which too often characterizes the home missionary activity, even when it does not degenerate into a mere scramble for denominational advantage. The results in very many cases have been sadly disproportionate to the expenditures.[39]

Not all the forces, however, have been centrifugal; the divided body of Lutherans has attempted, with varying success, to effect permanent union. Since 1890 the centripetal reaction has been strong, gaining impetus from the highly significant efforts of the branches of the Norwegian Lutherans in a synod held in that year in Minneapolis, to create a single organization. The United Norwegian Lutheran Church, formed June 13, 1890, was made up of the Norwegian Augustana Synod, the Norwegian-Danish Conference, and the Anti-Missourian Brotherhood, thus becoming the strongest of all the American Norwegian churches, numbering 1,122 congregations, about 120,000 members, and having property valued at more than $1,500,-000.[40] But old antagonisms and animosities, generated in the bitterness of religious controversy, were not easily

[38]*Annual Register of the University of Chicago*, 1904-5; 1912-1913, 311.

[39]Nelson (and Skordalsvold), "Historical Review of the Scandinavian Churches in Minnesota," *History of the Scandinavians*, I, 335-349.

[40]*Ibid.*, I, 236ff.; Jacobs, *History of the Evangelical Lutheran Church in the United States*, 513; *Minneapolis Tribune*, June 14, 1890.

overcome, and disputes soon arose to disturb the life of the United Church. The chief of these related to the control of certain educational institutions, especially Augsburg Seminary (theological) in Minneapolis. So acute was the factional quarrel that it was taken into the courts in 1893, and continued on until 1898, when the "Augsburg strife" was settled out of court by mutual agreement. Meantime the Augsburg party had withdrawn from the United Church, taking some 40,000 members, keeping the Seminary, worth about $60,000, but giving up to the United Church the endowment fund of about $40,000.[41] In spite of factions, secessions, and the expulsion of twelve congregations, the United Church as a whole prospered. Its annual report for 1905 gave the following statistics: congregations, more or less closely affiliated, 1,325; ministers and professors, 453; communicants, 267,000; property, $715,000.[42] While the United Church was the largest, there were no fewer than four other branches of Norwegian Lutherans in 1914.[43]

In contrast with the Norwegians, the Swedes have manifested a commendable unity in keeping the faith once delivered to them by the fathers, the chief exception being the Swedish Evangelical Mission Covenant, which can scarcely be called Lutheran. The great Swedish Lutheran Augustana Synod, one of the constituent members of the General Council of the Evangelical Lutheran Church in America, stood staunchly united in the midst of many changes in other branches of the church. Under the broad name of the Scandinavian Evangelical Lutheran Augustana Synod of North America, which comprised both Norwegians and Swedes down to 1870, it grew rapidly, setting its face sternly against the New Lutheranism which sought to modify the old rigidity of doctrine and practice. In

[41]Nelson, *History of the Scandinavians*, I, 217-224, 263; *U. S. Eleventh Census, 1890*, Churches, 452.

[42]*Beretning om det syttende Aarsmöde for den Forenede norsk lutherske Kirke i Amerika*, 140 and LVI.

[43]*World Almanac and Encyclopedia*, 1914, 538-539.

1894 the word Scandinavian was dropped.[44] By 1899 the Synod represented 900 congregations, 200,000 members, and a material estate of $4,200,000.[45]

The break-up of the Lutheran church is not wholly to be regretted when viewed in relation to the process of Americanization, for the church has usually been a stronghold of traditionalism and conservatism. Perhaps, too, the vigorous religious and ecclesiastical disputes, wasteful of energy and of money as they sometimes seem, have contributed to a wholesome and pervasive intellectual activity not altogether unlike the results of the Puritan disputations. So careful a student of Northwestern immigrants as Mr. O. N. Nelson is inclined to the opinion that the contentions of the Lutherans may have benefited the church. "Close observation has convinced us that if there had been peace instead of war, the Norwegian Lutherans in the State (Minnesota) would have numbered several thousand less than they do. It may not seem pious to say so, but many a worldly-minded Viking has become so interested in the fight that he has joined the faction with which he sympathized in order to assist in beating the opposing party."[46]

The church services in the great majority of cases are still conducted in the mother-tongue. In the United Norwegian Lutheran Church, in 1905, for example, the services in Norwegian numbered 30,407 as against 1,542 in English, and out of 1,300 congregations reporting, no more than six held services in English only, including two large congregations in Chicago and Milwaukee.[47] Five other congregations conducted more services in English than in Norwegian; in ten localities the numbers were equal; and in twenty-two, they were about equal, making a total of

[44]Nelson, *History of the Scandinavians*, I, 219.

[45]*Ibid.*, I, 217; Carroll, *The Religious Forces of the United States* (rev. ed.) 190.

[46]Nelson, *History of the Scandinavians*, I, 339.

[47]*Beretning om det syttende Aarsmöde for den Forenede norsk lutherske Kirke i Amerika, 1906*, XLIV.

forty-three in which English figured prominently.[48] The Hon. N. P. Haugen, speaking on Norway Day at the World's Columbian Exposition, in Chicago, commented on the fact that a Lutheran church had just been dedicated, in which English alone would be used, and said significantly: "Twenty years ago our theologians would not have entertained such a proposition."[49] Now the younger Lutheran preachers are expected to be able to preach both in their mother-tongue and in English.

The conduct of services in non-English languages will and should continue so long as there is a considerable body of men and women who emigrated too late to learn the new language well enough to stand that final linguistic test, the power to worship genuinely and satisfyingly in the adopted speech. This means that the churches will use the foreign speech until the generation of the foreign-born ceases to be predominant, and in the cities, perhaps while the second generation is in the majority; but children who receive their education in the public schools or other English speaking schools, will require that their religious instruction and their devotional exercises be conducted in English.

The children and grandchildren of the immigrants, except in certain large and compact settlements, chiefly in the cities, prefer English, and commonly use that language in conversation and in correspondence with each other. In the Swedish and Norwegian wards of such cities as Chicago, Minneapolis, St. Paul, and Rockford, and in a county like Goodhue in Minnesota, where the presence of large numbers of the foreign-born makes the use of the foreign tongue imperative in the homes, streets, markets, and places of business, and where the news is read in a Scandinavian daily or weekly, the tendency to keep to the speech of their ancestors is strong. The preacher and the politician alike understand this, and the literature, speeches, and even the music, in the campaigns for per-

[48]*Ibid.,* II-LV.
[49]*Daily Skandinaven,* May 24, 1893.

sonal and civic righteousness are presented in no unknown tongue, as the theological seminaries and Scandinavian departments in other institutions, and the Swedish and Norwegian political orators in critical years, bear abundant witness.

Co-ordinate with the school and the church, as a social force to be estimated, is the press. Newspapers and periodicals of various sorts in foreign languages inevitably follow the settlement of any considerable number of aliens in a given community, for people of education and ambition will look in a familiar medium for their news and gossip, their instruction in commerce and politics, as well as their teaching in religion. So the Chinese and Japanese on the Pacific Coast, no less than the Germans, Italians, and Greeks on the Atlantic, have their dailies and their magazines. Since the three Norse peoples, practically without illiteracy and with active and ambitious minds, have settled in a large number of moderate-sized communities, frequently isolated from each other, and since their differences of opinion in matters religious and ecclesiastical are often positive and aggressive, the number of their publications of all kinds since the middle of the last century is curiously large, and quite as remarkable for their migratory and short-lived character.

The newspapers usually serve as the chief means of keeping informed concerning the general news of the European home-lands, as well as of the United States. Nearly all the larger papers publish regular European correspondence, summaries of events, letters, and clippings, under such headings as "Sverige," "Fra Norge," etc.[50]

The newspapers and magazines render another service by the publication, on the instalment plan, either as a part of the regular columns or as inserted sheets, of standard works of the great Scandinavian writers or of translations of the masterpieces of English and American authors. Since these novels, essays, and histories are so printed that they may be folded up and form a pamphlet for preserva-

[50]*Gamla och Nya Hemlandet,* Apr. 8, 1903.

tion, the periodical serves both as newspaper and library. "It was the Swedish-American press which caused the Swedish literature, as it is in America, to spring up."[51]

The dailies of Chicago, Minneapolis, and Duluth, in particular, publish every week scores of communications from subscribers in all parts of the Northwest, in a department devoted to neighborhood news or gossip. The old settler writes his reminiscences, sometimes a brief letter called out by some event, sometimes at great length, like the Rev. J. A. Ottesen's "Contribution to the History of our Settlements and Congregations," which ran through eleven numbers of the weekly paper *Amerika*, from April to September of 1894, and gave very minute details of immigrant families unto the third and fourth generation, as they had passed under the kindly eye of the patriarchal old pastor in his service of forty years among them.[52] Great numbers of these communications relate to the conditions and prospects of local settlements as viewed from the settler's standpoint—crop conditions, market prices, wages, opportunities for labor, nature and prices of near-by land, schools, religion. As a revelation of the real mind of a community or of an element of the population, showing the inducements and motives operating upon the immigrant, and his response, they are exceedingly valuable, and in some important respects almost unique.

The editors and business agents of the larger and more enterprising Scandinavian papers very early began making journeys about the country, especially into the newer parts, in the interests of their papers; incidentally they were spying out the land for themselves, but indirectly they were furnishing first-hand observations of frontier conditions to the hundreds who were moved to reinvest themselves and their small accumulations. One of these "circuit riders" was Johan Schröder, editor of *Fædrelandet og Emigranten*, founded at La Crosse, in 1864, who published a little book of information for immi-

[51]*Gamla och Nya Hemlandet*, April 8, 1903 (translated).
[52]"Bidrag til vore Settlementers og Menigheders Historie."

grants in 1867, after one of his extensive journeys among the settlements.[53] Three years later he made a trip into Minnesota as far as Otter Tail County—"En Snartur i Nordvesten"—and was deeply impressed with the possibilities of that fertile section, to which many men of his nationality were already looking, as the Newtown folk in Massachusetts Bay looked in 1636 toward the Connecticut country, with a "strong bent of their spirits to move thither." Such words as these were as seed sown in good soil: "So far as I have journeyed about in the prairie counties of Minnesota and Iowa, I have not yet met with any county which in multiplicity of natural resources can come up with Otter Tail. Immigration this year is very strong. Both newcomers direct from Norway, and older farmers from Iowa, Wisconsin and Southern Minnesota take their various ways thither."[54] The "America fever" of the Old World was now the "West fever," and again more of the "West fever."[55] These articles were not mere generalizations, but often, as in those just quoted from, they gave the exact and practical information the reader would desire—break-up of the prairie would cost $25 or $30 for five acres on which to grow wheat and potatoes, cash to be had by working on the nearby railroad at $2.50 per day, salt to be had at five cents per pound, butter could be sold for ten cents per pound, fish and game were abundant,—also mosquitoes![56]

The first of a long line of Swedish, Norwegian, and Danish periodicals in the west, was a little paper called *Nordlyset* (Northern Light), which began publication in the Norwegian colony in Racine county, Wisconsin, in 1847, with James D. Reymert as editor. It was a small

[53]This valuable little book bore the title *Skandinaverne i de Forenede Stater og Canada, med Indberetninger og Oplysninger fra 200 Skandinaviske Settlementer. En Ledetraad for Emigranten fra det gamle Land og for Nybyggeren in Amerika.*

[54]Translated from *Fæderelandet og Emigranten,* July 21, 1870.

[55]Schröder, *Skandinaverne i de Forenede Stater og Canada* (1867), 53.

[56]*Ibid.,* 53; also a two-and-a-half-column article "Vink til Nysettlere i Minnesota," in *Fædrelandet og Emigranten,* June 29, 1871.

four-page sheet which at the start espoused the cause of the Free Soil party. In 1850 it changed hands, and was re-christened *Demokraten;* tho its subscription list increased to three hundred, the venture proved a failure.[57]

After 1850 the number of Scandinavian newspapers and religious periodicals multiplied rapidly. Langeland, himself an editor and publisher of the time, mentions five of these publications on the Norwegian side alone in the decade following 1850.[58] *Skandinaven,* whose foundation marks an era in the Scandinavian press, dates back to this period. From its small beginnings has grown a great metropolitan daily, with a circulation of 20,000, besides its semi-weekly and weekly editions which have a circulation all over the Northwest of nearly 50,000.[59] In the ten years after 1870, a second expansion in the number of publications took place, tho the fifteen Scandinavian papers given in the list published in the standard newspaper directory for 1870, make an almost insignificant showing by the side of the two hundred and fifty or more printed in America in German.[60]

The Swedish press in the United States began somewhat later than the Norwegian, but it manifested a stability and steadiness of progress which the latter too often lacked. *Hemlandet* was founded in 1855 as an organ of Swedish Lutheranism, but in 1870 it was a political as well as a religious journal, with 4,000 subscribers to the

[57]Langeland, *Nordmændene i Amerika*, 94-107. Langeland succeeded Reymert as editor of *Nordlyset*. A few copies of *Nordlyset, Demokraten, Emigranten*, and some fifteen other early Norwegian papers were found some years ago in the hands of an old Norwegian, Christopher Hanson of St. Ansgar, Iowa. By him they were turned over to Rasmus B. Anderson, then editor of *Amerika*. *Amerika*, Jan. 4, 1899. Anderson sold the collection for $100 to the United Church in whose Seminary Library it now rests. "Raport fra Komiteen til Indsamling af historiske Documenter," *Beretning om det syttende Aarsmöde for den Forenede norsk lutherke Kirke i Amerika* (1906), 126-128.

[58]Langeland, *Nordmændene i Amerika*, 96-112.

[59]"Den skandinaviske tidnings-pressens barndom i Amerika," *Hemlandet*, Feb. 25, March 4, 1913; Hansen and Wist, "Den Norsk-Amerikanske Presse". *Norsk-Amerikanernes Festskrift*, 1914, 9-203.

[60]Rowell, *American Newspaper Directory*, 1870, 948.

weekly edition, and 2,000 to the monthly,—"the largest circulation of any Swedish political newspaper in this country."[61]

The high-water mark in the number of these publications in the Northern tongues seems to have been in 1892 or 1893, when Rowell mentions 146, of which Minnesota is credited with 33, Illinois with 30, Iowa with 13, and Wisconsin with 10, a total for these four States of 86, with a reported total of 140,000 subscribers, out of 550,000 subscribers for all the Scandinavian papers in the country. By 1901, the number of papers had fallen off—many suspended in the hard times after 1893[62]—but the number of subscribers increased for the whole country to more than 800,000, and for the four States just enumerated, to more than 650,000.[63]

The politics and religion of the papers reflected the variegated opinions of different parties and sects, and of men who would found new parties and denominations, but Lutheranism and Republicanism have been from the start the dominating influences. A historian of Lutheranism named 16 Swedish Evangelical Lutheran periodicals in existence in the United States in 1896.[64] About the same time a Democratic paper remarks grudgingly and sourly: "It is worthy of note that of the fifty or sixty Norwegian papers in the United States, including two dailies, all are Republican tho at rare intervals some may bolt individual nominations. Generally, however, they are amazingly steadfast to party—moss-backed and hide-bound, in fact."[65]

The strong hold which this press exercises upon its subscribers is excellently illustrated in the large sums of

[61]*Ibid.*, 633.

[62]*The North*, Aug. 9, 1893, reports six weeklies "suspended within the past few weeks."

[63]Rowell, *American Newspaper Directory* for years named; *Hemlandet*, Mar. 4, 1903: "De svenska tidningarne i Amerika har nu sammenlagt en prenumerantsiffra som uppgår till 400,000."

[64]Lenker, *Lutherans in all Lands*, 771.

[65]*Madison Democrat*, Oct. 6, 1898.

money raised from time to time through its agency in
behalf of sufferers from fire and famine in the North European peninsulas. By editorials and special correspondence, by subscriptions and the publications of lists of contributors, by stimulating concerts for raising relief
moneys, these journals have pursued the shrewd, enterprising, and, at the same time, benevolent schemes of advertising, followed by their American contemporaries. In
1893 *Skandinaven* received and remitted to Norway for
the relief of sufferers from a landslide in Thelemark more
than $2,700.[66] When a great fire nearly destroyed the city
of Aalesund, that journal in the winter and spring of 1904
gathered and sent to Norway $19,000, mostly in sums
ranging from $.25 to $2.00; at the same time *Decorah
Posten* remitted more than $12,000 for the same purpose.[67]
The great famine in northern Sweden and Finland in
1902-3 gave rise to a similar collection of money; the editor
of the *Svenska Amerikanska Posten*, the powerful Swedish
newspaper of Minneapolis, headed the list for his paper,
and at the end of several months the contributions through
this one journal reached the total of approximately $18,-
000.[68] Of course not all the money so liberally poured out
to aid the unfortunate by the Baltic or the North Sea, was
transmitted through the agents of the newspapers, but it
is true that almost the sole inspiration for the gifts came
more or less directly from the Scandinavian press. Probably out of $175,000 sent from the United States to the
famine sufferers in 1903,—and America's quota was about
one-half of the total handled by the Swedish central committee in Stockholm—the newspapers were instrumental
in raising fifty per-cent.[69]

[66]*Skandinaven*, May 3, May 31, 1893.
[67]*Ibid.*, Jan. 27-April 30, 1904; *Dannevirke*, March 30, 1904.
[68]*Svenska Amerikanska Posten*, Feb. 17, June 30, 1903.
[69]*Hemlandet*, Feb. 25 (quoting from *Nya Dagligt Allehanda* of
Stockholm for Feb. 7), July 15, Aug. 19, 1903.

CHAPTER X.

SOCIAL RELATIONS AND CHARACTERISTICS

While the normal unit in Scandinavian immigration is the family, a considerable proportion of the immigrants has consisted of young, unmarried men and women. Not infrequently the young man left behind him a sweetheart who followed a little later when a solid foundation was laid for the prospective family; or perchance, if sufficiently prosperous, he went back at some Christmastide to marry her and bring her to America. In any case, the farm meant a home, and the marriage back of it was generally between two of the same nationality. Still, intermarriages between Scandinavians and persons of American or of other alien stock, are not infrequent, tho the number and significance of such marriages is more a matter of personal opinion and estimate than of exact statistics, since the latter are lacking. The opinions expressed in this chapter are based upon the inconclusive figures of the census reports, upon a study of a large number of brief biographies, and upon a considerable acquaintance with conditions in the Northwest. The biographies, it should be noted, are almost exclusively of men of Scandinavian birth, whose intermarriage with American women is less common than that of American men with Scandinavian women.[1]

Before the flood tide of immigration in the period beginning about 1880 brought to America so many young, unmarried women, intermarriages were more infrequent than in the later time. Hence the discussion of the matter in the Census Report of 1880 would not necessarily hold true for the subsequent period: "There is but one im-

[1]Bremer, *Homes of the New World,* II, 222, 227, 236; Nelson, *History of the Scandinavians,* I, 372, 380, 384, 404, 423, 429, 438, 504, 530.

portant element (other than the Irish) which manifests an equally strong indisposition to intermarriage, viz., the Scandinavian. This element appears in an important degree in but few of the States and Territories embraced in the following tables, but in these the effects of inter-marriage are slight. Thus in Wisconsin, while there are 42,728 persons born on our soil having both Scandinavian father and Scandinavian mother, there are but 2,083 per-sons having a Scandinavian father and an American mother. In Dakota, the respective numbers are 10,071 and 418; in Minnesota 69,492 and 1,906. . . . It will be noted that in some of the States and Territories where the Scandinavians are few and where it is notorious that they are thoroly mingled with the general population, the pro-portion of intermarriages is not a low one."[2] The figures for the children of such mixed marriages given in the reports of the Twelfth Census certainly reveal a decided increase in the number, especially when the necessary allowance is made for the decreasing birthrate naturally incident to the development of urban communities and to filling up of States, which took place between 1880 and 1900.[3]

In these two decades, large numbers of young un-married women, moved by the same economic motives as the young men, came to the United States and took ser-vice among the Americans as domestic servants. The de-mand for capable and well-trained servants far exceeded, and still exceeds, the visible supply, and the wages which seemed high to the American housewife seemed trebly high to the girl who received in cash wages in the old home only $20 or $30 per year.[4] In the new service the girls must perforce learn English rapidly or fail, so they learned the language and also the ways of the American house-hold. In return they gave an honest, good-tempered, and

[2] U. S. Tenth Census, 1880, I, 676.

[3] U. S. Twelfth Census Reports, 1900, I, Population, Pt. I, CXCIII, and Tables 43, 46, 56.

[4] U. S. Consular Reports (1887) No. 76, 148; Young, Labor in Europe and America, 681.

trustworthy if sometimes clumsy service. If they were not always evidently grateful for the instruction and patience of the mistress of the household, if frequently they married soon after they were trained into efficient and satisfactory servants, they should not be condemned wholesale! While the marriages of these strong, healthy, intelligent, domestically capable young women with non-Scandinavian young men of the middle and lower classes constitute the larger proportion of intermarriages, the intermarriage of the American-born Scandinavian girls, trained in the public schools and colleges, with American men is also frequent, and no reservation as to the mixture of social classes needs to be made.

Large families have been a promient characteristic of the home life of the Northmen in America's Northwest. Race suicide should not be charged against the Scandinavians either in their new homes or in their old, for in spite of the steady drain which emigration has made upon the population of Sweden, Norway, and Denmark for fifty years, each country in each decade has shown an increase of population, due solely to natural increase.[5] In America this natural fecundity was re-enforced by the conditions under which settlement was made, for large families are characteristic of the early years of a developing agricultural frontier. So when the Scandinavians entered the newly-opened regions of the Great West and found land and food abundant, both immediately and prospectively, they felt no necessity for enforcing prudential or other checks upon the increase of population. Putting the case more positively, circumstances put a premium upon families with numerous children; the farmer welcomed additions to his circle of boys and girls who would grow up into helpers upon the expanding cultivated acreage of the farm, and later take up land near the original homestead, buttressing it with prosperous allied homes. Families of ten and twelve were common, while others reached sixteen,

[5]*Special Reports, Bureau of the Census,* "Supplementary Analysis and Derivative Tables" (1906), 32-33.

eighteen, and even twenty-four.[6] In his remarkably detailed reminiscences of Norwegian settlers in Wisconsin and the further Northwest, the Rev. J. A. Ottesen refers to families of his friends and acquaintances, sometimes in exact figures, as seven, ten, or fourteen children, and sometimes in such general phrases as "many children," or "several children," making use of these phrases no less than seventeen times in three columns of a single article.[7]

An examination of several thousand biographical sketches of Danes, Norwegians, and Swedes who have attained some degree of success in the American West, the very class which would first begin to limit the size of the family, leads to the conclusion that the average number of children per family among them is between four and five. In other words the average is nearly double that of the United States taken as a whole.[8]

Closely connected with this immigration of so many young, unmarried girls of the servant class, is the question of sex morality and illegitimacy. The statistics relating to this question are particularly unsatisfactory so far as the United States is concerned, even for a land where the scientific statistician is a recent product, and where the collection of social statistics, left mainly to the States and to local authorities, is very loosely carried on. The motives for concealment and for prevarication are obvious, and the records of municipal courts, even if closely inspected, would not give much more than a scant minimum of information applicable to an estimate of the Scandinavian element in the population.

[6]Sparks, *History of Winneshiek County, Iowa*, 110; *History of Fillmore County* (Minnesota), 377 ff., 434 ff.

[7]J. O. Ottesen, "Bidrag til vore Settlementers og Menigheders Historie," *Amerika*, April-September, 1894, especially July 4.

[8]These biographies are numerous in the many county histories which appeared between 1880 and 1890 as the work of a syndicate of publishers; they are also the staple of the latter half of such works as Johnson and Peterson, *Svenskarne i Illinois*, and Nelson, *History of the Scandinavians*, I, and II. All the Scandinavian newspapers print many similar sketches, biographical, autobiographical, and obituary.

To judge from the figures given for certain cities in Norway and Sweden, it would be natural to expect a much higher percentage of illegitimate births among the immigrants from those countries than among persons of American ancestry. The United States Consul at Stockholm reported for 1884 for the whole of Sweden that 10.2% of all births were illegitimate; for the city of Stockholm alone, 29.3%.[9] Twelve years later the figure for the whole kingdom was 11%.[10] For Norway, the figure for the kingdom was 7.2% for 1896; in the city of Christiania, 15.4% of the 5,349 births in 1895 were illegitimate.[11]

Such statistics are certainly ominous, whatever the allowance which should be made for peculiar social conditions in Europe, which make the begetting of children after betrothal and before actual wedlock a less heinous offence against good order and morality than in America. But over against these startling figures stands the fact that it does not seem to be harder to maintain order and decency in cities like Minneapolis and St. Paul, or in the Scandinavian wards of Chicago, than it is in Detroit or Boston, or in the other alien quarters of Chicago itself. Nor does an inspection of the court and police records of cities of the Northwest for crimes and offences against decency, or against women, give cause for any special alarm for the future morality of the Scandinavians of that section.

For a safe and conclusive estimate of the contributions made by the Scandinavian element to the delinquent and defective classes of society, no very complete or satisfactory data are at present to be had. A detailed study of the statistics of these classes in Wisconsin and Minnesota warrants the judgment that the immigrants from Northern Europe, and their immediate descendants, have

[9]U. S. Consular Reports (1887), No. 76, 151; Young, Labor in Europe, 689. C. C. Andrews, U. S. Minister to Sweden, 1873, states: "The proportion of illegitimate births, including the whole kingdom was 5.85%, but including only cities, the proportion of illegitimates was 14.32%."

[10]Statesman's Year Book, 1900, 1048.

[11]Ibid., 1062; Folkebladet, Feb. 5, 1896.

a much smaller percentage of paupers and criminals and a much larger percentage of insane, than do either the Germans or the Irish, the two other alien elements which approach the Scandinavians in importance in those States.[12] But these statistics are at best unconvincing, because they are acknowledgedly incomplete, and because in them little attempt is made to distinguish between the children of American descent and those born of immigrant parents in America.

The experts working out the interpretation of the results of the Twelfth Census (1900) have made distinct progress towards a fair comparative judgment in matters relating to social classes and conditions. John Koren, for example, the son of the veteran Norwegian Lutheran pastor, the Rev. V. Koren, and an investigator and writer of unusual weight, points out that the insane in hospitals are at least ten years of age, while there are few children under fifteen among the immigrants as compared with the number under that age among the native whites, and he accordingly concludes that "Of the whites at least 10 years of age in the general population of the United States in 1900, 80.5% were native and 19.5% were foreign-born; while of the white insane of known nativity enumerated in hospitals on December 31, 1903, 65.7% were native and 34.3% were foreign-born. Relatively, therefore, the insane are more numerous among the foreign born whites than among the native."[13] How much more convincing is such a cautious and careful estimate than the sweeping generalizations of another recent writer: "Roughly speaking, the foreigners furnish more than twice as many criminals, two and one-third times as many insane, and three times as many paupers as the native element."[14]

[12]A discussion of these statistics for 1885-1890 is given in *The Forum*, XIV, 103. The reports of the superintendents of some of the institutions give more or less of the history of each case. See Nelson, *History of the Scandinavians*, II, 1-23.

[13]*Special Reports, Bureau of the Census*, 1904, "Insane and Feeble-minded in Hospitals and Institutions," 20.

[14]Hall, *Immigration*, 166.

The statistics for the insane in hospitals at the end of 1903 and of those admitted during 1904, as given by Mr. Koren, show a strikingly high percentage of insane persons of foreign parentage in Wisconsin, Minnesota, North Dakota, and Iowa. No other State comes within ten per-cent of the ratio of the first three. Of those enumerated in December, 1903, 56% in Wisconsin, 48% in Minnesota, 52% in North Dakota, and 34% in Iowa, were of foreign parentage; the percentages of the admissions for 1904 were 53% in Wisconsin, 55% in Minnesota, and 33% in Iowa.[15] In all these States the Scandinavian element has been numerous for at least two generations. Figures gathered for this study for the period between 1885 and 1895, before the children of the Scandinavian immigrants reached in very considerable numbers what might be termed the age for acquiring insanity, gave similarly significant conclusions. Of the inmates of the state hospitals for the insane in Minnesota, the foreign-born Scandinavians were 28% in 1886 and 30.7% in 1890; of the admissions to the state hospital at St. Peter in 1890, 35% were Norse. Of the total admissions for the State in 1900, 23% were Scandinavians, while in the Fergus Falls hospital, located in the heart of a more recently settled Scandinavian area, 40% were of that nationality; Wisconsin reports show like percentages.[16] All of these statistics warrant the general conclusion that of all the foreign-born, the Scandinavians are the most prone to insanity.[17]

[15]*Special Reports, Bureau of the Census,* "Insane and Feebleminded," 21.

[16]*Minnesota Executive Documents, 1900*—statistics for the insane for 1890, 1896, and 1900; *The North,* Dec. 18, 1889; *Wisconsin State Board of Control* [biennial], 1890 to 1902.

[17]*Special Reports, Bureau of the Census, 1904,* "Insane, etc., in Hospitals," 21. Nelson, *History of the Scandinavians,* II, ch. i, makes a conscientious, but rather lame, attempt at analyzing available statistics of insanity, and gives his conclusions for two periods, 1881-2 and 1890-4: ratio of insane in total population, 1 :2718 and 1 :1719; in American-born, 1 :4120 and 1 :3009; in foreign-born 1 :1480 and 1 :1144; in Irish, 1 :1061 and 1 :769; in German, 1 :1461 and 1 :1439, in Scandinamian, 1 :1588 and 1 :819.

If one seeks for adequate reasons for this unusual tendency to insanity, he will not find ready satisfaction. Undoubtedly the difference of environment and the severer strain upon muscle and nerve imposed by American industrial conditions, by which the machinery of the individual must run at a higher and unwonted speed, will account for part of the phenomena, but these causes operate alike upon all classes of immigrants. The change from the mountains of Norway, or from the rugged sea-coast of the great Northern peninsula, to the rolling prairies and the vast silent plains of the interior of the United States, has also its depressing effect. The very flatness of the land, its extremes of temperature, the fierce tornadoes of wind, the bewildering, imprisoning storms of snow, with no friendly mountain or forest to offer a body of protection or a face of comfort, and the isolation of the life of the frontier farmer and his family, together with the severity of their labor—all these are causes operating with peculiar force in the case of the Norwegian and Swedish immigrants. Dr. Gronvald, writing in 1887, stated his conviction that the women of these classes, especially the Norwegians, were predisposed to nervous disorders and insanity by early and frequent child-bearing, and from early rising from child-bed.[18]

Since the Norse immigrants have rarely if ever been charged with illiteracy, dependency, pauperism or mendicancy, the remaining social test, usually considered co-ordinate with that for insanity, is the proportion of criminals contributed to the total of delinquents.[19] Earlier computations must undergo the same severe correction as do the estimates regarding the insane. By 1885 there were

[18]Gronvald, "The Effects of the Immigration on the Norwegian Immigrants," *Sixth Annual Report of the State Board of Health of Minnesota,* 520.

[19]For an interesting background for this discussion, see Grellet, *Memoirs,* I, 324. He wrote in 1818 of a parish named Stavanger, having a population of some 7,000: "We visited their prison and their schools; the former kept by an old woman. She had but one prisoner in it, and had so much confidence in him that the door of his cell was kept open."

in the Northwest large communities made up of the older Norwegian and Swedish settlers and their descendants, and other communities comprising great numbers of recently arrived immigrants. According to the State census of 1885 in Minnesota, the Scandinavians formed 16.5% of the population, and the Germans, 11.5%. The reports of the wardens of the State's prisons for 1886 show 8.7% of the prisoners to be Scandinavian, and 7.4% German. The population of the State during the next five years grew rapidly; the Scandinavian element increased faster than the German and nearly twice as fast as the native American. Yet in 1890 the percentage of the prisoners who could be identified as Scandinavian was only 7.1%.[20]

In Wisconsin, where the increase of population in the last ten years of the nineteenth century was in the native-born of Scandinavian parentage, rather than in the number of immigrants, the reports of the Waupun State Prison may be supplemented by those of the State Industrial School, the reformatory for first offenders between the ages of fifteen and thirty. In 1900, the foreign-born Scandinavian population of Wisconsin was 5% of the total, and the Scandinavian population of foreign-born parentage was 10% of the total.[21] Of the prisoners received at Waupun, the Scandinavians were: 1891, 4.1%; 1898, 4.4%; 1900, 3.7%. Of boys and young men received at the Industrial School, those of Scandinavian parentage were: 1890-1892, 7%; 1896-1898, 6.5%; 1900-1902, 6.6%.[22]

In the matter of petty offences which are usually tried in the police courts, particularly cases arising out of intemperance, the records of convictions in Minneapolis, St. Paul, and Chicago, together with the statistics of city

[20]*Minnesota Executive Documents*, biennial reports of State Prisons for the years mentioned.

[21]*U. S. Twelfth Census*, I, *Population*, Pt. I, Tables 25, 38, 40.

[22]*Reports of the Wisconsin. State Board of Control* for the years mentioned.

prisons and workhouses, indicate that the Northmen are clearly the chief offenders.[23]

[23]*Minnesota Executive Documents,* Reports of the State Board of Charities and Corrections, especially for 1884, 1890, 1896; *The North,* Dec. 18, 1889. Nelson, *History of the Scandinavians,* II, ch. i, tabulates his estimates of criminality as he does those of insanity; for the years 1880-1882 and 1892-1894:

Ratio of criminals in the whole population	1 :2302	1 :1999
American-born population	1 :2413	1 :2013
Foreign-born population	1 :2035	1 :1887
Irish population	1 :1600	1 :860
German population	1 :2713	1 :2715
Scandinavian population	1 :3706	1 :5933

CHAPTER XI.

The Scandinavian in Local and State Politics

The Scandinavian usually entered the field of politics rather slowly; he took out his "first papers" for the purpose of acquiring land, not that he might vote in the next election. In the early years of his settlement he was too busy building and paying for a home, learning English, and adopting American customs, to give much time or attention to public affairs. The clearing of woodland, the breaking up of the prairie, and the transformation of a one-room shack into a frame dwelling required severe labor and all his energies. Not until the leisure of some degree of success was his, did he yield to his natural inclination for politics of the larger sort.

The Norwegian, of all the men of the Northern lands, has the strongest liking for the political arena, and has had the most thoro political training at home. Since 1814 he has lived and acted in a community markedly democratic. He understands the meaning of the Fourth of July all the better because he, and his ancestors for two or three generations in their home by the North Sea, celebrated on the Seventeenth of May the independence of Norway and the advent of republicanism. His sense of individuality and equality is stronger than that of his cousins to the east or south, and he steadily and stubbornly fights for the recognition and maintenance of his rights. In 1821, before the first real immigrants sailed for the United States, Norway abolished nobility, while Sweden and Denmark still retain the institution. Equipped thus, and educated in such a vigorous school, it is the Norwegian rather than the Swede or Dane who figures most largely in the political activities of the American Northwest.

Several causes operating on the western side of the Atlantic augmented these natural advantages of the Norwegians. In their settlements they had ten or fifteen years the start of the Swedes, and in the formative period of Wisconsin, Iowa, Minnesota, and Dakota they greatly outnumbered both the Swedes and Danes. They went into new States and territories, and, settling on farms, profited by the power which the rural portion of a developing region usually exercises in politics. On the other hand, tho the Swedes in Illinois since the early fifties, and in Kansas since the late sixties, have formed decidedly the larger part of the Scandinavian population of those two States, they have by no means taken a part in politics equal to that taken by the Norwegians. In 1890 the foreign-born Swedes in Iowa were more numerous than the foreign-born Norwegians, and in Minnesota about equal in number, but these figures do not fairly represent the political strength of the two elements, for to the foreign-born Norwegians must be added those of the second and third generation of persons of purely Norwegian extraction.[1] The sons, and even the grandsons of the early Norwegian settlers were voters before the Swedish immigration greatly exceeded the Norwegian.[2] Broadly speaking, the early political pre-eminence of the Norwegians has never been overcome.

For the common people of Sweden and Denmark, political experience practically began with the agitation for the reforms of 1866 and 1867. The peasants and burghers thus came to think definitely and decisively about what they desired and of the means for securing the

[1]Statistics for foreign-born in 1890:

	Iowa	Minnesota
Norwegians	27,078	101,169
Swedes	30,276	99,913
Danes	15,519	14,133

[2]In 1850 the total of foreign-born Scandinavians was 12,678, of whom 3,559 were Swedes. In 1860 the corresponding figures were 43,995 and 18,625. In 1880 the Swedes numbered 194,337, and the Norwegians, 181,729. *United States Census Reports* for the years 1850, 1860, 1880.

wished-for reforms. It may therefore be asserted without reservation that after 1870 the average Scandinavian immigrant brought to America a fairly clear understanding of the meaning of republicanism; elections, representation, local self-government, and constitutions, are neither novel nor meaningless terms to him; he is ready to fill his place, play his part, and cast his vote, as "a citizen of no mean city." In the discharge of their civic duties, the Scandinavian voters have had the aid of several unusually well edited newspapers in their own languages. Since active participation in politics and patriotism are not always synonymous, one branch of the Scandinavian peoples may be just as patriotic as another. Certain it is that in the Civil War the Swedes were every whit as prompt and hearty in their response to calls for men, and as thoro in their efficiency and courage as soldiers, as were the Norwegians.

From a political view-point, the importance of the Norse immigrants in the agricultural regions of the West has not been fully recognized. At first thought, it would seem that location in a city or town, with its intimate associations and sharper competitions, with its friction of frequent contact with Americans, should be more conducive to rapid Americanization of immigrants, than the life of the farm or of the rural village, with its isolation and narrow horizon. More careful consideration will make clear that the opportunities for political action beyond merely casting a vote, are really much better in a new, thinly-settled township than in a ward of a large town or city. It surely was not a hunger for the sweets of political influence or official place which led the Scandinavians into frontier regions; but once there, with the old political ties forever severed by taking out their "first papers," with partial title to land entered by preemption or by homesteading, their first and greatest steps in Americanization were safely made, and each one carried certain political consequences. Local political organization had to be effected somehow as a given locality filled up, and it happened frequently that there were none but Scandinavians to undertake the task. No matter what their political inclinations, no matter what form of organization they would have preferred, only one course was open to them: to get information as to the laws and customs of the United States and of the States in which they were settled, to prepare for the elections, and to assume the responsibilities of the necessary offices. Over and over again these things were done promptly and well by men in whose veins coursed only Viking blood, by men but recently transplanted from Norway, Sweden, and Denmark.

Whenever a township became populous enough to have a name as well as a number on the surveyor's map, that question was likely to be determined by the people on the ground, and such names as Christiana, Swede Plain, Numedal, Throndhjem, and Vasa leave no doubt that Scandinavians officiated at the christening.[3] Besides the names of townships, Minnesota alone has no fewer than seventy-five postoffices whose names are unmistakably Norse,—Malmö, Ringbo, Ibsen, Tordenskjold, and the like. It was in organizing these new townships, working the town machinery, carrying on elections, levying and collecting taxes, and laying out roads, that the Scandinavian immigrants learned the rudiments of American politics.[4] In studying the accounts of the formation of scores of towns inhabited wholly or in major part by Norwegians or Swedes—accounts usually written by Americans, and often going into minute details—not one was found which describes any noteworthy irregularity. Except for the peculiar names no one would suspect that the townmakers were born elsewhere than in Massachusetts or New York. In some cases probably more than one-fifth of the

<hr />

[3]Christiana got its name through the carelessness of Gunnul Vindæg, who desired to name the town after the Norwegian capital, but omitted the "i" in the last syllable. *Billed Magazin*, I, 388.

[4]Mattson, *Story of an Emigrant*, 50-51 ; *History of Goodhue County, Minnesota*, 248.

men of the community shared in the actual administration of town affairs; and while this ratio decreased with the growth of the town, the tendency of the Scandinavian settlers to move on from one new region to another gave many of them continuing opportunities to gain political experience. Had the same number of men located in the larger towns or cities, their active duties as citizens would generally have ended with the casting of their annual ballot. A few might have become policemen, commissioners, or even aldermen, but they would have made an insignificant percentage; the management or mismanagement of finances, schools, streets, sanitation, and public services would go on without their efforts or participation.

A few illustrations selected almost at random, will give a concrete idea of the process just described. Two townships in Fillmore County, Minnesota, were organized in 1860, and received the familiar Old World names, Norway and Arendahl; at the first election, all the officers chosen in both townships were Norwegians, and for twenty years and more, the Norwegians continued to fill nearly all the offices.[5] Another and later example is found in Nicollet County, Minnesota, farther west than Fillmore County, where the township of New Sweden was formed in 1864. Thirty votes were cast at the first election, and at the first town-meeting, held three months later, all the offices were filled by the election of six Swedes and four Norwegians.[6] Five years later this township was divided and the name Bernadotte was given to the new township; by the first election, all ten offices were filled by Swedes.[7] Other Minnesota towns, Johnsonville in Redwood County (1879), Wang in Renville County (1875), and Stockholm in Wright County (1868), were similarly organized and officered by Norwegians and Swedes.[8]

[5]History of Fillmore County, Minnesota, 346,378.
[6]History of the Minnesota Valley, 688, 690, 693.
[7]Ibid., 688.
[8]Ibid., 790; 837; History of the Upper Mississippi Valley, 572.

As the townships developed, and the villages grew into cities with large foreign-born elements, the familiar and characteristic Northern names continue to fill the official records. Stoughton, Wisconsin, the capital, so to speak, of the solid old Dane County settlement, is a case in point. So late as 1901 the roster of the city ran as follows:

Mayor, O. K. Roe, born in Dane County of Norwegian parents

President of the Council, J. S. Liebe, born in Laurvik, Norway

Aldermen, four born in different parts of Norway, two born in Dane County of Norwegian parents.[9]

Much of the business in these new communities in their first years was carried on in a foreign tongue. Certainly election notices and documents of that sort were issued in Norwegian or Swedish, and sometimes orders, ordinances, and laws. No evidence, however, has come to hand to prove that any official records were ever kept in any other language than English, even in villages composed almost exclusively of Norwegians or Swedes.[10]

One of the first offices that had to be filled in the growing settlement was that of postmaster; for no considerable number of people, educated and intelligent, will long be content with a postoffice twenty miles away.[11]   In 1856 there were five Scandinavian postmasters in Minnesota alone.[12]   Thus the immigrant settlers came in contact with the national government at the postoffice more directly and frequently than they did at the land-office.

Township affairs shade off almost imperceptibly into

[9]*Amerika,* May 20, 1901.

[10]"The Norwegians of Wisconsin", *Phillips Times* (Wis.), April 22, 1905.

[11]The nearest postoffice to the early settlers in Fillmore County, Minnesota, was twenty miles away at Decorah, Iowa. *History of Fillmore County, Minnesota* 429.

[12]From the list transcribed from the books of the Appointment Office of the Post Office Department, Dec., 1856. Andrews, *Minnesota and Dakota,* 191.

county affairs in the western States, and the Scandinavians soon began to take part in the latter. No records are at hand for the Wisconsin settlements, but in 1858 the first Norwegian was elected to the board of supervisors in Goodhue County, Minnesota, and in the following year Hans Mattson, who was active in building up the town of Vasa, where he filled various town offices, was elected auditor of the county.[13] He continued to fill the office until July, 1862, tho in name only for the last months, for in the minutes of Board of Supervisors of Goodhue County appears the resolution that "because the County Auditor, Hans Mattson, has voluntarily gone to the war with a company of soldiers, a leave of absence shall be extended to him, and that the office shall not be declared vacant so long as the deputy properly performs the duties of the place."[14]

Hans Mattson was only one of many who found Goodhue County politics and a term of service in the army excellent fitting schools for larger activity in State affairs. One of the Norwegians who served an apprenticeship in Wisconsin, a journeymanship in Iowa, and came to the master-grade of citizenship—office-holding—in Minnesota, was Lars K. Aaker, who represented Goodhue County in the Minnesota Legislature in 1859-1860. After service as first lieutenant in Mattson's Scandinavian Company, he again sat in the Legislature in 1862, 1867, and 1869. Again after twelve years of residence in Goodhue County he moved to Otter Tail County, and represented that county in the State Senate, later becoming Register of the United States Land Office. In 1864, he moved again, to Crookston, in the extreme northwestern corner of Minnesota, where he served as Receiver of the Land Office from 1884 to 1893.[15] As the counties and towns have

[13]Mattson, *The Story of An Emigrant*, 50.
[14]Mattson, *The Story of an Emigrant*, 62.
[15]Personal interview with Mr. Aaker, May, 1890. He was school teacher, in English, and school district clerk in Wisconsin before moving to Iowa and Minnesota. See also *Minnesota Legislative Manual*, 1893, 89-92; Nelson, *History of the Scandinavians*, I, 365.

multiplied, by the biological process of division, in Minnesota and the Dakotas, Scandinavian names recur more
and more frequently in their records, tho it is not always
easy, especially since 1880, to identify such names, for the
Norsemen have had a habit of Americanizing their original
names or changing them altogether either with or without
legal process.[16]

The county offices which seem to be most attractive
to the Scandinavians are those of sheriff, treasurer, auditor, and register of deeds. The lists of county officers for
several years in Wisconsin, Minnesota, and the Dakotas,
show that the number of Swedes and Norwegians in the
four offices just mentioned was closely proportioned to
their percentage in the population of the States named.[17]
Because the Scandinavians are less numerous in the other
county offices, their proportion of the total offices in the
counties of the States falls considerably below their proportion of the population. Estimating on the basis of a
sure minimum, with the difficulties in identifying names
eliminated, the Scandinavians for several years about 1895
filled approximately one-fifth of the 1235 county offices
in Minnesota, one-fifth of the 268 in North Dakota- and
one-tenth of the 702 in Wisconsin. Their numbers relative
to the population in each State were respectively one-
fourth in Minnesota, two-fifths in North Dakota, one-
eighth in Wisconsin, and one-fifth in South Dakota. More
recent illustrations are to be found in the election of 1904.
In Traill County, North Dakota, the sixth in size of the
forty counties in the State, the sheriff, judge, treasurer,

---

[16]By these changes Johanson became Johnson; Hanson, Jackson;
Fjeld, Field; Larson, Lawson (as Victor F. Lawson, the great newspaper
owner of Chicago). By taking the homestead name, the too common name
of Olson was changed to Tuve in one case, while Adolf Olson became
Adolf Olson Bjelland in another.

[17]*Minnesota Legislative Manual,* 1893, 341-366 (naming 16 officers for
most counties); *Wisconsin Blue Book,* 1895, 630 (naming 10); *North Dakota Legislative Manual,* 1895; Basford, *South Dakota Handbook and Official and Legislative Manual,* 1894, 16-120.

auditor, register, surveyor, coroner, and superintendent of schools were of Scandinavian origin; in Lac Qui Parle County, Minnesota, a similar clean sweep was made; while in Yellow Medicine County seven out of ten principal officers were Scandinavians.[18]

The first Scandinavian to enter the field of State politics, was James D. Reymert, a Norwegian, who represented Racine County in the second constitutional convention of Wisconsin in 1847, and later in the Assembly of that State, first from Racine County and then from Milwaukee County in 1857.[19] He was also a candidate for presidential elector on the Free Soil ticket in 1840.[20] The son of a Scotch mother, and receiving part of his education in Scotland, he was better prepared than other Norwegians for taking part in politics, and for the work of editing the first Norwegian newspaper in America, *Nordlyset*—"The Northern Light"—which appeared in 1847 as a Free Soil organ.[21] In the constitutional convention he was not active in the debates, tho he advocated a six-months' residence as a qualification for voting, saying, "as to foreigners, the sooner they were entitled to vote, the better citizens they would make."[22] For one provision of the Wisconsin constitution he was personally responsible: Article VII, section 16, which directed the legislature to establish courts or tribunals of conciliation.[23] But in spite of the command, "The legislature shall pass laws" for these courts, no such law was ever passed in Wisconsin.

Down to the close of the Civil War the Scandinavians exercised very little influence in State politics. Here and there one or two of them appeared as members of conven-

[18]*Amerika*, Nov. 18, 1904.

[19]*Journal of the Second Convention*, 18; Tenney, *Fathers of Wisconsin*, 249; Langeland,*Nordmændene i Amerika*, 94-96; *Wisconsin Blue Book*, (1895), 141, 173.

[20]Langeland, *Nordmændene i Amerika*, 96.

[21]*Ibid.*, 95.

[22]*Journal of the Second Convention*, 31, 129.

[23]*Ibid.*, 422, 638; Poore, *Charters and Constitutions* (2nd ed.), 2037.

tions or of the legislatures, but even in Wisconsin the number rarely went above two in a single session of the legislature.[24] By 1870 many of the Norwegians and Swedes were well-to-do, while others who had served in the Civil War returned to their homes with the prestige conferred by honorable service in that great struggle. Furthermore, the suspicion with which foreign-born citizens had been viewed was greatly reduced, if not dissipated, by the highest evidence which any man can give of his patriotism and loyalty to his adopted country. No one might thenceforth deny them any of the rights, privileges, and honors of the political gild. Accordingly the number of them elected to the legislatures in the Northwest after 1870 increases noticeably both in Wisconsin and Minnesota, and in the Dakotas, where rapid material development and growth of population furnished unusual political opportunities which the Norwegians and Swedes were not slow to improve.

In the Wisconsin legislature of 1868 sat 2 Norwegians; in 1869, 3; in 1871, 4.[25] In Minnesota, the figures are striking: 1868, 2 Scandinavians; 1870, 4; 1872, 9; and 1873, 13.[26] Since then the percentage of Norse representatives has steadily grown, tho it is not always easy to determine the racial stock from which a native-born officer came. Recent Wisconsin legislatures had apparently out of a total membership of 133, in 1895, 5 Scandinavians; in 1901, 10 (1 Dane, 1 Swede, and 8 Norwegians) ; in 1903, 6.[27] The Minnesota legislature of 1893 had 9 out of 54 senators, and 20 out of 114 representatives, who were of Viking origin—fully one-sixth of the total membership.

[24]*Wisconsin Blue Book*, 1895, 136ff; *Minnesota Legislative Manual*, 1893, 87-92; *History of the Upper Mississippi Valley*, 573; Nelson, *History of the Scandinavians*, I, 390.

[25]*Wisconsin Blue Book*, 1895, 136ff. For the more recent legislatures it is possible to be fairly exact in these data, since the blue books and manuals give biographical sketches.

[26]*Minnesota Legislative Manual*, 1895, 573 ff.

[27]*Wisconsin Blue Books*, 1895, 66; 1901, 733ff; 1903, 740ff.

In the legislatures of 1899 and 1905 the numbers were as follows :[28]

1899

Senate 63 members	Norwegian	7	(3 American born)
	Swede	2	
House 119 members	Norwegian	16	(3 American born)
	Swede	9	(4 American born)
	Dane	1	

1905

Senate 63 members	Norwegian	7	
	Swede	4	
House 119 members	Norwegian	20	(7 American born)
	Swede	9	

In the newer States to the West, the percentages rise still higher. In North Dakota, the legislature of 93 members contained 17 men of Scandinavian parentage in 1895, and 18 in 1901—16 Norwegians (4 American born), one Dane, and one Icelander.[29] Unofficial figures for 1904 gave the Scandinavians 38 out of 140 members.[30] South Dakota in 1894 had 15 Norwegians (5 native-born) and 5 Swedes, in a legislative body of 127; in 1897, 17; in 1903, 16; and in 1904, 17.[31]

In the executive and administrative departments of State government, as distinguished from the legislative, the participation of the Scandinavians notably increased after 1869. In the summer of that year, a Scandinavian convention was held in Minneapolis for the express purpose of booming Colonel Hans Mattson for the office of Secretary of State in Minnesota. Of his fitness there was no doubt, for in addition to holding local offices in Goodhue County and his service in the army, he had for two years served as Commissioner of Emigration. The Repub-

[28]*Minnesota Legislative Manuals* for 1893, 1899, 1905.

[29]*Legislative Manual of North Dakota,* 1895, 18; *North Dakota Senate Journal,* 1901, 1; *North Dakota House Journal,* 1901, 1.

[30]*Amerika,* Nov. 18, 1904.

[31]Basford, *Political Handbook* (South Dakota), 149-197; *Senate Journal* and *House Journal,* 1897, 1903; *Amerika,* Nov. 18, 1904.

licans took the hint and nominated him almost unanimously in September, and his election followed. He served one term at this time and by re-elections filled the same office from 1887 to 1891.[32] So frequently have Swedes and Norwegians been elected to this office both in Minnesota and in the Dakotas that it might almost be said that they have a prescriptive right to it.[33] In the thirty-seven years ending in January, 1907, the Swedes filled the office in Minnesota sixteen years and the Norwegians four years.[34] Other State offices like those of Treasurer, Auditor, and Lieutenant Governor, not to mention commissionerships and appointments to boards, have also been frequently filled by Scandinavians in the States of the Northwest.[35]

The first Scandinavian to reach the eminence of a governorship was Knute Nelson, an emigrant from Voss, near Bergen in Norway, in 1849, who, after service in the Civil War, was elected in succession to the legislatures of Wisconsin and Minnesota and to the Congress of the United States. Nominated by acclamation for governor of Minnesota on the Republican ticket in 1892, he was elected by a plurality of 14,620 votes; two years later he was unanimously re-nominated, and re-elected by a plurality of more than 60,000 votes.[36] He served only one month of his second term, accepting election to the United States Senate, to the disappointment, not to say the disgust, of many who had voted for him for Governor, who considered him in duty bound to serve in that capacity after accepting their suffrages.

[32]Mattson, *The Story of an Emigrant,* 115; *Minnesota Legislative Manual,* 1905, 99.

[33]*Minnesota Legislative Manual,* 1905, 99; *North Dakota Legislative Manual,* 1895, 66; *South Dakota Legislative Manual,* 1894, 130, 134.

[34]*Minnesota Legislative Manual,* 1905, 99, 627.

[35]*Ibid.,* 99-106, 627-637; *Wisconsin Blue Book,* 1895, 662ff; *South Dakota Political Handbook,* 1894, 130ff; *The Viking,* I, 3 (1906).

[36]Stenholt, *Knute Nelson,* 68-78; Nelson, *History of the Scandinavians,* I, 451; *Minnesota Legislative Manual,* 1893, 549.

The second Scandinavian governor was a Swede born in Smaaland, who landed in the United States in 1868 at the age of fourteen—John Lind. Passing up through such political gradations as county superintendent of schools, receiver of the United States Land Office, and Republican representative in Congress, he allied himself with the free-silver movement of 1896 and became the Fusion candidate for governor of Minnesota. Opposed by the leading Swedes who remained loyal to the Republican party, he was defeated by a small majority, tho supported by many of the Norwegians. The Spanish War, in which he served as quartermaster of volunteers, gave him a new claim to popular favor, and when he again ran for governor in 1898 he was elected by a combination of Democrats and Populists, turning his former deficiency of 3,496 into a plurality of 20,399.[37] This victory was due more to a revolt against the Republican candidate than to clannish support of a Swede by Swedes, for the two strongholds of the Swedes, Chisago and Goodhue Counties, went Republican as usual, while the German and Irish wards of St. Paul and Minneapolis gave majorities for Lind.

The third of Minnesota's Scandinavian governors came into office under circumstances of distinctly dramatic character. John A. Johnson was born of Swedish parents in the State over which he was to be made ruler; at the age of fourteen he became the support of his mother and of the family, save the inebriate father who was sent to an almshouse where he died. When nominated by the Democrats in 1904, Johnson had been for eighteen years editor of a country newspaper printed in English. The Republicans, especially their candidate for governor, a coarse-grained distrusted, machine politician, endeavored to make political capital out of the fact that Johnson's father died in the poorhouse. The Democratic leaders persuaded Johnson with some difficulty to let the plain truth be told, and told on the stump—and Johnson, the son of a Swedish immi-

[37]*Svenska Amerikanska Posten,* Nov. 22, 1898; *World Almanac,* 1899; Nelson, *History of the Scandinavians,* I, 432.

grant, a man from a small, interior city, a Democrat in a State strongly Republican as a rule, won by a plurality of 6,352 votes in a Presidential year, when Theodore Roose-velt carried the State by 161,464.[38] Two years of vigorous but quiet administration brought the reward of a renomi-nation and reelection in 1906 by a plurality of 76,000.[39] Again in 1908, another presidential year, Governor John-son was reelected by 20,000 plurality, though Taft received a plurality of 85,000.[40]

The death of Governor Johnson in October, 1909, made the Republican Lieutenant Governor, Adolph Olson Eber-hardt, the fourth Scandinavian executive of Minnesota. He was born in Sweden, the son of Andrew Olson, and came to America in his eleventh year. He added Eberhardt to his name by permission of the proper court in 1898 be-cause several other persons in his community also bore the name of Adolph Olson. Governor Eberhardt reached the governor's chair by various business and political experi-ences—as a lawyer, contractor, United States Commis-sioner, deputy clerk of the United States District and Cir-cuit Courts, State senator, and lieutenant governor. He was reelected in his own right in 1910 by a plurality of 60,000, and again in 1912 by 30,000.[41]

James O. Davidson rose to the governorship of Wis-consin through long service in subordinate capacities. Of Norwegian birth, immigrating in 1872, he was elected to the Wisconsin legislatures of 1893, 1895, 1897; twice chosen State Treasurer; elected Lieutenant Governor on the ticket with R. M. LaFollette, and upon the election of the latter to the United States Senate succeeded him as gov-ernor in January, 1906. In the summer of that year Sena-tor LaFollette vainly stumped the State to prevent David-son's nomination for Governor on the Republican ticket,

[38]*Minnesota Legislative Manual,* 1905, 506, 520. 'In this election of 1904, P. E. Hanson, a Swedish immigrant of 1857, was elected on the Republican ticket as Secretary of State by a plurality of more than 96,000.
[39]*World Almanac,* 1907, 487.
[40]*Ibid.,* 1909, 639.
[41]*Ibid.,* 1911, 673; 1913, 741; *Who's Who in America,* 1914-15.

and in the election that followed the Norwegian-born, soundly-experienced Governor was chosen by the handsome plurality of 80,247 votes.[42] In 1908 he was reelected by a plurality of 76,958.

Still further up the political scale, men from Northwestern Europe have been taking an active part in national affairs. Sixteen of them have been elected to the House of Representatives of the Federal Congress. The first one to achieve this high position was Knute Nelson who sat in the House from 1883 to 1889 as the Representative of the Fifth Minnesota District. In 1895 he was chosen United States Senator and has served continuously since March 4, 1895.[43] Others who have served for several terms in the House are: Nils P. Haugen, a Norwegian representing a Wisconsin district from 1887 to 1895; John Lind, a Swede, who represented the Second Minnesota District from 1887 to 1893; Asle J. Gronna, who was a member of the House from 1905 to 1909, and succeeded Johnson as Senator from North Dakota, serving up to the present time; Gilbert N. Haugen, another Wisconsin-born Norwegian, who has represented the Fourth Iowa District since 1899; Andrew J. Volstead, a Minnesota-born Norwegian, who has sat for the Seventh Minnesota District since 1903; and Halvor Steenerson, born in Dane County, Wisconsin, of Norwegian stock, who has represented the Ninth Minnesota District since 1903.[44] Martin N. Johnson, who was born of Norwegian parents in Wisconsin, had his first legislative

---

[42]*Wisconsin Blue Book* (1903), 1070; *World Almanac,* 1907, 513.

[43]*Minnesota Legislative Manual* (1895), 325-6, 648; *Congressional Directory,* May, 1914.

[44]*Wisconsin Bluebook* (1895), 191-2; *Congressional Directories,* 1887 to 1914, which contain brief biographies of Representatives and Senators. Other Representatives for briefer terms than those mentioned above are: from Minnesota, Kittle Halvorson (Norwegian), 1891 to 1895; Halvor E. Boen (Norwegian), 1893 to 1895; Charles A. Lindbergh (Swede), since 1906; from Wisconsin, H. B. Dahle (Norwegian), 1899 to 1901; John M. Nelson (Norwegian), since 1906; and Irvine L. Lenroot (born of Swedish parents in Wisconsin), since 1909; from North Dakota, Henry T. Helgesen (Norwegian, born in Iowa), since 1911; and from Utah, Jacob Johnson (the only Dane who has sat in the House), since 1913.

experience in the Iowa legislature, sat in the House as representative at large from the new State of North Dakota from 1891 to 1899, and then, after a period of retirement, was sent to the United States Senate from the same State, serving from March, 1909, until his death in October of the same year.

An analysis of this list of Representatives shows that eleven of the sixteen were Norwegians of the first or second generation of immigrant stock, four were Swedes, and one a Dane. Six of the eleven were born in America, three of them in the old Wisconsin settlements; only one of these represented the district in which he was born, the rest receiving their reward in the newer western sections into which they had migrated with the movement of population beyond the Mississippi.

Different Federal administrations have deemed it wise to "recognize" the Scandinavian among other elements of the political population, in making appointments in the diplomatic and consular services of the United States. One of the most notable instances is that of the selection of John Lind, the former governor of Minnesota as the personal representative of President Wilson in Mexico during the troubled months of 1913 and 1914 and as adviser to the United States embassy in Mexico City during the period following the recall of Ambassador Henry Lane Wilson. Another instance of appointment in this service is that of Lauritz Selmer Swenson, a Norwegian of the second generation, born in Minnesota, who was minister to Denmark from 1897 to 1906, and later received appointments as minister to Switzerland and to Norway, terminating the latter in 1913.[45] Rasmus B. Anderson represented the United States at the Danish court from 1885 to 1889, being at that time a Democrat. He was born in Wisconsin of pure Norse parentage, and had served as professor of the Scandinavian languages in the University of Wisconsin.[46]

[45]*Who's Who in America,* 1914-5.
[46]*Ibid.;* Anderson, *Norwegian Immigration,* quoting from the *Madison Democrat.*

The appointment of Nicolay A. Grevstad as minister to Uruguay and Paraguay in 1911 was a fitting recognition of ability combined with long and able service to the people of the older, or middle, Northwest as editor of the *Minneapolis Tribune*, the *Minneapolis Times*, and the great Chicago daily, *Skandinaven* (1902-1911). Hans Mattson, a Swedish veteran of the Civil War, was consul general at Calcutta from 1883 to 1885;[47] Soren Listoe, the Danish editor of *Nordvesten* of St. Paul, Minnesota, was consul at Düsseldorf, 1882-3, consul at Rotterdam, 1897-1902, and consul general at the same city, 1902-1914.[48] At Rotterdam he succeeded L. S Reque, a Norwegian from Iowa. Several other men have served for long terms in minor positions in the foreign service.[49]

[47]Mattson, *The Story of an Emigrant*, 143-145.
[48]*Congressional Directory*, 1897, 1907, 1914; Nelson, *History of the Scandinavians*, I, 435, 480, 503; II, 195.
[49]Peterson, *Svenskarne i Illinois*, 389.

CHAPTER XII.

The great majority of the Scandinavians, prior to 1884, were thoro-going and uncompromising Republicans, and tho the party still holds most of them, profiting largely from their natural conservatism and their loyalty to a principle, it can by no means depend upon them with the assurance it had in the "good old days" when to find a Scandinavian voter in the Northwest was to find a Republican.

The causes which determined the early party affiliations of the naturalized sons of the Vikings, in the broad area of State and Federal affairs, are to be found in the character of the immigrants themselves and in the great questions agitating the country at the time they became citizens. Coming to the United States with an endowment of natural independence, with an innate respect for government, and with an inclination for public concerns, their interest was at once actively aroused in the great problem of slavery that vexed national life from the time of the Sloop Folk to the Civil War. As their information about the slave system grew more exact, and as the tremendous significance of the restriction of the slave area as a cardinal political issue was made clear to their minds, they became of one mind in the mighty agitation. Neither they nor their ancestors for hundreds of years had held slaves; few of them had ever seen a slave, for their numerous traders and sailors, with slight exceptions, had no smell of blood of the African slave trade on their hands.[1] It was not chance, therefore, which kept the stream of North European immigrants from flowing into the South and Southwest; no attractiveness of climate or soil could compensate for the presence of Negro slavery. A horror and hatred of slavery colored their thinking from their first month in the New World; it was first a moral, then a

[1] DuBois, *Suppression of the African Slave-Trade*, 90 n 5, 131, 143 n 1.

political, conviction, not the sentiment of individuals, but the well-reasoned opinion of the whole community·

Bound together on this great question, then so dominant, they naturally maintained unity on other political questions as well as on slavery; and when once their ideas were fixed, any change would be effected slowly and with difficulty. The newcomers, in their first months in the older settlements, were speedily indoctrinated with anti-slavery sentiment. Thus it came about that one party received and retained the vast majority of the Scandinavians down to 1884, simply because a bent that way was given in the early years of immigration from the Northern peninsulas, and because the question of the status of the Negro, in one form or another, continued to be a political issue.

The first appearance of the Norwegians in State politics in Wisconsin, as already noted, was under the Free Soil banner between 1846 and 1848, when that State was endeavoring to form a constitution. The first constitution submitted to the people, in 1847, was rejected by a large majority, including a separately-submitted provision granting equal suffrage to Negroes. While the State decisively voted thus, the counties in which the Scandinavian vote was largest—Racine, Walworth, and Waukesha—showed large majorities in favor of giving the Negroes political privileges equal to those of the Whites. On the other hand, counties where the German votes were numerous stood solidly against equal suffrage, seemingly because in the constitutional convention the question of Negro suffrage was coupled with that of the granting of suffrage to foreign-born, in a way that greatly displeased the Germans.[2]   When the second convention finished its constitution, in 1848, resolutions were introduced to provide for printing and distributing translations of the document, 6000 copies in German, and 4000 copies in Norwegian, a hint of the relative strength of the two groups.[3]

[2]Baker, *History of the Elective Franchise in Wisconsin,* 9; including a reference to the *Wisconsin Banner,* Oct. 17, 1846.

[3]*Journal of the Second Convention,* 511, 584.

The relation of James Reymert and his *Nordlyset* to the Free Soil movement has been mentioned. When the Democratic papers mercilessly criticised the little sheet and poked fun at its name, the paper was sold by Reymert to Knud Langeland in 1849, and by him removed to Racine; the name was changed to *Demokraten*, but the politics of the paper were not affected.[4] As a political organ among the Norwegians, it was ahead of the times; the support of the paper was insufficient to pay the bills, and it was discontinued in 1850. The Norwegian immigrants were unaccustomed to a purely secular press; they preferred to have their politics wrapped up in papers labelled "religious." Langeland declares that many of them considered it a sin to read a political newspaper.[5] But the Free Soil sentiment was too strong to go without printed expression in Norwegian; and accordingly the propaganda continued in the form of speeches of Chase, Seward, Hale, Giddings, and other anti-slavery leaders, which were translated into Norwegian and mixed in with non-political matter in *Maanedstidende,* a paper whose publication, after the failure of *Demokraten,* Langeland undertook along with four clergymen, Clausen, Preuss, Stub, and Hatlestad.[6]

As they read these speeches of the great leaders, as they heard from Negroes themselves the evils of slavery, as they learned of the high-handed doings in Kansas, the zeal of the Scandinavians for human freedom increased. There were no old party traditions, feelings, or feuds, to keep them from judging the issue of slavery's expansion on its merits; no loyalty to the memories of dead heroes held them in mortmain. Some few of them voted for Cass in 1848 and for Pierce in 1852, but by 1856 there was only one issue for them: simply and straightforwardly and

[4]Langeland, *Nordmændene i Amerika,* 96.

[5]Langeland, *Nordmændene i Amerika,* 98: "Den första Indvandrerbefolkning hovedsagelig bestod af Folk fra Landsbygderne, som for en stor Del ikke var vant til at læse andet end Deres Religionsböger, og mange af dem ansaa det endog for en Synd at læse politiske Blade."

[6]*Ibid.,* 98.

almost to a man, they became Republicans.[7] The Democrats, of course, did not let the children of the North go without an effort to secure them in their ranks. In 1856 Elias Stangeland of Madison, Wisconsin, started a Norwegian paper, *Den Norske Amerikaner*, in support of James Buchanan. His efforts to get Langeland to undertake the editorship failed because the latter was an ardent admirer of Fremont. The paper had a short life, and probably Langeland is right in attributing its disappearance to the withdrawal of the Democratic subsidy.[8] A long time was to elapse before a successful attempt would be made to maintain a Democratic paper in Norwegian or Swedish.

What the anti-slavery agitation left undone towards making the Scandinavians unswervingly Republican, was accomplished by the Civil War. The lingering glories of the golden age of the Democracy of Jackson and Jefferson were entirely obscured by the attitude of the Democratic party toward the conduct of the war. Only when the memories of the Civil War grew less vivid and less influential with new arrivals from the Old World, and not until moral questions were superseded in political discussions by economic questions relating to the tariff, currency, and labor, did the Scandinavians begin to arrange themselves in any considerable numbers outside the Republican ranks.

Four times during the last thirty-five years the Scandinavian voters in large numbers, under varying circumstances and in different degrees in different States, have abjured Republican leadership. After each such excursion they have returned, for the most part, to their old party relations, but never with quite the same fervent, reliable zeal for Republican principles and candidates. The development of the bacillus of independence is unmistakable. One defection affected Wisconsin alone, the only instance where the Democrats profited directly by the votes of large

[7] Peterson, *Svenskarne i Illinois*, xii; Mattson, *The Story of an Emigrant*, 56; Nelson, *History of the Scandinavians*, I, 305, 310.

[8] *Langeland, Nordmændene i Amerika*, 110.

numbers of Scandinavians. At a later time, when the Free Silver and Populist ideas took strong hold on the Northwest, the Scandinavian vote re-enforced the personal popularity of John Lind, the Swedish candidate of the Populist-Democratic party, and secured his election, tho the rest of the Fusion ticket suffered defeat·

The first time Norse voters broke from the Republican ranks was in connection with the Greenback movement which began with the depression following the panic of 1873 and culminated in the election of 1880. Many of them, especially the Swedes in Illinois, became out-and-out Greenbackers or Independents. In his book on the Swedes in Illinois, published in 1880, C. F. Peterson gives brief biographies of some seven hundred Swedes, men of all walks of life above day laborer, who may be considered as representatives of the 40,000 Swedes in Illinois at that time.[9] At least they represent the classes which would be least likely to be led off into economic heresies. Of 628 whose party affiliations are stated, 472 were Republicans; 76, Independents; 55, Greenbackers; and 25, Democrats or Prohibitionists. In other words, out of the total number canvassed, more than twenty per-cent were dissenters from Republican orthodoxy.

The relation of political and religious sentiment is strikingly illustrated in analyzing these biographies, for those who were Lutherans or Methodists were usually Republicans in politics, and proud to belong to "the party of moral ideas."[10] Those stating their religious preferences as Lutheran numbered 388, and of these only 10 were Democrats, 16 were Greenbackers, and 19 were Independent. On the other hand, of 131 who belonged to the three political parties last mentioned, 87 were in religion also Independent, Free Thinkers, or "Ingersollites". For States other than Illinois, no such complete contemporary data are available; but since the Greenback vote in Minne-

[9]Peterson, *Svenskarne i Illinois,* part II.

[10]*Ibid.,* 353: "Medlem i de 'moralska ideernas' politska parti—det republikanska."

sota was only 2% of the total, and in Wisconsin 3%, it is fair to assume that the Scandinavians did not desert the Republican standard in very large numbers in those States.

The second case of considerable defection among the Republican Scandinavians occurred after the widespread development of agrarian discontent in the late eighties. The farmers and laborers, American and Scandinavian alike, felt the stress of hard times, turned to political agencies for relief, forsook the old parties, and formed the party called variously the Populist, People's, and Farmers' Alliance Party. Besides those Norwegians and Swedes who had been for years Republicans, whose political color was fixed by the mordant of slavery and the Civil War, there was then a very large number of men who arrived in the vast immigrant invasions between 1880 and 1885, and who were just coming into the full exercise of the rights of citizenship· An increasing proportion of these later arrivals went to the large cities and towns. All of them were moved less by the traditions of "moral ideas" and more by the contagious discontent of the older settlers and by the arguments of industrial and political agitators.

In the election of 1890 a serious break occurred in the Republican Party in Minnesota and in the Dakotas. There was a general impression in the rural districts of Minnesota that the Republican candidate for governor, William R. Merriam, a wealthy banker of St. Paul, was renominated for his second term by a political ring composed of lumber-kings, wheat dealers, and millers who combined to cheat and rob the farmer. Accordingly the Farmers' Alliance nominated a third ticket headed by S. M. Owen, the editor of an agricultural paper in Minneapolis, who polled a vote of 58,513, and reduced Merriam's vote of 1888 by about 46,000.[11] Merriam was re-elected by a plurality of

[11]*Minnesota Legislative Manual,* 1893, 482:

	1888	1890
Republican candidate	134,355	88,111
Democratic candidate	110,251	85,844
Prohibition candidate	17,026	8,424
Farmers' Alliance candidate		58,513

less than 2,500, tho he had had more than 24,000 two years before.

A careful examination of the votes for 1888 and 1890 in such strong Scandinavian counties as Otter Tail, Douglas, Chisago, Freeborn, Polk, and Norman leaves no doubt that the Swedes and Norwegians in very large numbers either voted for Owen, or refused to vote for Merriam.[12] In some cases the Republican vote fell off one-half and even two-thirds, and third-party Alliance candidates for the legislature were elected. A prominent Norwegian writer estimated that "25,000 Norwegian-born farmers turned their backs upon Mr. Merriam and voted for Mr. Owen for governor," disregarding the injunction of the Scandinavian Republican press to "stick to the grand old party, for the grand old party is particularly favorable to the Scandinavians, and the best political party in America."[13]

At the next state election in the presidential year, 1892, a Norwegian ran for governor on the Republican ticket, and a large part of the Scandinavian deserters wheeled into line and voted the Republican ticket. With a total vote only 15,000 greater than in 1890, the vote for the Republican candidate for governor increased in round number 20,000, for the Democratic candidate, 9,000, and for the Prohibition candidate, 4,000, while the vote of the Alliance or People's party fell off 20,000.[14]

Conditions in North Dakota and South Dakota were even more favorable to the new party than in Minnesota.

[12]*Minnesota Legislative Manual,* 1889, 397; 1893, 472.

[13]Mr. J. J. Skordalsvold in *The North,* Aug. 10, 1892.

[14]The ticket in Minneapolis, Hennepin County, Minnesota, in this year, 1892, is an interesting illustration of "recognition" of the power of the recent deserters. The Scandinavians had:

	Republican	Democrat	Populist
Presidential elector	1	2	2
Governor or Lieutenant Governor	1	—	1
Secretary of State	1	1	1
Legislative ticket	2	2	—
County officers	2	1	—
City officers	4	1	—

Minneapolis Journal, Nov. 3, 1892.

Estimates based on a study of statistics .and newspapers have been confirmed by prominent officials of those States, one of whom declares that "in some localities quite a percent has joined the Populist party; but it is very rare indeed to find a Scandinavian Democrat."[15] Another believes that a considerable portion of the Scandinavians voted the Populist ticket in 1892 and in 1894, but that they were normally believers in the protective principle and therefore naturally affiliated with the Republican party.[16] A German lawyer of Valley City, North Dakota, a Democrat, practically agreed with the Norwegian city attorney of Devil's Lake in the same State, the one saying that a large part of the Norse voters were Populists, the other declaring that the Populist party was largely composed of Scandinavians.[17] All agreed that these voters later tended to return to their former Republican alliance. It may be doubted, however, whether the hold of the protection idea is one of the primary reasons for Scandinavian Republicanism. At any rate the vote of the Hon. Knute Nelson for the Mills Bill for tariff revision in 1888—one of six Republican votes for the measure—did not make him politically *persona non grata* or a suspicious character among his Norwegian or Swedish brethren.

Another index of the shifting of political sentiment among the Norse voters is found in the changes in the party affiliations of Scandinavian newspapers, tho the varying importance of these journals imposes special caution in interpreting these figures. It would be obviously unfair to offset the staunch and well-supported Republicanism of the ably-edited and widely-circulated *Skandinaven* of Chicago with the less stable *Normannen* of Stoughton, Wisconsin, which had not one-third the circulation nor

[15]Letter of Thomas Thorson, Secretary of State of South Dakota, April 9, 1906.

[16]Letter of C. M. Dahl, Secretary of State of North Dakota, March 24, 1896.

[17]Letter of E. Winterer, Valley City, March 21, 1896, and of Siver Serumgard, March 24, 1896.

one-tenth of the influence of the metropolitan journal.[18] The "mugwump spirit" of the press is well illustrated by the case of *Norden,* a Norwegian weekly of Chicago, Republican up to 1884, when it took an independent attitude. In 1888 it became avowedly Democratic and supported Grover Cleveland for the presidency· This move was made only after the proprietor and editor assured themselves that the patrons of the paper would sustain them in the proposed change.[19]

Of the secular political Scandinavian papers published in Minnesota in 1889 nine were Republican—five Norwegian or Norwegian-Danish, four Swedish; three were Democratic,—all Norwegian; two were Prohibitionist, one Norwegian and one Swedish; and one was Labor,— Norwegian.[20]   In the next five years, the independent press in Minnesota and other states increased in numbers at least, and included such influential journals as *Amerika* and *Folkebladet.*   George Taylor Rygh, professor of Scandinavian languages in the University of North Dakota, estimated in 1893 that "until a few years ago over four-fifths of the [Scandinavian] secular press were strictly Republican in politics.   One after another has ceased to defend the Republican party, and today not more than one-third of the whole number are strictly Republican."[21] While this personal opinion or impression is probably exaggerated, it may represent approximately the temporary state of that year if proper emphasis be laid on the word "strictly." Since there appears to be no evidence that these papers, with two or three exceptions, were subsidized to induce their change of political creed, it is reasonable to conclude that they had behind them a solidified constitu-

[18]Rowell, *American Newspaper Directory* for 1896, 1901, 1906; *Cosmopolitan,* Oct., 1890, 689.

[19]Interview in 1890 with the editor of *Norden,* Mr. P. O. Strömme. He said that the change was an excellent move for the paper.

[20]*Minnesota Legislative Manual,* 1889, 432-445.

[21]G. T. Rygh, "The Scandinavian American," *Literary Northwest,* Feb., 1893.   He estimated the total number of papers at "about 125."

ency, for they were run neither for personal amusement, pure philanthropy, nor mere partisan propaganda.

The third defection occurred in Wisconsin alone, and took its rise in a purely local question. Its interest lies in the peculiar and remarkable temporary alliance to which it led. The Wisconsin Legislature passed an act, approved April 18, 1889, "concerning the education and employment of children."[22] To the ordinary provisions for coercing parents and children, so that all children between the ages of seven and fourteen years should attend at least twelve weeks in some public or private school in the city or town or district in which they lived, nobody objected. But the fifth section of the act, which was known as the Bennett Law, was in certain church circles, like a dash of vitriol in the face:

"No school shall be regarded as a school under this act unless there shall be taught therein as a part of the elementary education of the children, reading, writing, arithmetic, and United States history, in the English language."

The last four words of this section, innocent and reasonable as they look to the average American, stirred up one of the bitterest political fights ever known in Wisconsin. The Roman Catholic church, unalterably committed to a system of parochial schools in many of which instruction is given in a foreign language, was for once in accord with the German and Scandinavian Lutherans who maintained similar schools. The compulsory use of English in instructing pupils in specified subjects turned priests and pastors and whole congregations into active, vociferous politicians, for Germans, Norwegians, Poles, and Bohemians claimed the right to educate their children in parochial schools of their own choosing. Was not education education, whether carried on in English or German or Polish or Norwegian? Were not the graduates of church schools, even tho they spoke English brokenly or with brogue, just as intelligent, just as capable, just as indus-

[22]*Laws of Wisconsin,* 1889, ch. 519.

trious, and just as honest, as those educated in the "little red school house" and the public high school?[23]   The chairman of the Lutheran Committee on School Legislation stated the matter clearly from the standpoint of the churches:

"The Lutherans of Wisconsin do not oppose the Bennett Law because they are the enemies of the English language. . . .   The Lutherans oppose the present compulsory school law because—whether designedly or not—it in fact infringes on the rights of conscience guaranteed by the constitution, and the right of parents to educate according to their convictions, their own children. . . . .   In short, the Lutherans insist upon their right to establish private schools at their own expense, and regulate them, without any intereference on the part of the State, ... that their children may become Lutheran Christians as well as loyal and good citizens."[24]   The official circular of the State Superintendent of Public Instruction of Wisconsin, dated January 25, 1890, almost a year after the passage of the act, was a statement of the opposite point of view, and a justification of attempts to enforce the law.   Incidentally it was a political pamphlet as well.   Superintendent Thayer said: "The thing that is antagonized by this law is the practice of allowing children of this State of proper school age, to pass that period of life without acquiring the minimum of education in elementary branches; without acquiring the ability to think in the language of the country, to express themselves intelligibly in that language, orally, in writing, and in business forms."

All through the latter part of 1889 and the first ten months of 1890, the agitation went on.   The press gave great space to it; some papers through several months, both in Wisconsin and in the neighboring States where

[23]*The Bennett Law Analyzed,* a campaign pamphlet issued by the Republicans in 1890, in English, German, Polish, and Norwegian, had for its heading a picture of a district school house labelled "The Little School House," and underneath, "Stand by It."

[24]See F. W. A. Notz, "Parochial School System" in Stearns (editor), *The Columbian History of Education in Wisconsin* (1893).

Lutherans and Catholics were numerous, offered "symposiums" which printed arguments on both sides.[25] *Public Opinion* summarized the sentiment for the larger world.[26] Church assemblies took action, and finally an Anti-Bennett Law convention was held in Milwaukee, June 4, 1890.

The Democrats were not slow in seizing the advantage offered, and managed their campaign of 1890 very shrewdly. The combination of sternly anti-Catholic German and Norwegian Lutherans, usually Republican, with Roman Catholics, under the Democratic banner, was irresistible. In spite of the frantic appeals of the Republican press and speakers for loyalty to the American flag and to the "little red school house," the Democrats elected their candidate for governor, and a legislature pledged to give the desired relief. By the six-line act of February 5, 1891, the Bennett Law was repealed, and two months later another compulsory education act was passed without the offensive and troublesome four words.[27] The work of the Lutheran-Catholic alliance was done; the heterogeneous, naturally antagonistic elements fell apart; and in a few years old party lines were re-established. The plurality of 28,000 by which the Democratic Governor, G. W. Peck, was elected in 1890, overcoming the usual Republican plurality of about 20,000, was reduced at his re-election in 1892 to 7,700. In 1894 the Republican candidate defeated Governor Peck by the handsome plurality of 50,000 votes.[28]

While the Bennett Law agitation was going on in Wisconsin, a similar, but milder disturbance occurred in Illinois. The compulsory education act of the latter State, which went into effect July 1, 1889, was closely, if not deliberately, modelled after the Wisconsin statute, and enacted that "no school shall be regarded as a school under this act, unless there shall be taught therein in the English language, reading, writing, arithmetic, history of the

[25]*The North,* Apr. 30, May 7, 14, 21, 28, June 4, 25, July 2, 1890.
[26]*Public Opinion,* IX, no. 1, Apr. 12, 1890.
[27]*Laws of Wisconsin,* 1891, chaps. 4, 187.
[28]*Wisconsin Bluebook* (1895), 342-342, 347.

United States, and geography.[29] In the campaign of 1890, the Republican candidate for State Superintendent of Education, favoring the new compulsory education law, was defeated by some 36,000 votes by Raab, the Democratic candidate who opposed the law. The Norwegians and Danes in the city of Chicago probably voted for Raab in large numbers, tho he won the Swedish wards of that city by small pluralities. In such counties as Knox, with its two thousand Swedish voters, and Winnebago (in which is situated the city of Rockford, with about fifteen hundred Swedish voters), where one-third of the foreign born population was at that time Scandinavian, the Republican candidate received large majorities. A writer for *America,* the periodical published in English for Scandinavian readers, claimed proudly that "the large Swedish settlements in Henry, Rock Island, Bureau, De Kalb, Henderson, Warren, Mercer, Ford, Whiteside, and other counties cast a solid vote for Edwards. . . . . . The Swedes were in favor of compulsory education almost to a man.[30] In the city of Chicago, the County Superintendent of Schools for Cook County was re-elected by a plurality of 23,000 tho he favored the compulsory law. The repeal of the law of 1889 was not so prompt in Illinois as it was in Wisconsin, for it was not until 1893 that a new and expurgated compulsory education measure took its place.[31]

A close and detailed examination of the legislative journals and the statutes of the Northwestern States does not reveal above a half-dozen laws which can be said to be due to the leadership and direct influence of the Scandinavians as such. On the other hand, in the field of general legislation these men have been indistinguishable from the native-born in ability, efficiency, and uprightness; the gross and net products of the labors of those legislatures with many Scandinavian representatives in such states as Minnesota and North Dakota, are not perceptibly different

[29]*Laws of Illinois,* 1889, Act of May 24.

[30]*America.* V. 201, (Nov. 20, 1890). See also editorial in the same volume, 172-174 (Nov. 13, 1890).

[31]*Laws of Illinois,* 1893, Acts of February 17 and June 19, 1893.

from the output of legislatures in which no Swede or Norwegian ever sat, as in Michigan or Colorado. Scarcely a law has been passed for the purpose of catering to the preferences, or of catching the vote, of the sons of the Northlands.

An exception to this general statement is the Minnesota law of 1883 providing for the establishment of a "professorship of Scandinavian language and literature in the State University, with the same salary as is paid in said University to other professors of the same grade." The man to be chosen must be "some person learned in the Scandinavian language and literature, and at the same time skilled and capable of teaching the dead languages so called."[32]

The motives of the makers of the law were benevolent enough, and circumstances warranted its passage, but nothing could better illustrate the utter carelessness and looseness with which American State legislators do their work, than this simple statute. It was drawn up by a distinguished American lawyer, Gordon E. Cole of St. Paul at the request of Truls Paulsen by whom it was introduced into the legislature.[33] It created a chair of "Scandinavian language," when there is no such language, living or dead; the professorship was established "in the State University," when the laws of the State recognize no institution bearing such a name. The Norwegian who presented the bill, the legislature (including twenty-one other Norwegians and Swedes) which passed it, and the Governor who signed it, all showed the same quality of ignorance and neglect of fact, law, and English. A second law, undoubtedly based directly upon the first, even to copying its confusion of terms, was the act passed by the legislature of North Dakota in 1891, creating a chair of Scandinavian language and literature in the University of North Dakota.[34]

[32]*The General Statutes of the State of Minnesota*, 1894, secs. 3908-3909 (*Laws of 1883,* Chap. 140.)

[33]Nelson, *Scandinavians in the United States* (1st ed.), I, 541-542.

[34]*Revised Codes of North Dakota*, 1895, sec. 887 (*Laws of 1891,* chap. 60).

Another statute having still more distinct Scandinavian earmarks was passed by the legislature of North Dakota in 1893, providing for tribunals of conciliation, to be composed of four commissioners of conciliation elected in each town, incorporated village, and city. The measure was modelled in a feeble and tentative fashion after a statute of Norway, where such courts have been in operation since 1824, proving especially efficient in securing amicable adjustment of petty neighborhood difficulties.[35] But the law in North Dakota speedily fell into "innocuous desuetude," in spite of the enormous percentage of Norwegians in that State; its construction was defective; its constitutionality was questioned; its machinery was cumbersome and expensive. During its first two years, many communities failed to elect commissioners, and no serious attempt was made to comply with its provisions; even the Norwegians themselves manifested no anxiety or haste to make use of this characteristically Norwegian court. Nor did the amendment of 1895, substituting for compulsory use of the tribunal hearings at the request of one party and with the consent of both parties, improve matters. One Norwegian attorney pronounced the law "an unmitigated absurdity under present conditions," because most suits in the United States arise out of contracts, debts, titles, etc., rather than out of neighborhood quarrels, slanders, and the like.

In all matters relating to temperance and temperance legislation, the Scandinavian voters have almost invariably been on the side of restriction of the saloon and the liquor traffic. They have supported prohibition in Iowa and in the Dakotas, high license in Minnesota, and the patrol-limit system in Minneapolis.[36] The prohibition State and local tickets, especially in Minnesota, and in the Dakotas,

[35]Letter of Siver Serumgard, City Attorney of Devil's Lake, N. D., March 24, 1896, and various other letters.
[36]*Minneapolis Journal,* Jan. 16, 1891. In Dakota "the reform was asked for more earnestly by the Scandinavian element than by any others." Ralph, *Our Great West,* 152.

always have a large proportion of Norwegians and Swedes among their nominees.[37]   The best illustration of this sentiment, however, is to be found in the history of prohibition in North Dakota.   When the new constitution for the proposed State was made and presented to the people in 1889, the section which provided for the absolute prohibition of both the manufacture and sale of intoxicating liquors was submitted separately to the voters.   Thus the prohibition issue was presented fairly and squarely to every man in the State.   The constitution itself was carried by a majority approximating twenty thousand in a total vote of upwards of thirty-five thousand; the prohibitionist section received a majority of 1159.   Analysis of the vote by counties makes it clear that in every county where the Scandinavians predominated, with a single exception, the section was carried by fair majorities.[38]   The question of re-submission of this section to the vote of the people of the State came up in 1895, and was postponed indefinitely by the House of Representatives of the State of North Dakota by a vote of twenty-six to twenty-two, fourteen of the sixteen Scandinavian members of the House voting with the twenty-six.[39]   This seems to justify the opinion of the Secretary of State of North Dakota: "Nearly all Scandinavian members of the legislature have invariably voted against the resubmission of the question to the people. . . . It is safe to say that at least three-fourths of the Scandinavian population of this State favor prohibition, and one-half of them are earnest advocates of the law."[40]

The only remaining question as to the political influence of the Scandinavians is the claim of the Swedes and Norwegians for "recognition" at the hands of old parties;

[37]The ticket voted in Minneapolis in 1893, illustrates this tendency. Among the Prohobitionist nominees were two Scandinavian presidential electors, the lieutenant governor, secretary of state, county treasurer, one candidate for the legislature, and one for the city council!

[38]*Legislative Manual of North Dakota*, 1889-1890, 170, compared with the population tables of the census of 1890; Ralph, *Our Great West,* 152.

[39]*Ibid.,* 1895, 19-20; *Minneapolis Sunday Times,* Feb. 10, 1895.

[40]Letter from C. M. Dahl, March 24, 1896.

and the concessions which such claims have extorted. From the foregoing accounts, it is evident that the Scandinavians have been ready in fitting themselves into the political system of the United States. Altho they have not been guilty of that excessive and pernicious activity in the field of public affairs which has characterized some classes of immigrants settling by preference in the great cities, it must be admitted that they have now and then appealed to race pride and prejudice and jealousy, remarking boundary lines and distinctions which should be obliterated. The practical politicians, on their part, have not hesitated to stir up, for party advantage, the sensitiveness of naturalized citizens to real or imaginary slights and discriminations against them by "the other party."

The appeal of the Norwegian and Swedish press is not infrequently based frankly on the essential sentiment of clannishness: "Scandinavians in Superior and other places should always support a country man for election to public office," and if he is in all ways worthy, "we should all together rally around him, lay aside all small considerations, and honor him with our trust and esteem."[41] Ridiculing the narrowness of these "demands," another editor, under the heading "From Norway, Birthplace of Giants," suggests a full Republican ticket of Norwegians, including Rasmus B. Anderson, "Republican pro tem.," and also a full Democratic ticket of Norwegians, including Rasmus B. Anderson, "thinking that he may next year be a Democrat again."[42] This trick of asserting their political importance in the Northwestern States was very early learned; and so long as party managers bid for votes in the tongues of the aliens, bribing them with nominations of the foreign-born, just so long will these groups of adopted citizens reiterate and multiply their demands, just so long will they capitalize their voting power and collect a generous interest in the shape of nominations and appointments. It must not be supposed that the Norwegian and

[41]Editorial in *Superior Tidende* (Wisconsin), Feb. 2, 1898. See also *Vikingen,* Aug. 18. 1888.
[42]P. O. Strömme in *Amerika og Norden,* Feb. 2, 1898.

Swedish party papers in America exist for the primary purpose of forwarding the political interests of people of those nationalities as such, for they do not, any more than do the partisan papers printed in English, but the Scandinavian groups are so large and so definite that appeals to them to stand together as a race for their own interests are inevitable.

So early as 1870, one of the leading Norwegian newspapers declared that it was time for the Norwegians to get a Representative in Congress just as well as other nationalities—*"ligesaavel som andre nationaliteter."*[43] The editor suggested that the eight thousand Norse voters in the southern Minnesota district hold a convention the day before the regular Republican convention, and agree upon a candidate for the Congressional nomination: if the Republicans refused to nominate him, put on the screws! About twenty years later this very method was resorted to in North Dakota, when the Scandinavians of that State "in mass convention assembled," proceeded to pass resolutions and to organize the Scandinavian Union of North Dakota, to secure for themselves "that share in the government to which their competency, their character and numerical strength, and their rank as pioneers in all matters of civilization entitle them." While declaring that it believed that every man should stand or fall on his own merits, the convention resolved "that we have seen with deep regret the disposition of a large number of our fellow citizens in some parts of North Dakota to discriminate against us, because we are Scandinavians, and that an unprovoked war has been waged against us."[44] The Hon. M. N. Johnson, presiding officer, presumptive beneficiary of the Union, an aspirant for nomination as Representative, stated the case very frankly: "The Scandinavians

[43]*Fædrelandet og Emigranten,* July 10, 1870. See also an editorial in *The North,* June 12, 1889, regretting that the question of national proportions and groups should be raised "but the principle having been recognized, we consider it our plain duty to see that it is fairly and squarely enforced."

[44]*The North,* July 10, 1889.

constitute a majority of the Republican party in North Dakota. Under the territorial government they have not received many official favors, but with the opening of statehood it is proper that they should have some recognition. The Scandinavians are not disposed to leave the Republican Party. They are heartily loyal to the organization and its principles. . . . . We have the numerical strength to demand and secure justice, and all we ask is fair play. . . . We are simply organizing our forces for united action in urging our just demands."[45] Their just demands consisted in "from three to five of the State officers, and if they stand together and attend the primaries, there is no doubt but that they will get what they ask for."[46]

The effectiveness of this movement is sarcastically summed up by a correspondent of *The North,* in reporting the Republican convention: "M. N. Johnson's Scandinavian League has evidently come out of the small end of the horn. To be sure M. N. was made the chairman of the convention and the dear Scandinavians got honorary mention in the resolutions: but M. N.'s chairmanship was evidently devoid of results beneficial to the Scandinavians, and as for resolutions—talk is cheap!"[47]

In an editorial in English *Skandinaven* discussed "Governor Sheldon's Mistake" in 1893: "Upwards of one-third of the population of South Dakota is of Scandinavian birth or origin, while Scandinavians furnish not less than one-half of the Republican vote of the State. Governor Sheldon is apparently oblivious to this fact; for in making his appointments he saw fit to ignore the Scandinavian-American citizens of South Dakota. For the sake of the Republican party of the State this mistake is very much to be regretted. The Scandinavians are sensitive of their

[45]*The North,* July 10, 1889, including translations from *Posten og Vesten* of Fargo.

[46]*Ibid.,* letter of Sigurd Syr.

[47]*Ibid.,* Aug. 28, 1889. After the fall election the same paper, October 9, announced: "The Scandinavian Union thus seems barren of results. . . . Peace be with its ashes!"—because it secured only 5 senators and 18 representatives in the State legislature.

rights as American citizens. . . . . . What has the Republican party of South Dakota done to Governor Sheldon that he should deal it such a dangerous blow?"[48] Five years later the governor of Minnesota was accused of a like offence in that, on the State boards appointed by Governor Merriam, the Scandinavians were "insufficiently represented," having only five out of one hundred members, or one-twenty-fifth, when they constituted one-third of the population of the State.[49]

The pettiness of these squabbles over political "recognition" and spoils is well illustrated by a letter written in Oshkosh, Wisconsin, to a Minneapolis newspaper in 1889: "While our people here number over 3000, and the Irish only 1400, the latter hold a still larger percentage of offices than they do in your city. This year for the first time the Scandinavians (or more correctly speaking, the Danes) have succeeded in obtaining a place on the police force"![50]

These insistent demands do not stop with simple recognition of the Scandinavian race: different sections must be satisfied. The most influential Swedish paper of the Northwest announced in 1890 that "what we on the other hand with full propriety and without the least danger of transgression can demand, is a man of Swedish descent at the head of one of our State departments. . . . . To deny them (Swedes) this just recognition would stir up bad feeling, and would be looked upon as a slight, not to say contempt. . . . . Our brethren, the Norwegians, are a little more numerous in Minnesota, than the Swedes, although not equaly good Republicans. They, too, are entitled to a place on the State ticket, and for a long time have had one [Lieutenant Governor Rice]."[51]

The failure of the Scandinavians to receive what some of them consider a just and due reward, one in proportion

[48]*Skandinaven,* April 5, 1893.

[49]*The North,* Jan. 22, 1890, quoting in translation from *Fædrelandet og Emigranten.*

[50]*The North,* July 17, 1889.

[51]Translated from *Svenska Folkets Tidning* (Minneapolis), April 20, 1890.

to their numbers and their devotion to one party, is not to be attributed wholly to the hardness of heart of the party leaders, nor to their shortsightedness. Nor can it be fairly charged to any strong dislike of Swedes, Norwegians, and Danes for each other: the Swedes, for example, have never bolted a ticket because it happened to be headed by a Norwegian.[52] In addition to the extension of religious antagonism into politics, "there is still another reason for the limited success of the Scandinavians in the political field, and that is their natural apathy [antipathy?] to following a leader. Each one considers himself competent to work on his own hook. To follow a leader seems incompatible with their ideas of liberty. Yet without union and without leaders, victory is impossible. . . . . . 'Everybody for himself, and the Devil for the hindmost' is the law governing American life, and this the Irish have learned, while the Scandinavian is generally waiting for someone to come along and offer something with the polite 'if you please.' But he has to wait."[53]

The Scandinavian press, in complaining of "a failure to get a due share of offices," in declaring that Norwegians are "entitled to ten seats" in the Wisconsin legislature when they happen to have but three, or in insinuating that they have never been fittingly recognized in Iowa, resorts to political claptrap, often quite unworthy of the journal printing it. The facts so easily forgotten are that the counties and legislative districts in which the Scandinavians are a ruling majority are comparatively few, while the districts in which they are an influential minority are very many.[54] The system of representation in the United

[52]Boyeson, "The Scandinavians in the United States," *North American Review,* CLV, 531; *Rockford Register* (Ill.), Sept. 16, 1889.

[53]*The North,* Aug. 14, 1889, translating from *Skandinavia* (Worcester, Mass.)

[54]*Billed Magazin,* I, 139 (1869); *Skandinaven,* Feb. 5, 1896—an editorial printed, like many others, in English and evidently designed for the consumption of editors of English papers. It is also evident that *Skandinaven's* readers understood English. Söderström, *Minneapolis Minnen,* 132, gives a fairly complete list of all the Swedes, Norwegians, and Danes

States is not based on any racial divisions or class distinctions, and not until some scheme of minority representation is adopted can any foreign element get its "share" of the political plums. It would be hard to suggest a more dangerous and disrupting experiment, in these decades when aliens by the hundreds of thousands, not to say millions, enter the country and are incorporated into the body politic, than to attempt to "recognize" the various alien factors in complex public affairs, even if they were all as adaptable as the men from the Northlands. Nothing would do more, for example, to develop the latent religious and racial antipathies between the Scandinavians and the Irish. The fundamental assumption, therefore, which lies back of all claims for "recognition" of Swedish-Americans, or other hyphenated Americans, as such, savors of ward politics and the machine, rather than of political equity or right, and just so far as it does this it menaces social and political safety.

elected or appointed to city, state or county office, even including policemen. For similar list for a rural county, see Tew, *Illustrated History and Descriptive and Biographical Review of Kandiyohi County, Minnesota* (1905).

CHAPTER XIII.

CONCLUSION

The meaning of the word American as applied to the inhabitants of the United States, has undergone a great change as they have multiplied fifteenfold in numbers and many times in varieties of nationalities in the course of a century. In that progress the Norwegians, Swedes, and Danes have played a conspicuous and constructive part. As late as 1840, American ordinarily meant a white person of English descent, born in America or resident in the United States long enough to understand and accept as fundamental and vital certain political and social ideals and ideas. That simple and definite significance applies no more. The American race is already alarmingly complex, tho the old type has been more closely adhered to than would be expected from an enumeration of the elements which have gone into the crucible.

In temperament, early training, and ideals, the Scandinavians more nearly approach the American type than any other class of immigrants, except those from Great Britain. In such features as adaptability and loyalty without reservation, no exceptions need be made. They have not come to the New World merely to get away from Europe, nor to escape Siberian exile or an Abyssinian war; nor has their motive been one of ordinary adventure-seeking. Theirs has been a determined purpose and a serious resolve to "arrive" somewhere in America, and, finding their places, to fill them with honorable endeavor and steady ambition. They have come as families, or with a wholesome desire to establish families for themselves. Most of them have fallen considerably below the best types of their own nationalities; their conservatism has sometimes been of the degenerate sort bordering on stolidity; their independence and individualism has come painfully near stubbornness; and their shrewdness has not infrequently developed into insincerity. They have now and then manifested a clannishness which led them into disagreeable, if temporary, complications.

The fact that this characteristic or that tendency exists in an immigrant or alien element, should not cause disturbance of mind to the good citizen, the statesman, or the scholar; the real question is whether this characteristic or tendency is growing stronger or disappearing more or less rapidly. For example, is the stolidity of a group deepening, or does mental agility develop in the second and third generation? That the Scandinavians have readily outgrown much of their clannishness, perceptibly quickened their energies in the new environment, and developed notably in social, commercial, and political efficiency cannot be seriously questioned by any one who studies their activities as a whole, or who has observed them for two generations.

The immigrants from the North are decently educated, able-bodied, law-abiding men and women, not illiterates, paupers, or criminals. They are not here as exiles from home and country for a few years, after which they purpose to return to their native lands, there to enjoy a cheap and narrow idleness. They are in the United States as citizens, to become thoroly and loyally American. Their ingrained habits of industry and economy, coupled with a natural conservatism and shrewdness, have given them material success and contributed in large measure to the prosperity of the States in which they have made their settlements. They have ever striven for homes, and while some of them have been content for a few years to serve others, the proletariat has not been largely recruited from them. Mere wage-earning has not been a permanent condition, but a stepping stone to a greater or less degree of independence. In politics and in war they have evidenced their ability to stand side by side with the native-born of New England, Pennsylvania, Ohio, and Indiana, and, with real faithfulness and efficiency to fill such places, low or high, as shall be opened to them.

Tho as Swedes, Norwegians, and Danes they will gradually disappear, becoming indistinguishable from other Americans, their fundamental characteristics cannot be blotted out even in the third and fourth generation. Men do not change so readily, even under the most favorable conditions. Fresh additions from Europe will continue to re-enforce the old stock; but they too will be sturdy, independent, and Protestant. It is not too much to expect that their virtues of intelligence, patience, persistence, and thrift, will be preserved as they mingle in the current of national life. The demand for these qualities will be steady; the supply on the part of the Scandinavians will not be readily exhausted. The intermarriage and amalgamation of two peoples so closely allied as the Scandinavians and Americans connotes much of promise and little of danger.

Several forces will continue to operate in the future, as they have in the past, against perpetuating any distinctively Scandinavian influence on the population or institutions of the United States. All three Northern peoples are particuarly free from other than traditional ties and sentimental attachments binding them to the mother countries. No one of the three kingdoms is great or powerful in the affairs of Europe; the heroes of the past, like Gustavus Adolphus, are too far away in time to affect powerfully the imaginations of today. Patriotism with them in the Old World is quite as much a sentiment or love for the parish or the homestead as it is a fierce and militant passion for the power and leadership of the nation. No dramatic outbursts of national feeling, or antagonisms to ancient enemies, will rekindle old enthusiams in the American Scandinavians. Even the prospect of war between Norway and Sweden, when the former dissolved the Dual Monarchy, did not profoundly stir the Swedes or Norwegians in the Northwest; and had war broken out all the recruits from America could probably have been shipped across the Atlantic in one voyage of a small steamship.

Furthermore, no great and permanent causes centering in Europe continually demand their active and intense sympathy and financial aid, knitting them closely together, as in the case of the Irish or the Russians. The Scandinavian contributions to European causes have been filial and fraternal, never political, never revolutionary, never such as to raise a national issue in America. Their church organizations, decentralized, centrifugal rather than centripetal, recognizing no unity under a temporal head, cannot be turned into a keen, insinuating political weapon. They have no secret societies ramifying through their settlements, no Mafias, "Molly Maguires," anarchist lodges, or other badges of ancient servitude or foreign hates.

The Scandinavians, knowing the price of American citizenship, have paid it ungrudgingly, and are proud of the possession of the high prerogatives and privileges conferred. They fit readily into places among the best and most serviceable of the nation's citizens; without long hammering or costly chiseling they give strength and stability, if not beauty and the delicate refinements of culture, to the social and economic structure of the United States.

For all these reasons the difficulties of the United States in adjusting the life and ideals and institutions of the nation to the presence of foreigners are reduced in the case of the Scandinavians to a minimum. The Swedes, Norwegians, and Danes are not likely to furnish great leaders, but they will be in the front rank of those who follow with sturdy intelligence and conscience, striving to make the land of their adoption strong and prosperous,— "a blessing to the common man," according to the original vision of America seen by Sweden's great king Gustavus Adolphus. They will be builders, not destroyers; their greatest service will be as a mighty, silent, steadying influence, re-enforcing those high qualities which are sometimes called Puritan, sometimes American, but which in any case make for local and national peace, progress, and righteousness.

CHAPTER XIV.

The term bibliography does not accurately or fully describe the materials upon which this study of the Scandinavians in the Northwest is based. To the printed sources of all sorts,—official reports of European and American governments, autobiographies, travels, and the like—and to a wide range of secondary works, there must be added much matter relating to the subject gathered by means of personal interviews, correspondence, and observations extending over a series of years. The Scandinavian press is an inexhaustible mine of source material; its information, in nuggets, flakes, and fine particles, must be sought for diligently, extracted, refined, and shaped; but it is the purest source material, nevertheless, comprising brief autobiographies, letters, personal opinions, description of surroundings and movements, and contributions to current discussion in politics, religion, and education. The county and local histories which multiplied rapidly between 1880 and 1895, and which have not yet ceased to appear, are not far from the borderland of source material. Their sketches of men and women and settlements, tho for the most part of a crude, innocent, laudatory type based upon brief personal interviews by canvassers and elaborated according to the varying size of the subscriptions of individuals, are almost indispensable for certain statistical purposes.

The customary distinction between source material and secondary material is often hard to maintain, so recent is the Scandinavian immigration, and so numerous are the first-hand and second-hand accounts by contemporaries participating in or observing the phenomena under consideration. The Northern peoples settling in the United

States have had no William Bradford for a historian, but the work of Norelius and Mattson is in a class similar to that of *Plimouth Plantation*.

The best bibliography of immigration in general is that published by the Library of Congress, A. P. C. Griffin (compiler), *A List of Books (with References to Periodicals) on Immigration* (3rd issue, with additions, 1907), but this is not complete, especially as relating to Scandinavian immigration. It omits all state documents, but is strong in its list of Congressional and executive documents. For the Scandinavian movement, the bibliography in O. N. Nelson (editor), *History of the Scandinavians and Successful Scandinavians in the United States* (2nd ed., I, 265-295), is the most useful, though it is unfortunately arranged on a strictly chronological basis in two parts. It is, however, far from complete, omitting practically all Federal and State publications, and all periodicals save for specific mention of certain articles. In the field of periodicals, is *Bibliografi; Svensk-Amerikansk Periodisk Literatur* (being No. 8, *Kungl. Bibliothekets Handlingar*, Stockholm, 1886).

In a general way, the following bibliography includes only those books, pamphlets, periodicals, and newspapers which were directly used in the preparation of this volume. In the case of foreign publications, the place as well as the date of publication is usually given.

DOCUMENTARY SOURCES

1. *Official Publications of the United States.*

Five series of reports published by the Federal Government are of very great importance in the study of immigration, both for their scope and their accuracy: the *Reports* of the censuses from 1850 to 1910; the *Annual Statistical Abstracts* (36 vols., 1879-1913); *Annual Reports of the Commissioner-general of Immigration* (17 vols., 1891-1909); *Reports from the Consuls of the United States* (notably vol. 22, No. 76, 1887), particularly those from the consuls in Norway, Sweden, and Denmark; and

Special Consular Reports (particularly vol. 30, 1904). *The Report of the Industrial Commission* (especially vols. XV. (1901) and XIX (1902), contains a vast amount of recent, complete, and diversified material in the testimony taken by the Commission and in the well-digested reports prepared by experts like John R. Commons. The Bureau of Statistics of the Treasury Department, *Immigration into the United States, showing number, nationality, sex, age, destination* (etc.) *from 1820-1903* (in *Monthly Summary of Commerce and Finance*, June, 1903), gives general tables and a review in convenient form.

The following reports of committees of the House of Representatives and of the Senate include usually the "hearings" of the committees, if any have been held: *Report from the Committee on Immigration and Naturalization,* 51 Cong., 2 Sess., H. R. No. 3472 (Owen Report, 1891) ; 52 Cong., 1 Sess., H. R. No. 2090 (Stump Report, 1892) ; *Report of the Committee on Immigration,* 52 Cong., 2 Sess., S. R. No. 1333 (Chandler Report, 1893) ; 54 Cong., 1 Sess., S. R. No. 290 (Lodge Report, 1896) ; 57 Cong., 2 Sess., S. Doc. No. 62 (Penrose Report, 1902). Special reports of importance are: *Report of the Immigration Investigating Commission* (1895) ; Edward Young, Chief of the Bureau of Statistics, *Special Report on Immigration,* (42 Cong., 1 Sess., H. Mis. Doc. No. 19, (1871) ; and C. C. Andrews, *Report made to the Department of State on the Conditions of the Industrial Classes in Sweden and Norway* (1874).

In a class by itself is the recent elaborate *Report of the Immigration Commission,* S. Docs., 61 Cong., 2-3 Sess. (Dillingham Report, 1910-1911), 43 vols., of which vols. 1 and 2 (Abstract), 4, 34, and 36 are specially important for this study. The *Report* is by far the most scientific, thorough-going, and detailed study of the nature, extent, distribution and results of immigration to the United States, and to a few other countries like Canada, Australia, and Brazil, which has yet been produced.

Various volumes of the United States *Statutes at Large* and the *Congressional Directories* have also some material.

2. *Official Reports of Scandinavian countries.*

DENMARK: annual volumes of *Statistisk Aarbog.*

NORWAY: annual volumes of *Norges Officielle Statistik* (1870-1913), of *Norges Land og Folk* (1885-1906), and of *Meddelelser fra det Statistiske Centralbureau* (1883-1899); and *Oversigt over Kongeriget Norges civile, geistlige og judicielle Inddeling* (1893).

SWEDEN: annual issues of *Bidrag till Sveriges officiella statistik* (1857-1913), covering a wide range of topics. Gustav Sundbärg (editor), *Sweden, Its People and Its Industry* (1904), is a valuable "historical and statistical handbook published by the order of the Government" of Sweden, in Swedish, English, and French.

NORWAY,—*Official Publication for the Paris Exhibition, 1900* (Christiania, 1900) is a companion volume to that for Sweden just mentioned.

3. *Official Publications of Great Britain.*

The *Report of the Board of Trade on Alien Immigration* (into the United States) (London, 1893) is at once able, comprehensive, judicious.

4. *Official Publications of the Northwestern States.*

The various annual or biennial legislative handbooks contain useful biographies and statistics, especially the volumes since 1880: *The Legislative Manual of the State of Minnesota; Wisconsin Blue Book; The Legislative Manual of North Dakota; South Dakota Political Handbook and Official and Legislative Manual* (sometimes entitled *South Dakota Legislative, Executive, and Judicial Directory*). Of the great number and variety of official State documents and reports, those most directly useful for this study are the volumes of statistics of Wisconsin, Illinois, Iowa, Minnesota, North Dakota, and South Dakota; those relating to the State censuses, State institutions (a board

of control as in Wisconsin and Iowa, or a board of charities and corrections, for certain institutions, in Minnesota
and South Dakota), commissioners or boards of immigration, and boards of health. Reports of officers in charge of
immigration matters are in State documents as follows:
Wisconsin, 1853, 1854, 1869-1875, 1880-1882, 1884, 1886,
1897, 1900; Iowa, 1872; Minnesota, 1867-1872. The publications of certain institutions chiefly supported by the
States, like the Wisconsin Historical Society, the State
Historical Society of Iowa, especially vol. III (1905), and
the Minnesota Historical Society, really fall into this class
of sources.

GENERAL WORKS

The classical work on the broad subject of immigration, notable alike for the breadth and penetration of its
views, is Richmond Mayo-Smith, *Emigration and Immigration: a Study in Social Science* (1890). Two other works
by the same authority, are: *Immigration and the Foreign-
Born Population* (in vol. III of the *Publications of the
American Statistical Assn.*, 1893), and *Statistics and So-
ciology* (1895). The *Publications* of the Immigration Restriction League take a wide range in 63 pamphlets (1894-
1914). Next to these in importance come: Prescott F.
Hall, *Immigration and its Effects upon the United States*
(1906), an excellent and compact study, somewhat marred
by the bias of its author, who is secretary of the Restriction League; J. R. Commons, *Races and Immigrants in
America* (1907), a popular rather than profound statement, but the fresh work of a careful scholar; E. A. Steiner,
On the Trail of the Immigrant (1906); S. McLanahan, *Our
People of Foreign Speech . . . with particular reference
to religious work among them* (1904).

A group of more recent works by competent scholars
combining qualities of penetration and popular presenta-
tion in satisfying proportions are: H. P. Fairchild, *Immigration: a World Movement and its American Significance*
(1913); J. W. Jenks and W. J. Lauck, *The Immigration
Problem* (3d ed. revised and enlarged, 1913), by two men

intimately connected with the making of the Dillingham Report; E. A. Ross, *The Old World in the New: The significance of past and present immigration to the American people* (1914) ; especially ch. IV; F. J. Warne, *The Immigrant Invasion* (1913), ch. XII.

Of less direct bearing, but valuable: W. J. Bromwell, *History of Immigration to the United States* (1856) ; F. L. Dingley, *European Immigration* (1890) ; F. Kapp, *Immigration and the Commissioners of Immigration of the State of New York* (1870) ; R. M. LaFollette (editor), *The Making of America,* vols. II, and VIII (1906) ; F. A. Walker, *Discussions in Economics and Statistics,* vol. II (1899).

The great mass of periodical literature is listed in Griffin's bibliography, already cited. Including general and special articles and some speeches in the *Congressional Record,* nearly 700 titles are arranged chronologically. The list is incomplete, omitting several articles, dealing particularly with the Scandinavians.

SPECIAL HISTORIES

Three works deal with the history of the Scandinavian immigration in a large-spirited, comprehensive way, and by these characteristics stand out from the mass of less important works. O. N. Nelson (compiler and editor), *History of the Scandinavians and Successful Scandinavians in the United States* (2 vols., 2nd revised ed., 1904), is made up of specially prepared articles, reprinted articles, statistical tables, a bibliography, and some two hundred and eighty biographies of men in Minnesota, Wisconsin and Iowa. It is very uneven, and on almost every page betrays at once the zeal, honesty, and the inadequate training of the authors and the compiler. It might almost be characterized as a cyclopedia of the Scandinavians in America. E. Norelius, *De Svenska Luterska Församlingarnas och Svenskarnes Historia i Amerika* (1890), while nominally a church history is in reality an excellent history of Swedish settlement; George T. Flom, *A History of Norwegian Immigration to the United States from the Earliest*

Beginning down to the Year 1848 (1909), made up in part of articles mentioned elsewhere, is a painstaking, exhaustive, accurate account of Norwegian immigration of that period into Wisconsin, Iowa, and Illinois.

Other books dealing with special groups or States or localities are: Axel A. Ahlroth, *Svenskarne i Minnesota— Historiska Anteckningar* (Westervik, 1891); Rasmus B. Anderson, *The First Chapter of Norwegian Immigration, 1821-1840,* a prolix, padded, but valuable volume; and *Tale ved Femtiaarsfesten for den Norske Udvandring til Amerika* (1875); John H. Bille, *A History of the Danes in America* (*Trans. Wis. Acad. of Sciences, Arts, and Letters,* XI, 1896), a short pamphlet; Tancred Boissy, *Svenska Nationaliteten i Förenta Staterna* (Göteborg, 1882), a reprint of correspondence in *Sydsvenska Dagbl. Snällposten;* J. W. C. Dietrichson, *Reise blandt de Norske Emigranter i "de forenede Nordamerikanske Fristater"* (Stavanger 1846, and reprinted Madison, 1896), a historical and contemporary description of the early settlements, and *Nogle Ord fra Prædikestolen i Amerika og Norge* (1851); Robert Grönberger, *Svenskarne i St. Croix-Dalen, Minnesota* (1879), an early and reliable piece of work; George Kæding, *Rockfords Svenskar—Historiska Anteckningar* (1885); Knud Langeland, *Nordmændene i Amerika—Nogle Optegnelser om de Norskes Udvandring til Amerika* (1889),—one of the very best of the books on the Norwegians; C. F. Peterson (see also Eric Johnson), *Sverige i Amerika—Kulturhistoriska och Biografiska Teckningar* (1898); Johan Schroeder, *Skandinaverne i de Forenede Stater og Canada, med Indberetninger og Oplysninger fra 200 Skandinaviske Settlementer* (1867),—full of the most valuable information about life and conditions in the Northwest; Ole Rynning, *Sandfærdig Beretning om Amerika til Oplysning og Nytte for Bonde og Menigmand* (Christiania, 1838),—a remarkably clear, compact, and influential pamphlet; Carl Sundbeck, *Svenskarna i Amerika, Deras Land, Antal, och Kolonien* (Stockholm, 1900); Alfred Söderström, *Minneapolis Minnen* (1899), an excellent, extensive, newspaper-like description of the life and activities of the Scandinavians in that half-Norse city; Alfred Strömberg, *Minnen af Minneapolis* (1902); *Underretning om Amerika, fornemmeligen de Stater hvori udvandrede Normænd have nedsat sig, ... udgivne af X* (Skien, 1843); M. Ulvestad, *Normændene i Amerika, deres Historie og Record* (1907); P. S. Vig, *Danske i Amerika* (1900; Johs. B. Wist, *Den norske Indvandring til 1850, og Skandinaverne i Amerikas Politik* (1884?),—a small but suggestive pamphlet.

On the Bishop Hill colony, the best authorities are: Michael A. Mikkelsen, *The Bishop Hill Colony, a religious communistic Settlement in Henry County, Illinois* (*Johns Hopkins University Studies*, X, No. 1, 1892)—the most convenient work in English, based almost entirely on Norelius, and on Johnson and Peterson, *Svenskarne i Illinois*, Johnson being a son of the founder, Eric Janson; Emil Herlenius, *Erik-Jansismens Historia, ett Bidrag till Kännedomen om det Svenska Sektväsendet* (Jönköping, 1900); *History of Henry County, Illinois* (1877); *Erick Jansismen i Nord Amerika* (Gefle, 1845); Hiram Bigelow, *The Bishop Hill Colony* (No. 7 of the *Publications of the Illinois State Historical Library*, 1902); W. A. Hinds, *American Communities* (1902).

SELECT ARTICLES IN PERIODICALS

Articles in periodicals: R. B. Anderson, "Norwegian Immigration," "The Coming of the Danes," "Icelandic Immigration," *Chicago Record Herald* (June 19, 26, July 24, Aug. 21, 1901); K. C. Babcock, "The Scandinavians in the Northwest," *Forum*, XIV (1892), "The Scandinavian Contingent," *Atlantic*, LXVII (1896), "The Scandinavian Element in American Population", *American Historical Review*, XVI (1911); H. H. Boyesen, "Norse Americans," *The American*, I (1880), "The Scandinavians in the United States," *North American Review*, CLV 1892); G. T. Flam, "The Scandinavian Factor in the American Population," *Iowa Journal of History and Politics*, III (1905), and (in Norwegian translation) in *Vor Tid*, I (1905); A. H. Hyde, "The Foreign Element in

American Civilization," *Popular Science Mo.,* LII (1898) ; Juth Jæger, "The Scandinavian Element in the United States," *The North,* June, 1889,—with many other similar discussions in the same weekly paper, all of them excellent; Kristofer Janson, "Norsemen in the United States," *Cosmopolitan,* IX (1890) ; Axel Jarlson, "A Swedish Emigrant's Story," *Independent,* LV (1903) ; F. H. B. Mac-Dowell, "The Newer Scandinavia—a Sketch of the Growth and Progress of the Scandinavian Races in America," *Scandinavia,* III (1884) ; J. A. Ottesen, "Bidrag til vore Settlementers og Menigheders Historie," *Amerika* (Apr. to Nov., 1894),—an elaborate series of articles, full of genealogical and community details; E. A. Ross, "Scandinavians in America," *Century,* LXXXVIII (1914) ; Geo. T. Rygh, "The Scandinavian Americans," *The Literary Northwest,* II (1893) ; Albert Shaw, "The Scandinavians in the United States," *Chautauquan, VIII* (1887).

State and Local Histories

The number of historical books and pamphlets relating to the States, counties, cities, and settlements in the Northwest is very great, and for the larger part, unsatisfactory but indispensable. They have usually been written by ambitious but untrained persons, either as commercial ventures, advertising agencies, or as the pastime of retirement or old age; they are nevertheless full of suggestive data; now and then one is found which can be trusted throughout.

A. MINNESOTA

First in importance for the Scandinavian settlements in Minnesota are four county histories: *History of Fillmore County, including Explorers and Pioneers of Minnesota* (1882) ; *History of Goodhue County* (1882) ; *History of Houston County, etc.* (1882) ; Martin E. Tew and Victor E. Lawson and J. E. Nelson, *Illustrated History and Description and Biographical Review of Kandiyohi County, Minnesota* (1905),—easily the best local history relating to Scandinavian settlement, as well as one of the latest and most comprehensive. Closely connected with this last work in scope and value is Alfred Söderström, *Minneapolis Minnen: Kulturhistorisk Axplockning från Qvarnstaden vid Mississippi* (1899). Other works dealing with the State or sections: Isaac Atwater (editor), *History of the City of Minneapolis, Minnesota* (1893); Fredk. W. Harrington, *Geography, History, and Civil Government of Minnesota* (1883); Soren Listoe, *Staten Minnesota i Nord Amerika* (1869); *History of the Minnesota Valley* (1882); *History of the Upper Mississippi Valley* (1882).

W. A. Gates, *Alien and Non-resident Dependents in Minnesota* (in *Proceedings* of National Conference of Charities and Correction, (1899); F. H. B. MacDowell, "Minneapolis and her Scandinavian Population", *Scandinavia*, III (1884); Louis Pio, "The Sioux War, in 1862— a Leaf from the History of Scandinavian Settlers in Minnesota", *Scandinavia*, I (1883).

B. WISCONSIN

Of the State as a whole: J. W. Hunt, *Wisconsin Gazetteer, containing the Names, Locations, and Advantages of the Counties, Cities, Towns, Villages, Postoffices, and Settlements* (1853); Wm. R. Smith, *The History of Wisconsin, in three Parts: Historical, Documentary, and Descriptive* (1852); Alexander M. Thompson, *A Political History of Wisconsin* (1902); Charles R. Tuttle, *An Illustrated History of the State of Wisconsin* (1875); R. G. Thwaites, *Preliminary Notes on the Distribution of Foreign Groups in Wisconsin* (in *Annual Reports of State Historical Society of Wisconsin*, 1890); G. W. Peck (editor), *Cyclopedia of Wisconsin*, 2 vols. (1906).

For the localities: Spencer Carr, *A Brief Sketch of La Crosse, Wisconsin* (1854); Daniel S. Durrie, *A History of Madison, the Capital of Wisconsin . . . . with an Appendix of Notes on Dane County* (1874); E. W. Keyes, *History of Dane County, 3 vols.* (1906); *The History of Racine and Kenosha Counties* (1879); *The History of Rock County* (1879); *The History of Waukesha County* (1880); H. L. Skavlem, "Scandinavians in the Early Days of Rock County, Wisconsin", *Normands-Forbundet* (1909).

C. ILLINOIS

Charles A. Church, *History of Rockford and Winnebago County, Illinois, From its first Settlement in 1834 to the Civil War* (1900); *History of Henry County, Illinois* (1877); *The Past and Present of La Salle County* (1877); John M. Palmer, *The Bench and Bar of Illinois. Historical and Reminiscent* (1899).

Eric Johnson (Janson) and C. F. Peterson, *Scanskarne i Illinois, Historiska Anteckningar* (1880), is an early work of limited scope but judiciously written.

E. W. Olson (Editor with A. Schön and M. J. Engberg), *History of the Swedes of Illinois*, 2 vols. (1908), has some valuable chapters in the first volume, especially ch. IV on the Bishop Hill Colony, and the chapters dealing with Swedish churches; volume two is devoted to the usual illustrated biographies.

D. IOWA

Charles R. Tuttle, *An Illustrated History of the State of Iowa* (1876); W. E. Alexander, *History of Winneshiek and Allamakee Counties, Iowa* (1882); Charles H. Sparks, *History of Winneshiek County, with Biographical Sketches of its Eminent Men* (1877); J. J. Louis, *Shelby County;* Charles H. Fletcher, *The Centennial History of Jefferson County* (1876); *A Biographical Record of Boone County* (1902); A. Jacobson, *The Pioneer Norwegians* (1905).

G. T. Flom, "The Coming of the Norwegians to Iowa," *Iowa Jour. of Hist. and Politics*, III (1905); "The Early Swedish Immigration to Iowa," *Ibid.*, III (1905), "The Danish Contingent in the Population of early Iowa," *Ibid.*, IV (1906), and "The Growth of the Scandinavian Factor in the Population of Iowa," *Ibid.*, IV (1906); B. L. Wick, "The Earliest Scandinavian Settlement in Iowa," *Iowa Historical Record*, XVI (1900); F. A. Danborn, "Swede Point, or Madrid, Iowa", *Year-Book of the Swedish Historical Society of America*, 1911-1913.

E. OTHER STATES

North Dakota: H. V. Arnold, *History of Grand Forks County . . . . including an Historical Outline of the Red*

River Valley (1900) ; T. Haggerty, *The Territory of Dakota* (1889) ; *Compendium of the History and Biography of North Dakota* (1900).

Nebraska: History of the State of Nebraska (1882).

Kansas: John A. Martin, *Addresses* ("The Swedes in Kansas") (1888).

Utah: H. H. Bancroft, *Utah, 1540-1886* (in *History of the Pacific Coast States of North America*, vol. XXI, 1889).

New York: Arad Thomas, *Pioneer History of Orleans County, New York* (1871) ; G. J. Mason, "The Foreign Element in New York City," *Harper's Weekly* (Sept., 1888) ; S. Folkestad, "Norske i Brooklyn-New York", *Symra* (1908).

TRAVELS AND GUIDE BOOKS

Good accounts of conditions in the European kingdoms, as those conditions were related to emigration at different periods, are: Samuel Laing, *A Tour of Sweden in 1838: comprising Observations on the Moral, Political and Economic State of the Swedish Nation* (London 1839), and *Journal of a Residence in Norway during the Years 1834, 1835 and 1836* (2nd ed., 1837) ; Charles Loring Brace, *The Norsk Folk; or a Visit to the Homes of Norway and Sweden* (1857) ; Mrs. Woods Baker, *Pictures of Swedish Life, or Svea and her Children* (1894) ; J. F. Hanson, *Light and Shade from the Land of the Midnight Sun* (1903).

Of the numerous travelers through the American Northwest, noting the Scandinavian settlements or the conditions affecting them, the most significant is Frederika Bremer, *The Homes of the New World—Impressions of America* (In translation from the Swedish, 3 vols., London, 1853), the work of an educated, alert, sympathetic Swedish lady already noted as a writer. Others of special worth are C. C. Andrews, *Minnesota and Dakota: in Letters Descriptive of a Tour through the Northwest in the Autumn of 1856* (1857) ; Johan Bolin, *Beskrifning öfver Nord Amerikas Förenta Stater* (Wexjö, 1853) ; A. Budde, *Af et Brev om Amerika* (Stavanger, 1850) ; Basil Hall,

Travels in North America in the Years 1827-1828 (1829, Edinburgh, 3 vols.) ; Thorvald Klavenes, *Det Norske Amerika* (Kristiania, 1904) ; Harriet Martineau, *Society in Autumn of 1856* (1857) ; Johan Bolin, *Beskrifning öfver Amerika* (Göteborg, 1872) ; P. Waldenström, *Genom Norra Amerikas Förenta Stater: Reiseskildringar* (Stockholm, 1890) ; Victor Wickström, *Som Tidningsman Jorden Rundt* (Östersund, 1901).

Of guidebooks and handbooks for emigrants and immigrants there is a great number, in English, Swedish, and Norwegian; some issued from philanthropic motives, some by interested States, railroad companies, land companies, and counties, and some by the United States. Only those that directly affected the Scandinavians, or that are typical of a period, are mentioned, and the list is not meant to be exhaustive of titles or editions. Some of the publications by States, might well have been put under the heading of State documents.

One of the typical, widely circulated English handbooks is William Cobbett, *The Emigrant's Guide, in ten Letters addressed to the Taxpayers of England, containing Information of every Kind, necessary to Persons who are about to emigrate* (London, 1829). A similar Norwegian pamphlet is L. J. Fribert, *Haandbog for Emigranter til Amerikas Vest* (Christiania, 1847), or J. R. Reierson, *Veiviser for norske Emigranter til de forenede nordamerikanske Stater och Texas* (Christiania, 1844, reprinted in America, 1899). The United States issued a guide: Edward Young, *Special Report on Immigration; accompanying Information for Immigrants* (1871), reprinted in 1872, with editions in French and German. Other works are: Frederick B. Goddard, *Where to Emigrate and Why* (1864) ; and Edward Young, *Information for Immigrants, relative to Prices and Rentals of Land, etc.* (1871).

For Wisconsin, the most significant and helpful are: *Beskrivelse over Staten Wisconsin: Dens Klimat, Jordbund, Agerdyrkning, samt Natur- og Kunstprodukter. Udgivet efter Legislaturens Ordre af Statens Immigrations*

Department (1870) ; K. K. Kennan (joint agent in Europe for the Wisconsin State Board of Immigration and the Wisconsin Central Railroad, without expense to the former), *Staten Wisconsin, dens Hjælpekilder og Fordele for Udvandreren* (1884)—in several editions, and also in Swedish; C. F. J. Moeller, *Staten Wisconsin, beskreven med særligt Hensyn til denne Stats fortrinlige Stilling som et fremtidigt Hjem for Emigranter fra Danmark, Norge, og Sverige* (1865) ; *Wisconsin,—What it offers to the Immigrant. An official Report published by the State Board of Immigration of Wisconsin* (1879)—many editions, and in various languages.

For Minnesota: Girart Hewitt, *Minnesota: Its Advantages to Settlers,* etc. (1868),—seven editions, one being published by the State; Hans Mattson, *Minnesota och dess Fordelar for Indvandreren* (1867) ; *Minnesota as a Home for Emigrants* (1886),—in Norwegian and Swedish also.

For other States: *Resources of Dakota,—an Official Publication compiled by the Commissioner of Immigration* (1887), later editions dealing with the two States formed from the Teritory of Dakota; Fred. Gerhard, *Illinois as it is: its History, Geography, Statistics,* etc. (1857) ; *Iowa: the Home for Immigrants* (1879), also in Swedish, Norwegian, German, and Dutch.

BIOGRAPHIES AND AUTOBIOGRAPHIES

Several of the books mentioned under special histories, like those of Norelius, Langeland, Dietrichson, and Schroeder, have much autobiographical material in them; while others, such as the volumes of O. N. Nelson and C. F. Peterson and the county histories, contain hundreds of brief biographies. The more important and illuminating autobiographies are: Hans Mattson, *Minnen* (Lund, 1890) and the same in translation, *Reminiscences, the Story of an Emigrant* (1891), an interestingly naïve account of the varied activities of a prominent politician and business man; Gustaf Unonius, *Minnen från en sjutton-årig Vistelse i Nordvestra Amerika* (2 vols., Upsala, 1862), a graphic

account of the first years of Swedish settlement, by one of
its highly educated leaders, and *Bihang till Minnen*
(Stockholm, 1891). With less direct bearing, is W. H. C.
Folsom, *Fifty Years in the Northwest* (1888) ; H. P. Hall,
*H. P. Hall's Observations, being more or less a History of
Political Contests in Minnesota from 1843 to 1904* (1904) ;
John Reynolds, *My Own Times, embracing also the History
of My Life* (Chicago, 1855) ; Stephen Grellet, *Memoirs*
(edited by Benj. Seebohm, 2 vols., 1860) ; and S. B. New-
man, *Pastor S. Newmans Sjelfbiografi* (1890).

Four biographies stand out above the others: T. N.
Hasselquist, *Lefnadsteckning af E. Norelius;* L. A. Sten-
holt, *En Studie af Knute Nelson* (1896) ; Chr. O. Brohough,
and I. Eisteinsen, *Kortfattet Beretning om Elling Eielsens Liv og Virksomhed* (1883) ; and L. M. Björn, *Pastor
P. A. Rasmussen* (1905). Other biographies of less significance for this study are: C. J. Rosenberg, *Jenny Lind
in America* (1851) ; Sara C. Bull, *Ole Bull* (1883) ; W. C.
Church, *Life of John Ericsson* (2 vols., 1890).

Other collected biographies, including Scandinavians,
are: J. C. Jensson, *American Lutheran Biographies*
(1890) ; *Men of Minnesota* (1902) ; F. G. Flower, *Biographical Souvenir Book* (1899), relating to North Dakota alone; *Prominent Democrats of Illinois* (1899; H. A.
Tenney, and D. Atwood, *Fathers of Wisconsin* (1880) ;
C. J. A. Erickson, "Memories of a Swedish Immigrant,"
Annals of Iowa, April, 1907.

RELIGION, EDUCATION, AND THE PRESS

No attempt is made here at a bibliography of the
abundant polemical religious literature, nor of the sermons and proceedings of church conventions, nor of denominational year books, further than to show the material
contributing to this valume. In similar manner, a limit
is put upon the list of catalogs and publications of colleges
and seminaries, and upon the periodicals and newspapers
of which the number is very large.

A very recent and excellent volume dealing with Norwegian progress and culture in America is *Norsk-Ameri-*

kanernes Festskrift, 1914 (Chief Editor, Johs. B. Wist) which was prepared as an American contribution to the celebration of the centennial of Norwegian independence. Important chapters are devoted to the press (noted below), the churches, schools, literature, and men in public or political life, each being the work of a careful scholar.

The most valuable volumes dealing with the religious histories of Scandinavian settlement are E. Norelius, *De Svenska Luterska Församlingarnas och Svenskarnes Historia i Amerika* (1890) and, of almost equal worth, for Norwegian church history, Th. Bothne, *Kort Udsigt over det Lutherske Kirkearbeide blandt Nordmændene i Amerika* (1898), being a separate made up of a section of "Norske Kirkeforhold i Amerika," pp. 815-903, of H. G. Heggtveit, *Illustreret Kirkehistorie*. Good brief sketches of various denominations are embodied in O. N. Nelson, *History of the Scandinavians*, already noted. The most important of the other works are: R. Anderson, *Den Evangelisk Lutherske Kirkes Historie i Amerika* (1889); and *Emigrantmissjonen, Kirkelig Vejledning for Udvandrere* (1884); H. K. Carroll, *The Religious Forces of the United States, enumerated, classified, and described on the Basis of the Government Census of 1890 . . . Revised to 1896* (1896); Theodor H. Dahl, *Den Forenede Kirke: Fred og Strid eller Lidt Forenings Historie* (1894); O. Ellison, *Svenska Baptisternas i Wisconsin Missions Historia* (1902); Simon W. Harkey, *The Mission of the Lutheran Church in America* (1853); O. J. Hatlestad, *Historiske Meddelelser om den norske Augustana Synode* (1887); H. G. Heggtveit, *Illustreret Kirkehistorie* (1898); Chauncy Hobart, *History of Methodism in Minnesota* (1887); Henry E. Jacobs, *A History of the Evangelical Lutheran Church in the United States* (1893); J. N. Lenker, *Lutherans in all Lands* (1896); N. M. Liljengren and C. G. Wallenius, *Svenska Methodismen i Amerika* (1885); *Minde fra Jubelfesterne paa Koshkonong* (1894); M. W. Montgomery, *The Work among the Scandinavians* (1888) and "A Wind from the Holy Spirit," *Sweden and Norway* (1884); A. H. Newman, *History of the Baptist Churches in* the *United States* (1894), and *A Century of Baptist Achievement* (1901); E. Norelius, *Evangeliska Luterska Augustana Synoden i Nord Amerika och dess Mission* (1870); *Affidavits of Sven Oftedal, et al* (in Dist. Court of Minnesota, 4th Jud. Dist.) (1897); H. Olson, *Minnestal öfver framlidne pastorn O. G. Hedström* (1886); George Richardson, *The Rise and Progress of the Society of Friends in Norway* (London, 1849); Matthew Simpson (editor), *Cyclopedia of Methodism* (5th ed., 1882); E. J. Wolf, *The Lutherans in America* (1890); N. C. Brun, "Kort Omrids af den amerikansk-lutherske Kirkes Historie", *Vor Tid*, I (1905).

On the educational side are Kiddle and Schem, *Dictionary of Education* (1890); Chr. Koerner, *The Bennett Law and the German Parochial Schools of Wisconsin* (1890); J. W. Stearns (editor), *The Columbian History of Education in Wisconsin* (1893); *The Bennett Law Analyzed* (1890); A. Estrem, "A Norwegian-American College (Luther College)," *Midland Monthly*, I (1894); E. S. White, "Elk Horn College," *Midland Monthly*, II (1894); J. P. Uhler, "Scandinavian Studies in the United States," *Science*, IX (1887); G. Andreen, "Det svenska Språket i Amerika", *Studentföreningen Verdandis Småskrifter*, No. 87 (Stockholm, 1900); G. T. Flom, *A History of Scandinavian Studies in American Universities* (Bulletin of the State University of Iowa, No. 153, 1907), and "Det norsk sprogs bruk og utvikling i Amerika", *Normands-Forbundet*, IV (1912); G. Bothne, "Nordiske studier ved amerikanske universiteter", *Norsk-Amerikanernes Festkrift, 1914;* A. A. Stomberg, "Swedish in American Universities", *Year-Book of the Swedish Historical Society of America*, 1909-1910; C. G. Wallenius, "Den högre Skolverksamheten bland Svenskarne i Amerika", *Year-Book of the Swedish Historical Society of America*, 1911-1913.

University and college catalogs and registers need not be enumerated for each year; two typical years would be 1895 and 1905; Augustana College and Seminary, Rock Island, Ill.; Luther College, Decorah, Iowa; Bethany College, Lindsborg, Kansas; Gustavus Adolphus College, St. Peter, Minnesota; St. Olaf College, Northfield, Minnesota; Elk Horn College, Elk Horn, Iowa; Augsburg Seminary, Minneapolis, Minnesota; Red Wing Seminary, Red Wing, Minnesota; Northwestern University; University of Chicago; Chicago Theological Seminary; University of Wisconsin; University of Minnesota; University of North Dakota; University of Nebraska; State University of Iowa.

Exhaustive and scholarly discussions of the history and character of the Scandinavian newspapers and periodicals published in the United States are: Juul Dieserud, "Den norske presse i Amerika. En historisk oversigt", *Normands-Forbundet*, V (April 1912); Carl Hansen, "Et Stykke Norsk-Amerikanske Pressens-historie", *Kvartalskrift*, III (Jan. 1907), "Den norsk-amerikanske presse før borgerkrigen", *Symra: en Aarbog for Norske paa begge Sider af Havet*, IV (1908); and "Den norsk-amerikanske presse: Pressen til borgerkrigens slutning", *Norsk-Amerikanernes Festskrift, 1914;* Johs. B. Wist, "Den norsk-amerikanske press: Pressen efter borgerkrigen", *Norsk-Amerikanernes Festskrift, 1914*—remarkably full and complete in its details; E. W. Olson (editor), "Press and Literature", *History of the Swedes in Illinois* (1908), ch. 13. Less important is Eric Johnson, "The Swedish American Press", *The Viking*, I (July and Aug. 1906).

For statistics and ratings of newspapers, G. P. Rowell & Co., *American Newspaper Directories* (1869 to 1906); N. W. Ayer, *American Newspaper Annual* (1881-1914) (Philadelphia).

ECONOMIC, SOCIAL, AND POLITICAL QUESTIONS

Florence E. Baker, *A Brief History of the Elective Franchises in Wisconsin* (1894); Fremont O. Bennett, *Politics and Politicians of Chicago, Cook County, and Illinois* (1886); Eugene Brown and F. Fred Rowe (compilers), *Industrial and Picturesque Rockford, Illinois* (1891; Carlo De'Negri, *Appunti di Statistica Comparata dell' Emigrazione dell' Europa e della Immigrazione in America e in Australia* (in *Bulletin de l' Institute International de*

Statistique, 1888) ; John G. Gregory, *Foreign Immigration to Wisconsin* (1902) ; C. H. Gronvald, *The Effects of the Immigration on the Norwegian Immigrants* (in *Sixth Annual Report to the State Board of Health of Minnesota,* 1878) ; Hans Mattson (editor), *Two Hundred and Fiftieth Anniversary of the First Swedish Settlement in America, September 14, 1888* (1889) ; Robert P. Porter (and others), *The West: from the Census of 1880* (1882) ; Julian Ralph, *Our Great West: a Study of the Present Conditions and Future Possibilities of the New Commonwealths and Capitals of the United States* (1893) ; Gustav Sundbärg, *Bidrag till Utvandringsfrågen från Befolkningsstatistisk Synpunkt* (in *Upsala Universitets Årsskrift,* 1884 o. 1885) ; Carl Sundbeck, *Svensk-Amerikanerna, deras Materialla och Andliga Sträfvanden* (1904)—a good up-to-date summary of conditions in America; William W. Thomas, *Sweden and the Swedes* (1893) ; James D. Whelpley, *The Problem of the Immigrant* (1905) ; Edward Young, *Labor in Europe and America, a Special Report on the Rate of Wages, etc.* (1875),—a particularly valuable book, dealing with conditions in Europe on the eve of the great movement to America.

Two groups of Federal reports are very useful: *Emigration from Europe,* (*Reports from the Consuls of the United States,* No. 76, 1887), dealing with European conditions; and *Emigration to the United States* (*Special Consular Reports,* vol. XXX, 1904). Another exhaustive and scholarly investigation is embodied in *Reports of the Industrial Commission on Immigration, including testimony, with Review and Digest, and Special Reports,* being vol. XV of the Commission's *Reports* (1901).

The Civil War as related to immigration from Northern Europe is treated in: Ole A. Buslett, *Det Femtende Regiment Wisconsin Frivillige* (1895) ; P. G. Dietrichson, *En Kortfattet Skildring af det femtende Wisconsins Regiments Historie og Virksomhed under Borgerkrigen* (1884) ; J. A. Enander, *Borgerkrigen i de Forenede Stater i Nord Amerika* (1881) ; John A. Johnson, *Det Skandinaviske Regiments Historie* (1869).

Important articles in periodicals: F. W. Hewes, "Where our Immigrants Settle" (with excellent statistical maps), *World's Work*, VI (1903); G. G. Huebner, "The Americanization of the Immigrant," *Annals of the American Academy of Political and Social Science*, XXVII (1906); Richmond Mayo-Smith, "Control of Immigration", *Political Science Quarterly*, III, 46, 197, 404 (1888); G. H. Schwab, "A Practical Remedy for the Evils of Immigration," *Forum*, XVI (1893); Nicolay A. Grevstad, "Courts of Conciliation," and "Courts of Conciliation in America," *Atlantic*, LXVIII (1891), LXXII (1893).

Various numbers of *Normands-Forbundet*, published in Christiania, have contained noteworthy articles, besides those mentioned elsewhere in this bibliography, dealing with American conditions: S. Sondresen, "Den norsk-amerikanske farmer" (1908); J. Dieserud, "Nordmændenes deltagelse i de Forenede Staters politiske liv" (1908); M. Alger, "Re-immigrationen" (1913); Av. Kand. Gottenborg, "Hjemvandte norsk-amerikanere, deres livsforhold i Amerika og i Norge efter hjemkomste" (1913); O. K. Winberg, "Degenererer Nordmaend i Amerika" (1910).

Three small novels contain particularly graphic accounts of the life and social conditions among the Norwegian settlers: P. O. Strömme, *Hvorledes Halvor blev Prest* (1893), one of the very best pictures of pioneer immigrant family life; H. A. Foss (translated by J. J. Skordalsvold), *Tobias, a Story of the Northwest*, an exaggerated account of intemperance; and Sigurd H. Severson, *Dei möttes ve Utica. En paa personlig Iagttagelse grundet Skildring af Livet i ældre Norsk-Amerikanske Settlementer* (1882).

NEWSPAPERS

The number of newspapers and other periodicals for the Scandinavians in the United States yearly given in G. P. Rowell & Co., *American Newspaper Directory*, has varied in recent years from 125 to 140, while the total of short-lived and long-lived publications of the same sort would pass 200. The following list includes those periodicals, chiefly newspapers, which were useful in some special degree in preparing this volume:

America, Chicago, an English monthly for Swedes and Norwegians.

American-Scandinavian Review, New York, 1913—Engl. bi-mo.

Amerika, Chicago & Madison, Wis., 1884 (united with *Norden,* 1897 q. v.), Norw. Wkly.

Billed-Magazin, Skandinavisk, Madison, Wis., 1868-1870. Norw. mo.

Budstikken, Minneapolis, 1872—. Norw. wkly.

Chicago Daily Tribune, Chicago, 1847—. dly.

Chicago Record-Herald, Chicago, 1854—. dly.

Dannevirke, Cedar Falls, Iowa, 1880—. Dan. wkly.

Danske Pioneer, Omaha, Neb., 1873—. Dan. wkly.

Decorah Posten, Decorah, Iowa, 1874—. Norw. wkly.

Fædrelandet og Emigranten, La Crosse, Wis., and Minneapolis, 1864-1888. (*Emigranten,* Inmansville, Wis., 1852; Janesville, 1856; Madison, 1857; La Crosse, 1864, and united with *Fædrelandet.*Q Norw. wkly.

Folkebladet, Minneapolis, 1878—. Norw. wkly.

Gamla och Nya Hemlandet, Chicago, 1855. Sw. wkly.

Korsbaneret, Rock Island, Ill., 1880. Sw. church annual.

Kvartalskrift, Minneapolis, 1903—. Nor. qtly.

Madison Democrat, Madison, Wis., 1852—. Eng. dly.

Milwaukee Daily Sentinel, Milwaukee, Wis., 1837—. Eng. dly.

Minneapolis Evening Journal, Minneapolis, 1878—Eng. dly.

Minneapolis Times, Minneapolis, 1889-1905. Eng. dly.

Minneapolis Tribune, Minneapolis, 1867—. Eng. dly.

Minneapolis Tidende, Minneapolis, 1887—. Norw. dly. and wkly.

Minnesota Stats Tidning, Minneapolis and St. Paul, 1877—. Sw. wkly.

Norden, Chicago, 1874-1897 (united with *Amerika*). Norw. wkly.

Nordvesten, St. Paul, 1883—. Norw.-Dan. wkly.

Nordmanden, Grand Forks, N. D., 1887—. Norw. wkly.

Nordmands-Forbundet, Christiania, Norway, 1908—. Nor.

Normannen, Stoughton, Wis., 1867. Norw. wkly.

The North, Minneapolis, 1889-1894. Eng. wkly. for Scandinavians.

Red River Posten (merged with *Dakota*), Fargo, N. D., 1879—. Norw. wkly.

Rockford Register, Rockford, Ill., 1867—. Eng. dly.

Rodhuggeren, Crookston, Minn., 1880-1884. Norw. wkly.

Scandinavia, Chicago, 1883-1886. Eng. mo. for Scandinavians.

Skandinaven, Chicago, 1866—. Norw. dly, wkly., and tri-wkly., the strongest and most influential Scandinavian paper in the United States.

St. Paul Pioneer-Press, St. Paul, 1849—. Eng. dly.

St. Paul Dispatch, St. Paul, 1868—. Eng. dly.

Superior Tidende (originally *Posten*), Superior, Wis., 1888—. Norw.-Dan. wkly.

Svensk-Amerikaneren, Chicago, Ill., 1866—. Sw. wkly.

Svenska Amerikanska Posten, Minneapolis, 1886—. Sw. wkly., a large and influential paper.

Svenska Folkets Tidning, Minneapolis, 1883—. Sw. wkly.

Svenska Tribunen, Chicago, 1868—. Sw. wkly.

Ugebladet, Chicago, later Minneapolis, 1888—. Norw. wkly.

Valdris-Helsing (*Valdris-Samband*), Iowa City, Ia., later Stillwater and Minneapolis, Minn., 1893—. Norw. mo. (since 1912) devoted to interests of immigrants from Valders.

The Viking, Fremont, Neb., 1906—? Eng. mo. for Scandinavians.

Vikingen, Minneapolis, 1906—- Norw.-Dan. mo.

Vor Tid, Minneapolis, 1905-1908. Norw. mo.

Wisconsin State Journal, Madison, 1897—. Eng. dly.

APPENDIX I
Statistical Tables

TABLE I

STATISTICS OF IMMIGRANTS FROM DENMARK, NORWAY AND SWEDEN.

The number of alien passengers and immigrants from the Scandinavian countries arriving in the United States, 1820-1913, together with the total number of alien arrivals according to the statistics of the United States, and, where available, of the Scandinavian kingdoms. The figures from 1820-1840 are at best a safe minimum. The earlier figures reported by the Scandinavian kingdoms, given in round numbers, are probably estimates based upon partial data. See United States Reports of the Bureau of Commerce and Navigation, Annual Statistical Abstracts and the report of the Dillingham Commission (1911); Sundbärg, Bidrag til Utvandringsfrågen från Befolkningsstatistisk Synpunkt; Nelson, Scandinavians in the United States, I, 253-264c; Bulletin de l'Institute Internationale de Statistique, III, ii, 125-127; Statesman's Year-Books, 1906-14.

	UNITED STATES STATISTICS					EUROPEAN STATISTICS			
	Denmark	Norway	Sweden	Total Scandinavian	Total Aliens	Denmark	Norway	Sweden	Total Scandinavian
1820	20		3	23	8,385				
1821	12		12	24	9,127			1	1
1822	18		10	28	6,911				
1823	6		1	7	6,354				
1824	11		9	20	7,912				
1825	14		4	18	10,199			53	53
1826	10		16	26	10,837				
1827	15		13	28	18,875				
1828	50		10	60	27,382				
1829	17		13	30	22,520				
1830	16		3	19	23,322				
1820-1830	189		94	283	151,824			54	54
1831	23		13	36	22,633				
1832	21		313	334	60,482				
1833	173		16	189	58,640				
1834	24		42	66	65,365				
1835	37		31	68	45,374				
1836	416		57	473	76,242			200	200
1837	109		290	399	79,340			200	200
1838	52		60	112	38,914			100	100
1839	56		324	380	68,069			400	400
1840	152		55	207	84,066			300	300
1831-40	1,063		1,201	2,264	599,125			1,200	1,200

TABLE 1 (Continued)

	UNITED STATES STATISTICS					EUROPEAN STATISTICS			
	Denmark	Norway	Sweden	Total Scandinavian	Total Aliens	Denmark	Norway	Sweden	Total Scandinavian
1841	31		195	226	80,289	....	400		400
1842	35		553	588	104,565	....	700		700
1843	29		1,748	1,777	52,496	....	1,600		1,600
1844	25		1,311	1,336	78,615	....	1,200		1,200
1845	54		928	982	114,371	....	1,100		1,100
1846	114		1,916	2,030	154,416	....	1,300		1,300
1847	13		1,307	1,320	234,968	....	1,600		1,600
1848	210		903	1,113	226,527	....	1,400		1,400
1849	8		3,473	3,481	297,024	....	4,000		4,000
1850	20		1,569	1,589	369,980	....	3,700		3,700
1841-50	539		13,903	14,442	1,713,251	....	17,000		17,000
1851	14		2,424	2,438	379,466	....	2,640	934	3,574
1852	3		4,103	4,106	371,601	....	4,030	3,031	7,061
1853	32		3,364	3,396	368,645	....	6,050	2,619	8,669
1854	691		3,531	4,222	427,833	....	5,950	3,980	9,930
1855	528		821	1,349	200,877	....	1,600	586	2,186
1856	173		1,157	1,330	200,436	....	3,200	959	4,159
1857	1,035		1,712	2,747	251,306	....	6,400	1,762	8,162
1858	232		2,430	2,662	123,126	....	2,500	512	3,012
1859	499		1,091	1,590	121,282	....	1,800	208	2,008
1860	542		298	840	153,640	....	1,900	266	2,166
1851-60	3,749		20,931	24,680	2,598,212	....	36,070	14,857	50,927
1861	234		616	850	91,918	....	8,900	1,087	9,987
1862	1,658		892	2,550	91,985	....	5,250	1,206	6,456
1863	1,492		1,627	3,119	176,282	....	1,100	1,485	2,585
1864	712		2,249	2,961	193,418	....	4,300	2,461	6,761
1865	1,149		6,109	7,258	248,120	....	4,000	3,180	7,180
1866	1,862		12,633	14,495	318,568	....	15,455	4,466	19,921
1867	1,436		7,055	8,491	315,722	....	12,829	5,893	18,722
1868	819		11,166	11,985	142,023	....	13,211	21,472	34,683
1861-68	9,362		42,347	51,709	1,578,036	....	65,045	41,250	106,295

TABLE 1 (Continued)

	UNITED STATES STATISTICS					EUROPEAN STATISTICS			
	Denmark	Norway	Sweden	Total Scandinavian	Total Aliens	Denmark	Norway	Sweden	Total Scandinavian
1869	3,649	16,068	24,224	43,941	352,768	4,340	18,070	32,050	54,460
1870	4,083	13,216	13,443	30,742	387,203	3,264	14,834	15,430	33,528
1871	2,015	9,418	10,699	22,132	321,350	3,249	12,276	12,985	28,510
1872	3,690	11,421	13,464	28,575	404,806	5,941	13,865	11,838	31,644
1873	4,931	16,247	14,303	35,481	459,803	5,926	10,352	9,486	25,764
1874	3,082	10,384	5,712	19,178	313,339	2,261	4,601	3,380	10,242
1875	2,656	6,093	5,573	14,322	227,498	1,678	4,048	3,591	9,317
1876	1,547	5,173	5,603	12,323	169,986	1,336	4,355	3,702	9,393
1877	1,695	4,588	4,991	11,274	141,857	1,374	3,206	2,921	7,501
1878	2,105	4,759	5,390	12,354	138,469	2,300	4,863	4,242	11,405
1879	3,474	7,345	11,001	21,820	177,826	2,845	7,608	12,761	23,214
1880	6,576	19,895	39,186	65,657	457,257	5,475	20,212	36,263	61,950
1869-80	39,503	124,607	153,589	317,699	3,552,162	39,989	170,124	148,649	306,928
1881	9,177	22,705	49,760	81,582	669,431	7,823	25,976	40,620	74,419
1882	11,618	29,101	64,607	105,326	788,992	11,385	28,804	44,359	84,548
1883	10,319	23,398	38,277	71,994	603,322	8,280	22,167	25,678	56,125
1884	9,202	16,974	26,552	52,728	518,592	6,149	14,776	17,664	38,589
1885	6,100	12,356	22,248	40,704	395,346	4,211	13,901	18,222	36,334
1886	6,225	12,759	27,751	46,735	334,203	5,558	15,116	27,913	48,587
1887	8,524	16,269	42,836	67,629	490,109	8,184	20,706	46,252	75,142
1888	8,962	18,264	54,698	81,924	546,889	8,269	21,348	45,561	75,178
1889	8,699	13,390	35,415	57,504	444,427	8,271	12,597	28,529	49,397
1890	9,366	11,370	29,632	50,368	455,302	9,524	10,898	29,487	49,909
1881-90	88,132	176,586	391,776	656,494	5,246,613	77,654	186,289	324,285	588,228

TABLE 1 (Continued)

	UNITED STATES STATISTICS					EUROPEAN STATISTICS			
	Denmark	Norway	Sweden	Total Scandinavian	Total Aliens	Denmark	Norway	Sweden	Total Scandinavian
1891	10,659	12,568	36,880	60,107	560,319	9,781	13,249	36,134	59,164
1892	10,593	14,462	43,247	68,302	623,084	9,763	16,814	40,990	67,567
1893	8,779	16,079	38,077	62,935	502,917	8,551	18,690	37,321	64,562
1894	5,581	8,867	18,608	33,056	314,467	4,105	5,591	9,529	19,225
1895	4,244	7,373	15,683	27,300	279,948	3,607	6,153	14,982	24,742
1896	3,167	8,855	21,177	33,229	343,267	2,876	6,584	14,874	24,334
1897	2,085	5,842	13,162	21,089	230,832	2,260	4,580	10,109	16,949
1898	1,946	4,938	12,398	19,282	229,299	2,340	4,805	8,534	15,679
1899	2,690	6,705	12,797	22,192	311,715	2,799	6,466	11,842	21,097
1900	2,926	9,575	18,650	31,151	448,572	3,570	10,931	16,209	30,710
1891-00	52,670	95,264	230,679	378,643	3,844,410	49,652	93,863	200,524	344,029
1901	3,655	12,248	23,331	39,234	487,918	4,657	12,488	20,306	37,451
1902	5,660	17,484	30,894	54,038	648,743	6,823	19,225	33,151	59,199
1903	7,158	24,461	46,028	79,647	857,046	8,214	24,998	35,439	68,651
1904	8,525	23,808	27,763	60,096	812,870	9,034	20,836	18,533	48,403
1905	8,970	25,064	26,591	60,625	1,026,499	8,051	19,638	20,520	48,209
1906	7,741	21,730	23,310	52,781	1,100,735	8,516	20,449	21,242	50,207
1907	7,243	22,133	20,589	49,965	1,285,349	7,890	20,615	19,325	47,830
1908	4,954	12,412	12,809	30,175	782,870	4,558	7,850	8,873	21,281
1909	4,395	13,627	14,474	32,496	751,786	6,782	15,237	18,331	40,350
1910	6,984	17,538	23,745	48,267	1,041,570	8,890	17,361	23,529	49,780
1901-10	65,285	190,505	249,534	505,234	8,795,386	73,415	178,697	219,249	471,361
1911	7,555	13,950	20,780	42,285	878,587	8,303	11,122	15,571	34,996
1912	6,191	8,675	12,688	27,554	838,172	8,636	7,776	13,896	30,308
1913	6,478	8,587	17,202	33,267	1,197,892				
Totals	278,277	696,401	1,071,835	2,047,513	30,833,643				

TABLE II

FOREIGN-BORN SCANDINAVIAN POPULATION, 1850

U. S. Census of 1850

States and Territories	Denmark	Norway	Sweden	Total Scandi-navians	Total Popu-lation
Alabama	18	3	51	72	771,623
Arkansas	7	1	1	9	209,897
California	92	124	162	378	92,597
Conecticut	16	1	13	30	370,792
Delaware	1	....	2	3	91,532
District of Columbia	6	....	5	11	51,687
Florida	21	17	33	71	87,445
Georgia	24	6	11	41	906,185
Illinois	93	2,415	1,123	3,631	851,470
Indiana	10	18	16	44	988,416
Iowa	19	361	231	611	192,214
Kentucky	7	18	20	45	982,405
Louisiana	288	64	249	601	517,762
Maine	47	12	55	114	583,169
Maryland	35	10	57	102	583,034
Massachusetts	181	69	253	503	994,514
Michigan	13	110	16	139	397,654
Minnesota Territory	1	7	4	12	6,077
Mississippi	24	8	14	46	606,526
Missouri	55	155	37	247	682,044
New Hampshire	3	2	12	17	317,976
New Jersey	28	4	34	66	489,555
New Mexico Territory	2	2	1	5	61,547
New York	429	392	753	1,574	3,097,394
North Carolina	6	....	9	15	869,039
Ohio	53	18	55	126	1,980,329
Oregon Territory	2	1	2	5	13,294
Pennsylvania	97	27	133	257	2,311,786
Rhode Island	15	25	17	57	147,545
South Carolina	24	7	29	60	668,507
Tennessee	8	....	8	16	1,002,717
Texas	49	105	48	202	212,592
Utah Territory	2	32	1	35	11,380
Vermont	....	8	....	8	314,120
Virginia	15	5	16	36	1,421,661
Wisconsin	146	8,651	88	8,885	305,391
Total	1,837	12,678	3,559	18,074	23,191,876

TABLE III

FOREIGN-BORN SCANDINAVIAN POPULATION, 1870
U. S. Census, 1870

States and Territories	Denmark	Norway	Sweden	Total Scandi-navians	Total Popu-lation
Alabama	80	21	105	206	996,992
Arkansas	55	19	134	208	484,471
California	1,837	1,000	1,944	4,781	560,247
Connecticut	116	72	323	511	537,454
Delaware	8	....	9	17	125,015
Florida	40	16	30	86	187,748
Georgia	42	14	35	91	1,184,109
Illinois	3,711	11,880	29,979	45,570	2,539,891
Indiana	315	123	2,180	2,618	1,680,637
Iowa	2,827	17,554	10,796	31,177	1,194,020
Kansas	502	588	4,954	6.044	364,399
Kentucky	53	16	112	181	1,321,011
Louisiana	290	76	358	724	726,915
Maine	120	58	91	269	626,915
Maryland	106	17	100	223	780,894
Massachusetts	267	302	1,384	1,953	1,457,351
Michigan	1,354	1,516	2,406	5,276	1,184,059
Minnesota	1,910	35,940	20,987	58,837	439,706
Mississippi	193	78	970	1,241	827,922
Missouri	665	297	2,302	3,264	1,721,295
Nebraska	1,129	506	2,352	3,987	122,993
Nevada	208	80	217	505	42,491
New Hampshire	11	55	42	108	318,300
New Jersey	510	90	554	1,154	906,096
New York	1,698	975	5,522	8,195	4,382,759
North Carolina	8	5	38	51	1,071,361
Ohio	284	64	252	600	2,665,260
Oregon	87	76	205	368	90,923
Pennsylvania	561	115	2,266	2,942	3,521,951
Rhode Island	24	22	106	152	217,353
South Carolina	50	....	60	110	705,606
Tennessee	86	37	349	472	1,258,520
Texas	159	403	364	926	818,579
Vermont	21	34	83	138	330,551
Virginia	23	17	30	70	1,225,163
West Virginia	21	1	5	27	442,014
Wisconsin	5,212	40,046	2,799	48,057	1,054,670
Arizona Ter.	19	7	7	33	9,658
Colorado Ter.	77	40	180	297	39,864
Dakota Ter.	115	1,179	380	1,674	14,181
Dist. of Columbia	29	5	22	56	131,700
Idaho Ter.	88	61	91	240	14,999
Montana Ter.	95	88	141	324	20,595
New Mexico Ter.	15	5	6	26	91,874
Utah Ter.	4,957	613	1,790	7,360	! 86,786
Washington Ter.	84	104	158	346	23,955
Wyoming Ter.	54	28	109	191	9,118
Total	30,098	114,243	⁰97,327	241,686	38,558,371

TABLE IV

FOREIGN-BORN SCANDINAVIAN POPULATION, 1890

U. S. Census of 1890

States and Territories	Denmark	Norway	Sweden	Total Scandi-navians	Total Popu-lation
Alabama	71	47	294	412	1,513,017
Arizona Territory	180	59	168	407	59,620
Arkansas	125	60	333	518	1,128,179
California	7,764	3,702	10,923	22,389	1,208,130
Colorado	1,650	893	9,659	12,202	412,198
Connecticut	1,474	523	10,021	12,018	746,258
Delaware	41	14	246	301	168,493
District of Columbia	72	70	128	270	230,392
Florida	105	179	529	813	391,422
Georgia	61	88	191	340	1,837,353
Idaho	1,241	741	1,524	3,506	84,285
Illinois	12,044	30,339	86,514	128,897	3,826,351
Indiana	718	285	4,512	5,515	2,192,404
Iowa	15,519	27,078	30,276	72,873	1,911,896
Kansas	3,136	1,786	17,096	21,998	1,427,096
Kentucky	92	120	184	396	1,858,635
Louisiana	232	136	328	796	1,118,587
Maine	696	311	1,704	2,711	661,086
Maryland	130	164	305	599	1,042,390
Massachusetts	1,512	2,519	18,624	22,655	2,238,943
Michigan	6,335	7,795	27,366	41,496	2,093,889
Minnesota	14,133	101,169	99,913	215,215	1,301,826
Mississippi	90	54	305	449	1,289,600
Missouri	1,333	526	5,602	7,461	2,679,184
Montana	683	1,957	3,771	6,411	132,159
Nebraska	14,345	3,632	28,364	46,341	1,058,910
Nevada	332	69	314	715	45,761
New Hampshire	64	251	1,210	1,425	376,530
New Jersey	2,991	1,317	4,159	8,467	1,444,933
New Mexico Ter.	54	42	149	245	153,593
New York	6,238	8,602	28,430	43,270	5,997,753
North Dakota	2,860	25,773	5,583	34,216	182,719
North Carolina	26	13	51	90	1,617,947
Ohio	956	511	2,742	4,209	3,672,316
Oklahoma Ter.	37	36	138	211	61,834
Oregon	1,288	2,271	3,774	7,333	313,767
Pennsylvania	2,010	2,238	19,346	23,594	5,258,014
Rhode Island	154	285	3,392	3,831	345,506
South Dakota	4,369	19,257	7,746	31,372	328,808
South Carolina	36	23	60	119	1,151,149
Tennessee	92	41	332	465	1,767,518
Texas	649	1,313	2,806	4,768	2,235,523
Utah Territory	9,023	1,854	5,986	16,863	207,905
Vermont	58	38	870	966	332,422
Virginia	108	102	215	425	1,655,980
Washington	2,807	8,334	10,272	21,413	349,390
West Virginia	44	7	72	123	762,794
Wisconsin	13,885	65,696	20,157	99,738	1,686,880
Wyoming	680	345	1,357	2,382	60,705
Total	132,543	322,665	478,041	933,249	62,622,250

TABLE V

FOREIGN WHITE STOCK OF SCANDINAVIAN ORIGIN, 1910

13th **Census**, I, Chapter viii, Table 29

Under each state the figures represent
  (1) foreign born, corresponding to the figures given for 1850, 1870, and 1890
  (2) native white of foreign parentage
  (3) native white of mixed parentage

	Norway	Sweden	Denmark	Totals	Grand Total
Alabama	266	752	197	1,215	
	114	481	105	700	
	168	274	128	570	2,485
Arizona	272	845	284	1,401	
	164	427	172	763	
	106	302	246	654	2,818
Arkansas	76	385	178	639	
	49	176	72	297	
	77	374	198	649	1,585
California	9,952	26,210	14,208	50,370	
	4,666	14,797	8,244	27,707	
	2,528	5,464	4,043	12,035	90,112
Colorado	1,787	12,445	2,755	16,987	
	1,421	9,681	1,894	12,996	
	826	3,287	1,061	5,174	35,157
Connecticut	1,265	18,208	2,722	22,195	
	499	14,508	1,845	16,852	
	204	1,788	418	2,410	41,457
Delaware	38	332	52	422	
	15	208	17	240	
	12	85	19	116	778
Florida	303	728	295	1,326	
	158	387	110	655	
	303	412	161	876	2,857
Georgia	145	289	112	546	
	56	153	33	242	
	85	196	72	353	1,141
Idaho	2,566	4,985	2,254	9,805	
	2,221	3,876	2,680	8,777	
	1,289	2,124	2,532	5,945	24,527
Illinois	32,913	115,422	17,368	165,703	
	26,572	94,830	11,551	132,953	
	8,953	19,879	4,600	33,432	332,088
Indiana	531	5,081	900	6,512	
	363	4,824	692	5,879	
	299	1,896	582	2,777	15,168

TABLE V (Continued)

	Norway	Sweden	Denmark	Totals	Grand Total
Iowa	21,924	26,763	17,961	66,648	
	30,392	28,859	17,814	77,065	
	14,586	10,573	5,966	31,125	174,838
Kansas	1,294	13,309	2,759	17,362	
	1,371	15,911	2,635	19,917	
	1,031	6,411	1,822	9,264	46,543
Kentucky	53	190	78	321	
	39	104	40	183	
	40	148	96	284	788
Louisiana	294	344	239	877	
	92	154	125	371	
	252	438	392	1,082	2,330
Maine	580	2,203	929	3,712	
	288	1,478	715	2,481	
	218	627	340	1,185	7,378
Maryland	363	421	237	1,021	
	144	209	88	441	
	164	261	158	583	2,045
Massachusetts	5,432	39,560	3,403	48,395	
	2,170	25,149	1,706	29,025	
	768	3,759	963	5,490	82,910
Michigan	7,638	26,374	6,313	40,325	
	6,778	25,624	6,055	38,457	
	2,358	4,939	2,431	9,728	88,510
Minnesota	105,302	122,427	16,137	243,866	
	126,549	118,083	15,430	260,062	
	47,755	27,508	5,957	81,220	585,148
Mississippi	91	292	119	502	
	32	178	51	261	
	116	280	122	518	1,281
Missouri	660	5,654	1,729	8,043	
	543	4,937	1,147	6,627	
	537	2,936	1,380	4,853	19,523
Montana	7,169	6,410	1,943	15,522	
	4,859	3,865	1,302	10,026	
	1,914	1,527	696	4,137	29,685
Nebraska	2,750	23,219	13,673	39,643	
	2,989	26,599	13,957	43,545	
	1,968	8,668	4,932	15,568	98,755
Nevada	254	708	616	1,578	
	107	293	393	793	
	92	192	307	591	2,962
New Hampshire	491	2,068	131	2,690	
	292	1,172	55	1,519	
	69	316	69	454	4,663

TABLE V (Continued)

	Norway	Sweden	Denmark	Totals	Grand Total
New Jersey..........	5,351	10,547	5,056	20,954	
	2,256	5,899	3,350	11,505	
	745	1,902	1,261	3,908	36,367
New Mexico........	151	365	116	632	
	109	240	75	424	
	71	144	91	306	1,362
New York............	25,012	53,703	12,536	91,251	
	10,171	29,284	5,006	44,461	
	2,221	7,248	3,167	12,636	148,348
North Carolina....	39	112	36	187	
	13	36	13	62	
	28	70	28	126	375
North Dakota......	45,937	12,160	5,355	63,452	
	56,577	10,533	5,043	72,153	
	20,770	4,107	1,805	26,682	162,287
Ohio	1,109	5,522	1,837	8,468	
	571	4,075	1,150	5,796	
	351	1,458	808	2,617	16,881
Oklahoma	351	1,028	550	1,929	
	425	943	518	1,886	
	432	1,058	577	2,067	5,882
Oregon	6,843	10,099	3,215	20,157	
	4,643	5,866	2,167	12,676	
	1,949	2,233	1,391	5,573	38,406
Pennsylvania	2,317	23,467	3,033	28,817	
	995	22,803	1,656	25,454	
	651	5,415	1,261	7,327	61,598
Rhode Island......	577	7,404	328	8,309	
	230	5,174	153	5,557	
	109	636	108	853	14,719
South Carolina....	82	95	51	228	
	19	20	9	48	
	40	68	68	176	452
South Dakota......	20,918	9,998	6,294	37,210	
	27,803	9,640	6,396	43,839	
	12,025	3,654	2,273	17,952	99,001
Tennessee	89	363	163	615	
	74	237	87	398	
	79	281	119	479	1,492
Texas	1,784	4,703	1,287	7,774	
	1,649	4,724	844	7,217	
	1,012	2,171	942	4,125	19,116
Utah	2,304	7,227	8,300	17,831	
	1,562	5,906	10,169	17,637	
	1,643	3,930	8,142	13,715	49,183

TABLE V (Continued)

	Norway	Sweden	Denmark	Totals	Grand Total
Vermont	102	1,331	172	1,605	
	41	905	74	1,020	
	32	185	68	285	2,910
Virginia	311	368	239	918	
	222	215	140	577	
	164	138	95	397	1,892
Washington	28,363	32,195	7,804	68,362	
	18,486	18,244	4,988	41,718	
	5,875	5,640	2,286	13,801	123,881
West Virginia......	38	278	67	383	
	10	196	51	257	
	31	124	48	203	843
Wisconsin	56,999	25,739	16,454	99,192	
	71,681	23,268	15,903	110,852	
	29,020	6,379	5,958	41,357	251,401
Wyoming	623	2,497	962	4,082	
	381	1,455	866	2,702	
	245	598	521	1,364	8,148

APPENDIX II

STATISTICS OF THREE MINNESOTA COUNTIES
From the U. S. Census Reports

Chisago County	1860	1870	1880	1890	1900
White population	1,729	4,358	7,982	10,359	13,248
White native-born	1,209	2,164	4,017	5,613	8,230
White foreign-born	734	2,194	3,965	4,746	5,018
White foreign Danish	....	14	50	67	55
White foreign Norwegian	....	1,674	3,160	50	69
White foreign Swedish	....	....	....	3,955	4,215
Acres in farms					
Improved	3,468	8,004	31,198	43,476	85,277
Unimproved	18,484	34,593	72,595	101,649	129,501
Cash value of farms	$124,019	$477,720	$1,171,426	$2,563,630	$3,419,310

Fillmore County					
White population	13,542	24,887	28,162	25,966	28,238
White native-born	9,045	15,178	19,243	19,034	22,378
White foreign-born	4,497	9,709	8,919	6,932	5,860
White foreign Danish	....	13	96	68	59
White foreign Norwegian	....	6,612	5,191	4,171	3,593
White foreign Swedish	....	....	....	66	53
Acres in farms					
Improved	75,542	185,087	361,100	357,083	389,386
Unimproved	216,454	214,459	134,333	117,670	131,875
Cash value of farms	$1,844,797	$6,636,880	$9,535,815	$9,935,202	$14,240,595

Otter Tail County					
White population	178	1,968	18,675	34,232	45,375
White native-born	178	888	11,249	20,884	30,988
White foreign-born	....	1,080	7,426	13,348	14,387
White foreign Danish	....	41	214	345	372
White foreign Norwegian	....	889	4,772	5,955	5,738
White foreign Swedish	....	....	....	2,470	3,038
Acres in farms					
Improved	306	3,632	131,804	311,175	505,358
Unimproved	2,118	28,898	340,355	405,380	439,374
Cash value of farms	$17,550	$151,281	$3,650,223	$8,511,465	$12,478,640

INDEX